Meditation: This Book Includes: Chakra and Reiki Healing for Beginners, Buddhism for Beginners, Third Eye Awakening.

D1362002

Kimberly Empath

BOOK 4

THIRD EYE AWAKENING:

Book 1

Chakra Healing For Beginners: A Complete Guide to Balance and Discover Self-Healing Awakening Techniques through Crystals, Kundalini & Guided Meditation as a true Buddhist to Attract Positive Energy

Introduction

Words Chakra was originated from the Sanskrit word chakra meaning "wheel." Words refer to a spinning wheel of light or a wheel or time, as well as stands for celestial peace as well as order. The Chakra system was first defined in the ancient Hindu message Vedas, the earliest written practice in India. It is believed, nonetheless, that the Chakra system is an approach that originated from the Aryans, the Indo-European invaders of India.

The Chakras defined in Hindu customs are recognized as the key Chakras. These Chakras have no particular kinds or locations and are believed to be symbolic. In the western world, nonetheless, a different Chakra system dominates; it is called the New Age Chakra system.

New Age Chakras, unlike their primary counterparts, have certain types and locations in the body. They stand for energy centers, power joints, and points of power entrance in the body.

The New Age Chakra system consists of Chakras situated along the back cord. Each Chakra represents a specific shade, which describes the visible light range linked with it.

Chakras are not physical items but rather power patterns shaped like funnels and are frequently explained as "whirlpools of power."

Researchers considering that Einstein (that theorized

that all issues are power as well as whatever in the cosmos is accumulated by the internet of interconnecting energy) have actually understood concerning and also researched power fields. Sheldrake's Morphogenic Resonance Theory, the clinical research of individuals like Einthoven and also Berger, who have developed those body organs, such as the heart and brain, create bioelectric areas.

When conductors like cords or living cells lug electric currents, the surrounding space produces a magnetic field. The space around the living cells of the human body is currently being called the biomagnetic fields. Or more simply - energy fields.

Within these biomagnetic fields are rotating whirlpools of this energy. And there are plenty of varieties of these throughout the body- all feeding right into the 7 biggest vortices. These seven are what we generally call the Chakras, and they have actually been associated with the colors of the light range.

Each chakra properly attracts right into the body's power area energy from the 'interconnecting internet' Einstein talked of, as well as after that sucks out 'old' power from our body's are

\-   a little bit like just how air-conditioning jobs.

If our chakras functioned effectively constantly after that, we would certainly all be delighted and also completely healthy and balanced. The trouble is they do not and also, so we aren't.

Frequently the chakras end up being blocked by the particles of our lives- emotions, environmental stress, physical misuse like toxic substances in our food ... they all include up to those spinning vortexes not spinning the means they should.

So, just like our body needs to be cleaned up of particles by bathing, so the chakra system requires to be cleaned up as well as free from the particles that quit it performing its task properly.

There is a whole new type of healers who are dealing with the power fields to cause optimal wellness, and also, a great deal of their job entails these chakras.

Vibrational Medicine or Energy healing might appear a little bit airy-fairy, but the more we discover these energy areas as well as just how they function, the more the feeling behind these new kinds of holistic healing approaches makes.

However, you do not have to go to a specialist to remain healthy and balanced, although it's probably a great suggestion to see an excellent power healer if you aren't healthy to start

with. It functions actually well in combination with traditional clinical practices.

To keep your chakras, you can work with yourself vigorously by picturing these chakras and picturing them being cleansed. Those that have an idea in a Higher Power, such as Angels, can request their assistance to clear them.

The fact is, there is a great deal of high vibrational energy 'muscle' available simply waiting to help us with our power job. It's only a matter of requesting the assistance, and also locating the most effective means it works for you.

There Are Seven Major Chakras In The Human Body.

We all have seven major chakras, as well as several minor chakras. Each chakra associated with organs or parts of each demand and also the body to be looked after and balanced routinely. You can function on each chakra individually, starting with the base chakra, and also, after that, bring them all right into equilibrium, or you can work on all the chakras at the same time.

All chakras connect with one another. Each chakra corresponds to a certain color frequency and also with a certain gland or body organ.

In a healthy and balanced body, the chakras distribute and also soak up color power evenly, while in an undesirable person, contaminants might begin to collect triggering physical, psychological, and psychological troubles.

Each chakra can be stabilized, making use of colors, crystals, necessary oils, songs, affirmations, or altering what you do. It is additionally valuable to have a chakra balance to bring them all back into equilibrium. This can be done in your home on your own, or you can go to a crystal specialist or color specialist to have it done.

When all your chakras are well balanced - you should be healthy and also well balanced.

It is very important to have all your chakras in equilibrium; often, when people begin on the spiritual path, they focus on the pineal eye. However, it is essential to begin near the bottom. Our body is like a structure; you require to obtain the structures right before you deal with the top floors. So make sure your bottom chakras are well balanced as well as operating effectively.

- The First Chakra lies at the base of the spinal column and also stands for survival and also physical vigor. It is associated with the shade RED.

- The Second Chakra is located at the sacral as well as stands for a wish and also sexual power. It is connected with the shade ORANGE.

- The Third Chakra lies at the solar plexus and represents self-image. It is connected with the color YELLOW.

- The Fourth Chakra is located at heart and represents love, empathy, as well as compassion. It is associated with the color GREEN.

- The Fifth Chakra is situated at the pit of the throat and stands for interaction and liberty of expression. It is related to the shade BLUE.

- The Sixth Chakra lies at the forehead (typically called the 3rd eye) as well as stands for psychic vision. It is linked with the shade INDIGO.

- The Seventh Chakra lies at the crown of the head and also stands for the completeness of the being as well as spiritual perfection. It is connected with the color VIOLET.

The seven Chakras align in the spine. Energy normally moves upwards in the body, depending upon a person's specific life experience. The lower Chakras represent the physical existence, and also power ascends as a person participates in more spiritual features.

The Chakra system is a holistic entity that suggests that when the one chakra is interrupted, the energy circulation of the whole system is affected. An unbalanced Chakra system causes

an unbalanced life; it causes poor physical, psychological, psychological, and spiritual wellness.

Energy healing is a topic that often concerns those who

understand the importance of maintaining a stable chakra network. There are several examples and theories of how the chakra mechanism is restored. However, all lead to total well- being, as a balanced chakra system represents the complete harmony of body and spirit.

Chapter 1. Awakening The Chakra Within

The benefits of balancing your chakras are connected to yoga and its philosophies. Blocked chakras are believed to lead to illnesses in the areas of the body experiencing that blockage, especially if it is happening with your seven major chakras. If you have ever felt tired, lethargic and had those "off days" when everything feels like a monumental effort, that is what blocked chakras can do to your body.

No one can keep their chakras perfectly balanced all the time. The struggles and frustrations of dealing with everyday life, in general, make it exceedingly difficult to keep your chakras aligned throughout the day. Some days may be easier than others, but most of the time like everyone else, keeping your chakra pathways open and flowing is going to be a challenge. Everyone has their reasons why their chakras might be blocked, which is why those who believe in this practice advocate the practice of chakra healing through finding balance.

What Does Balancing Your Chakra

Mean?

When you restore your chakras to their relaxed, healthy and natural flow, you are balancing them. Since it is nearly impossible to remain relaxed or calm all the time in our daily lives, our chakras go out of balance from the anxious emotions, thoughts, and feelings that we experience. This overload of emotions disrupts your natural chakra flow, which can easily happen if you are someone who is not naturally expressive. Keeping your emotions bottled up inside is the surest way to throw your chakra out of sync. To find balance once more, you must release all the tension you are holding onto the inside and allow the energy within your body to flow freely the way that it was meant to.

An Unbalance In Your Chakra Energy

Your chakra could become unbalanced when there is too much extreme going on in your life. Being extremely stressed for example or prolonged periods in the fight or flight response. Being surrounded by toxic individuals, repressing your emotions for years, these are all extremes of negative behavior that could hinder our chakra's natural flow. Your chakras can be thrown off balance if you experience blocks in the following aspects of your life:

• Physical Blocks - Quite literally, your chakras are restricted in their flow when your body is not physically healthy. Fatty deposits, blocked arteries, cysts, tumors or excess toxins in your body can disrupt the flow of your chakras. Poor dietary choices, sedentary lifestyles, excessive alcohol consumption, lack of sleep and exercise, chronic stress, tiredness, being overworked and overexerting yourself will make it hard to maintain a balanced chakra flow because your physical activities are not balanced.

• Spiritual Blocks - The spiritual side of life is something that must be honored and respected. Chakras are all about embracing your spirituality as a part of who you are and refusing to acknowledge that this part of you exists blocks your access to your higher chakras.

• Emotional Blocks - Bottling up your emotions, mental illnesses including anxiety, addiction and depression, and past emotional trauma contribute to the reasons why your chakras become blocked. This happens when emotions are not adequately dealt with. Trying to deny, ignore or dismiss your feelings like they do not exist will leave you with unresolved issues because they never truly go away. When these "emotional toxins" continue to linger, it is only a matter of time before your chakras start to feel the effects.

• Karmic Blocks - In Sanskrit, the action is the literal translation of the word karma. The actions that you partake in are either good, bad, harmful, nourishing or neutral. Good karmic action might be donating your money to charity or helping the poor. Bad karmic action could be intentional deception. A neutral karmic action could be acts that have no direct impact on you or anyone else, such as tidying up your desk or making your bed in the morning. Adages like "you reap what you sow", "don't do unto others what you don't want to be done unto yourself", or "what goes around comes around", are expressions which perfectly sum up the essence of what karma is. Whether you believe in karma or not, every action you take has consequences, and too much negative action will cause your chakras to pay the price.

Areas Where Chakra Blocks Occur

The Benefits Of Healing And Balancing Your Chakras

Chakras are your pillars of vitality and energy. Without them, getting anything done would be difficult when you lack the energy to do so. That is why those who are sick often find it even getting out of bed to be a monumental effort because their chakras are so severely blocked and outbalance they do not have the energy for anything else except to lie down until they feel better. Which brings us to the benefits of investing your time and energy into healing your chakras. Healing your chakras is going to benefit your:

• Health and Wellbeing (Physically) - Chakras directly impact the way that you feel overall. When nothing is blocked in your body, there's no reason not to have a spring in your step when everything is working perfectly, as it should.

• Your Inner Self - Your chakras are a part of who you are. Healing your chakras forces you to stop, slow down and take a good look at who you are. Taking the time to pay attention to each chakra, how it affects you is an exercise is getting to know the inner part of yourself that very often goes unnoticed. A deeper connection to who you are helps you realize what your true purpose in life may be, and why holding onto negative emotions like anger, jealousy, greed and more are only going to weigh you down. When you get to know who you are inside and out, that's when you start to tap into your full potential. That is what your zest and enthusiasm for life are renewed as your chakra energy grows stronger each day.

• Spirituality's Fitness - Everyone talks about how important it is to exercise and take care of our bodies physically. But what are you doing to take care of your body spiritually? Being spiritually fit is just as important as your physical fitness. When your spirit is weakened, it is harder to regulate your emotions and remain strong, steady and calm even when everything seems to be falling apart around you. With the multitude of stressors we deal with daily, spiritual strength for inner peace is more important than ever. Since your chakras are the bridge between your physical and spiritual side, you need to balance them out so both sides are reaping the rewards that come with a healthy, balanced body.

• Your Strengths - Negative experiences in the past

are responsible for a lot of the chakra blocks you experience today. It is hard to let go of the past at times, and not see those disappointing moments as weaknesses or failure. But clinging to those emotions only hinders your ability to heal emotionally and spiritually, the way that your chakras need. Balancing your chakras is an exercise in self-healing, and it is through this process that you learn to turn your strengths into weaknesses. Balanced chakras bring with it mental clarity and greater focus, and the ability to shift your mindset away from the negative once you see how it has been holding you back all this time.

Benefits of Healing & Balancing Your Chakras

Restoring Balance to Your Chakras

To begin restoring balance to your chakras, start by spending a few quiet moments alone and concentrate deeply on connecting with your body. As you start to connect and be mindfully aware of how you are feeling, ask yourself where in your body right now do you feel the most "active"? It could be an area (or several areas) where you are feeling particularly tense. Or it could be an area where the physical symptoms are manifesting the strongest (headaches, migraine, tension, stiff neck, and shoulders, etc). Focusing on the "activated" area heightens awareness about which of your seven chakras need some balance restored.

Connecting to your body and all that you are feeling is the very first step. Once you have done that and identified the chakras you think maybe blocked, use the following methods to begin slowly unblocking your energy one at a time:

Chakra Balancing Method #1: Breath Deeply

Close your eyes and focus on taking deep, measured breaths. Breath is as deep as you can, right from the diaphragm. Focus on feeling the airflow through your body as you inhale and exhale in a controlled, steady manner. Now, as you exhale, imagine the tension leaving your body with each breath of air that escapes. Allow your body to feel physically lighter as you continue, and visualize yourself letting go of everything that is weighing you down.

Try this simple energizing breathing exercise. This is a great technique to use whenever you are feeling stressed and anytime that you feel your chakras could use a little help.

• Step 1 - Begin by sitting in a comfortable position on the floor with your legs crossed, keeping your back straight and your palms pressed together at the heart center.

• Step 2 - Inhale by breathing into 4 breaths, completely filling the lungs on the 4th breath. Exhale and release again following the same 4 sequences, thoroughly emptying the lungs at the 4th exhale.

• Step 3 - Pull in your navel to the spine on both the inhale and exhale, taking about 7 seconds for each repetition. Do this for at least two to three minutes.

• Step 4 - Combine the breathing by chanting Sa-Ta-Na-Ma on both the exhale and inhale. You may repeat this chant either verbally or in your mind.

• Step 5 - Complete the exercise by once again, inhaling deeply and pressing your palms together for 10 to 15 seconds.

Chakra Balancing Method #2: Neutralizing the Soul

Certain chants can bring balance and restore the positive energy to your chakras by neutralizing your soul, reinforcing the mental, emotional and spiritual healing from within. As you close your eyes and connect to your mind, body, and soul, chant Sat Nam as you do to neutralize any tension you might have in your mind and body. The Sat Nam is a basic meditational chant to help you relax and find inner peace.

• Step 1 - Sit in a pleasant pose with your legs laced. Keep your back straight and your spine elongated.

• Step 2 - Bring your palm to the heart center, palms in front of the chest, left a hand over right. Place your left thumb in the center of the right palm, and then gently rest your hands against the chest.

• Step 3 - Keep your arms relaxed, there should be no tension or strain on any of your muscles. Inhale deeply and then exhale with a long and loud Saaaatttttt- naaaam. Allow yourself to relax and release together with the "AAAAAAA" sounds in your chant.

• Step 4 - Repeat this 3 times and keep your breath

slow and controlled for at least two minutes. At the conclusion of the meditation, deeply inhale, holding your breath for as long as you can.

Once you are done, sit quietly or lie down to relax.

Chakra Balancing Method #3: Mantras to Help Your Chakras

Use the following mantras for each corresponding chakra to unblock the ones that need it most. Remain seated in your comfortable cross-legged position and once your body is visibly relaxed after several deep breathing sessions chant the following mantras depending on which chakra needs your attention:

- Root Chakra Chant - Laa-hmmmm

- Sacral Chakra Chant - Vaa-hmmmm

- Solar Plexus Chakra Chant - Raa-hmmmm

- Heart Chakra Chant - Yaa-hmmmm

- Throat Chakra Chant - Haa-hmmmm

- Third Eye Chakra Chant - Ohm-mmmm

For the seventh chakra (Crown Chakra) sit in quiet, contemplative silence. Follow the same chanting methods like the Sat Nam, inhaling and exhaling on the chants as you elongate the "HMMMMMM" sounds for as long as possible.

Chakra Balancing Method #4: Affirmations

Your chakra affirmations can be anything you want, as long as the words or phrases you choose to you empower and infuse you with positivity. The affirmations can be recited anytime that you feel your chakras may be experiencing a blockage. You can choose to repeat these affirmations in front of a mirror, looking yourself in the eye as you say them out loud convincingly. Or, if you prefer, repeat these affirmations while you continue to remain seated in your cross-legged, meditative position. Here are some examples you could use as a guideline as to what your affirmations should be. You could even use them as part of your own affirmation practice if you want:

• As I exhale, I can feel my_____chakra (state the name of the chakra like root, heart or throat, etc.) unblocking. With each deep breath, I open myself to receiving positivity and I let go of all that weighs me down.

• My chakras are healing every day. I am mindfully focusing

on positivity to restore balance and harmony.

• My voice is becoming stronger, clearer and firmer as my throat chakra unblocks itself each day.

• I am one with my intuition and my vision as I connect with my third eye chakra.

• I am letting go of my pain and expectations so my

heart chakra can open once more.

Chakra Balancing Method #5: Dietary Changes

Despite is the heavily spiritual focus, chakra blocks can happen when your physical body is not adequately cared for. Sometimes, the cause for our blocks may not stem from within at all. The problem could be what we are doing externally to our bodies, and a simple dietary change could be the answer. Once you have identified which of your seven chakras need balance, try including the following foods into your regular diet:

• Root Chakra - Consume more tomatoes, strawberries, and raspberries.

• Sacral Chakra - Oranges, bell peppers, and parsley in as many meals as possible.

• Solar Plexus Chakra - Bananas, lemons and chamomile tea are great for restoring balance to the solar plexus.

• Heart Chakra - This chakra could benefit from

more greens in your diet, which means consuming more green veggies. Green apples are a good choice of fruit too.

•   Throat Chakra - Blueberries and black currants will help this chakra the most.

•   Third Eye Chakra - Vegetables again, but this time with a focus on indigo veggies instead.

•   Crown Chakra - Red grapes, thyme, and eggplant will restore balance if you are struggling with this chakra.

Chakra Balancing Method #6: Healing Through Reiki

You will come across the term reiki healing several times as you continuously learn about chakras. If you have not already heard, reiki healing is a practice where the reiki master or healer attempts to facilitate the transfer of positive energy by placing their hands on the different parts of the body. The aim of the practice is to remove negative energy by transferring it out of your body. To use this to aid in your chakra healing, you will need to either hold your palm above the area your chakra is located, or place your palm flat on your skin. This might be difficult to do by yourself in some areas, so you might need the help of a reiki healer with the hard to reach areas.

Reiki is a Japanese practice which first emerged somewhere in the late 1800s. Practitioners believe that the healing powers of this practice come from the universal transfer of power, which the practitioner would transfer to their patient. Reiki advocates believe that this practice works by manipulating the energy fields that surround our body. It's healing benefits have caused Reiki's popularity to soar over the years, and in a 2007 survey taken in the United States, approximately 1.2 million American adults participate in some form of Reiki therapy or similar at least once in the past year. A 2014 report in The Washington Post revealed that more than 60 hospitals supposedly offered Reiki healing as part of its services for patients who wanted it.

Ideally, this should be done in a quiet and peaceful setting, but if you need on-the-go healing, Reiki can be done anywhere for a quick fix. Once you have identified the blocked chakra area, it is time to focus. Concentrate on the healing process taking place over the chakra area. Place your hands over or on the specific area for approximately 2 to 5 minutes at a time. If you are attempting to do this on yourself, your hands should experience a warm, tingling sensation as you hold it over your body. Maintain the position until you feel the energy has stopped transitioning out of your body, which is usually when your hands have stopped feeling warm.

Our body is a beautiful, an intricate system of energy channels that are although not promptly seen with the naked eye, are exceptionally powerful. When we clear the energy blocks from our chakra as we enable what is known as the kundalini energy to surge through our bodies, invigorating and uplifting our psyche and our physique to a new pinnacle.

Kundalini is an ancient Sanskrit term which focuses on focuses on the rising of consciousness and energy. It identifies this energy as a force that is coiled at the base of the spine since birth, and it is the force of life. In yogic science, it is this kundalini energy that triggered the development of a child in the womb. In simpler terms, kundalini's energy is a transformative power. It is a power and belief that is rooted in the process of spiritual and self-development.

When Kundalini energy runs through the body, it spreads through the spine via a central channel, known as the Sushumna Nadi, which is located along the spine. Sushumna is a channel through which the energy travels from chakra to chakra, all the way up to the crown or top of the head. The Sushumna channel is akin to our body's central nervous system. The channel functions to connect the energy flow from the first to the last chakra.

A person's Kundalini is derived from their chakras or energy centers. To understand the connection between kundalini and your chakras, picture the chakra system in the body like a single, electrical circuit, which runs lengthwise up the spine. Imagine that there is a visible light is positioned at each of these chakras. The moment Kundalini energy travels up the spinal cord, the energy passes each chakra, giving each a boost and making it light up.

Chapter 2. Pairs

The splenic and the larynx work together and belong to creativity. The Solar Plexus and the Third Eye are related to vision and intelligence. The cardiac and coronary will express dimensions. Each chakra will express the same function at a lower frequency. Diseases are also related to the inability to absorb, transmute or integrate energy frequencies. When energy enters a chakra and is blocked, it will seek to express itself through a psychological dissociation. Instead, when energy is already inside a chakra but it is expressed negatively, it manifests itself eventually through physical problems.

Chromotherapy And The Chakras

One of the ways to restore our energy centers or chakras is through chromotherapy. With lights of different colors directed on each of them we achieve an external harmonization. It is clear at this point that it depends on us how we maintain our chakras. Whatever method we use, we will always notice an immediate improvement in all areas (physical, emotional and mental) but that well-being will last as long as we take care of ourselves.

An effective method of leveling chakras is with a strobe light. This light has the particularity of being able to blink at different speeds, with which, using different filters and colors, each chakra will increase its speed gradually. With this increase, it will be cleaning and restoring its own energy. When I say cleaning I mean that our moods, negative thoughts or self- demands, are getting worse and darkening their original color. Here is a list of the chakras and their respective etheric colors:

Coronary Chakra: Violet Third Eye Chakra: white Laryngeal chakra: turquoise Heart Chakra: green

Solar Plexus Chakra: Orange Splenic Chakra: Yellow Basic Chakra: Red

We will take an example to discuss in detail Fifth Chakra: Vishuddha

Color: Sky Blue

Crystals: Celestina, Aquamarine Location: Throat

Our fifth Chakra takes care of our creativity in its widest expression. When we talk about creativity, we are not only talking about art, because it is true that not everyone in this world is destined to be an artist even if he has an excellent balance in this Chakra.

Creativity develops, in any area in which we work, if you are an entrepreneur, you will have a "bombing" of ideas that will lead your company to success, if you are a housewife you will have enough "spark" to make the routine something special (serving food is not the same as decorating the table with flowers and details to make unique and comfortable, that moment). Anyway, any activity must be performed with creativity.

As the throat is the point where our fifth Chakra is located, it will also regulate our voice, but not only the physical voice, but our inner voice, which struggles to express its ideas without fear of others, without fear of being accepted, without fear that the people around us do not share our ideals It is speaking with the truth, our truth.

Here there is no passion or fanaticism, we only communicate our ideas and we do not worry about convincing anyone or imposing our thoughts, we simply enter an exchange of ideas for the need for expression. The philosophical and religious currents enter this point of expression and creativity, you will be attracted by knowledge, you will ask yourself questions about life, but you will not identify with any nor will you criticize others, because first of all there will be the understanding of each of them, the what of each way and far from rejecting them you will open to know them. Being within an endless plethora of questions about the mysteries of life, the "flashes of light" will come to your mind, you will begin to answer all your questions, or the answers will begin to reach you by other means (books, movies, facts in your life, etc.).

By balancing the expression and our inner voice, we also learn to control the scenic fear, the nervousness that invades us when we have to speak in public, we will know how to control it by way of using that energy to "create the best speech". It's not about drowning or hiding our energy, it's working with it and from a creative perspective.

The elevation to the fifth Chakra is a great leap of consciousness. This is the first of the upper Chakras and the combination of individual consciousness with the universal. Thought becomes innovative and individual, we are no longer concerned with labeling ourselves with a political idea, religious, or anything else, we simply choose to make decisions based on an independent perspective.

Our vision of the world is enlarged and we spread it to others so that they try the same. Any philosophical or religious trend goes beyond obedience or culture, we learn to appreciate the beauty of each one of them. We don't identify with any of them, we appreciate them. There are points of view to defend, but we share. We become the conduit of the universal mind. We are able to find the center of each ideology. We discern them and nothing is imposed on us.

Imbalance In Our Fifth Chakra

One of the points in imbalance is when we discover our need to express ourselves, but what we do to seek the acceptance and approval of others, we want to convince and impose our ideas because "they are the right ones". We begin to express the opposite of what most people say. If they say white, I say black and that is the universal truth! There is no discernment, there is an imposition. It should be stressed that the purpose of our fifth Chakra is not to impose but to express.

Another point is the fear of expressing ourselves. We can have all the ideas in mind and we can feel like bustling out, but stay inside! Stop the fear that people do not share the same opinion. This makes us stand as spectators in all the meetings in which we are and we will figure as a "ghost." If the fifth Chakra seeks freedom, there is only the prison. Once you had a great idea that you don't dare to start and soon you discover that "someone won "? That would be the result of fear of expressing oneself.

The lack of control of stage fright also illustrates an imbalance in this Chakra. When we try to mitigate this energy instead of exploiting it, so we get out of balance, the energy cannot be turned off or hidden because it is simply there! What we can do is control it and use it for our own benefit.

Maintaining The Balance

When we balance our fifth Chakra, we awaken in us a total discernment of the things; we see life with much joy and freshness. Creativity is reflected in each of your actions, and they flow continuously, they do not stop, if you are an artist, you are able to create quality and originality, if you are in love, you will fill your relationship with details that will avoid routine and custom, if you are a trader, you will have the vision to take your company to the summit.

This happens when you are sure of your own identity, when you are aware of yourself, of your own power, and there are no fears or insecurities. Your mind becomes free, open, untethered and independent, knows itself and does not feel threatened by the different opinions that are around.

At this point your social life may be different, it is sure

that you are bored with "superficial" issues, and start rejecting situations where this occurs, you will start looking for quality time, parties and everyday amusements will no longer be attractive, instead you will look for loneliness and introspection. You will no longer meet to watch the football game, you will seek to integrate with the people who question "the match of life."

The Purpose of the Soul of the Fifth Chakra

The upper Chakras are collective in nature, they connect us with the higher dimension of our species. This personal-collective mix makes you a source of creative insights. You can help many people to wake up from their sleep and instead of following preset paths, follow your own identity and your own road.

The one who looks for a free posture for the facts will make people see in you a pattern of life to follow. He will begin to question himself and this will lead them to find their own identity.

Exercises to Awaken the Fifth Chakra Exercise 1

If you are stage frightened or afraid to express your ideas consider the tradition of "the rod of talk ", which is used in

43

many groups. When you have something to say you ask for your wand to talk and everyone pays attention. You can do this through visualization, imagine that wand, every time and have something to say and be afraid to do it

Exercise 2

When your creativity is "blocked", imagine that you are creating a project and hit the wall of the blocked energy. This sometimes happens when we still have some minor Chakra in imbalance. Breathe deeply into the throat Chakra and let your creativity and energy flow.

Sixth Chakra: Aina Color: Indigo blue

Crystals: Fluorite, indigo tourmaline Location: Frown

When our sixth Chakra awakens in us, we are flooded by a great desire to live the magic of a transcendental reality. A reality that is out of the ordinary and every day, expansive and unlimited. Imagination is the vehicle of this transcendence, here mental images are mixed with an inner strength that demands to know everything, is an inspiration, and good luck.

The well-oriented imagination acts as an escape from the

usual reality, to connect with the divine and with sensations that go beyond the sensory. When we talk about leaks, we are also talking about risks, we can use our imagination as a form of expansion and transcendence, another way is to use television as a means of evasion and although it is not so harmful, it limits our field of action, since the time and energy dedicated to entertainment, it is the same time we could use to start putting together our projects.

Harmful means: vices such as drugs and alcohol.

When we wake up in our sixth Chakra, we also wake up our intuition, as a guide to follow our path by working with our imagination we can differentiate what we like and what fills us with energy and exhausts us, when we follow the paths that connect us with our nature and our identity, we can be sure that we are following our own light. When we insist on living what we don't want to live, what overwhelms and displeases us, then, we are wrong the way.

When we awaken our intuition we must do it with spiritual will, that is, will of faith, we can no longer afford to feel fear when deciding, our fears have to be reserved for signs of real danger, not as a system of life. Here what counts is our faith, faith in what we want, and the faith that we are in our true path.

In order to recognize what our intuition dictates, you just have to ask yourself if what you are doing or what you are going to decide connects you to your energy flow, if there is improvement or deterioration, if it is healthy or unhealthy.

Our sixth Chakra helps us create a collective consciousness, we begin to act as spectators or witnesses of what happens to us and of ideology in general, there are no longer judgments or criticisms, things stop being good or bad, we simply see them as a diversity of ways of being and of thinking.

The Imbalance in the Sixth Chakra

Fear is one of the main indicators of our sixth unbalanced Chakra. Living based on fear transforms our reality by putting thoughts, illusions, and sensations that do not exist, it only causes that fearing to make any decision or path, we paralyze and don't act in a positive way or even worse, we don't act!

Drug and alcohol dependence distort our reality, leading us to unreal and dangerous worlds, creating false and monstrous illusions that can end any life and intention of transcendence. Guilt is also part of the imbalance, this is sometimes imposed on us by the old religious dogmas which limited our actions and our thoughts by putting man as a being without courage in the eyes of God. This is where human suffering derives from accepting pain as self-punishment for being "sinners".

Another manifestation of imbalance is when we lose our site and instead of integrating as a whole within the Earth or the Universe, we "self-situate ourselves" as superior beings, think that because we meditate, practice yoga or pray we are better than those who do not lose reality. There is also the other extreme, believing that we will earn heaven by accepting suffering and the pain of "being good" is also the product of a separation. We are part of a whole and there is no better or worse, we all follow the path of evolution by different routes.

One way to become aware when there is an imbalance and we do not want to see it if there is suffering, discomfort or pain in any aspect of our life. The pain and suffering, either physical or spiritual, are indicative that something is wrong, something is failing in our life, we are on the wrong way and we have to learn something. If we accelerate learning, we accelerate the evolution.

The connection with the natural flow of life energy is a perfect balance. It is at this point that it seems that you are in the right place at the right time. You start connecting with the magic of life and miracles are part of you. The opportunities and the events come without looking for them. In the eyes of others, you can be a "star" person, a visionary or prophet and you only consider yourself an observer of life.

You have learned to live in the midst of peace and tranquility, far from conflict, in a state of continued happiness. You are in the middle of a world full of violence and evil, but nobody touches you. You attract your own nature.

There will be times when you feel confused and have "lost the ground" in these cases look for the voice of your subconscious to meet your path and the light. The practice of meditation and yoga are some of the options, you can also look for books that give you new incentives for your life, books that contribute to your knowledge, concepts of philosophy and a new era of life, authors of Masters and Spiritual Guides are some examples. There are other ways to "get the voice out" of our subconscious, divinatory arts like tarot or runes can also guide you.

As a complement to maintain the sixth Chakra, you can do this visualization exercise: Unification of Being.

The Purpose Of The Sixth Chakra Soul

By learning to see and live a reality beyond the everyday, expansive and transcendental, you seek help for others by showing them this other life scheme. People may be surprised at the ease with which you are given things, and the power of vision you have, this will make it approach you, learn from your wisdom and you will like to open new paths in your life.

Seventh chakra: Sahasrara Color: Violet

Crystals: Clear Quartz Location: La Coronilla

The seventh Chakra, located in the crown, is the total conjunction of energy, it is the union of our personal experiences with the collective. It is the expression of divinity. When we have activated this Chakra, everything divine is shown to us in every moment of our life, here we no longer settle for knowing about God, at this stage, but we want to integrate into him, live it. Here we see through the eyes of divinity, we no longer see people as before. We learn to see his soul. Every event we see through the eyes of spirituality, we are basically living the miracle every day.

At this stage, we start living weird things because our conscience is totally different, the spiritual guides, delivered to the spirit, belong to this group. Maintaining this awareness of divinity is not easy since any sign of fear will return us to our lower Chakras. We cannot activate this seventh Chakra if the lower ones have some imbalance. This Chakra is the most complex, the most difficult, it is the one that covers everything, for that demands the perfect balance of the other Chakras. Here is the total purpose of our soul.

When we accept to live through our seventh Chakra, we are accepting the responsibility that this knowledge gives us, the decision of whether we accept or reject this responsibility is what will stay at that level. If we reject it we will be returned to the lower Chakras, if we accept it, the inextinguishable energy of the divine will be with us, to carry out the realization of the purpose of our soul.

When you live through the spiritual, we tend to live alone contemplating nature and our spirit, but the people around us will feel brought by our energy and want to be with us for the peace we inspire, for learning, and for representing the example and the guide.

Being at this level we can do very well since we can give people what they ask us to, through divine energy. This occurs naturally because there will also be a taste in you to help others, and we will be provided with a special divine connection, and their energy, that is why it is important that we maintain the connection with the divine, and balance because when we get out of balance, people will continue asking us for help, and in that case, we will continue giving it, but not through the divine energy but through our own energy which will end up being exhausting ourselves.

The imbalance in the seventh chakra

Being at this level, an imbalance is quite dangerous.

Being living entirely spiritual experiences, we can stop having a relationship with everything mundane, making us no longer have a relationship with people or with regard to the material world, considering both points of inferior importance.

Fears represent another danger since they will manifest as threatening entities. At any other stage of our life, it would not be so important since fear does not take form, but in this case we will be seeing and perceiving beings that can alter our psychic tranquility, asking us to take, in extreme cases, to a hospital for the mentally ill.

Another imbalance is the "whim of asking," when we integrate into the knowledge of the new era, or metaphysical teachings, these tell us that making a list of what we need and asking for it as if it were already part of our reality. This may make everything materialize, but at the same time, this list is being written by our ego, and we tend to think that our ego knows more than God himself. In this case, it is best to surrender to God, the one who knows the most about us and what we need, even more than ourselves.

Maintaining The Balance

When we are already at this level, we live within a divine consciousness and we have consciousness of eternity, that is, we know the meaning of it and we know that the law causes and effects. It is true, therefore we care about being aligned with the divine and doing things well.

It is important to clarify that the opening of this Chakra is not given on its own, it is the Supreme Being who "authorizes" the opening and it gives itself, brief flashes of divine awareness are what we begin to live. Delivery to divine is an act of faith and eliminates any trace of suffering, here there is no sacrifice because we know that our actions are for the good of all, even of ourselves. Here, we must include the fact of giving ourselves to the divine with a faith that does not allow us to doubt the inner voice that dictates our desires or vocation is the right one and far from someone getting damaged is a benefit for everyone and everything including the flow of material prosperity. Although here, we are talking about money and the material things that this entails, there is no attachment to it, we can enjoy the benefits of having a comfortable economic position, but there is no dependence and attachment to it.

Time and patience become our best allies since we no longer have the same concept of time. At this point, we know that there is no time, that we have a lifetime to carry out our projects and that a few minutes here or in eternity make no difference. This brings out our patience because there is no longer any desperation to fulfill our wishes. We simply enjoy the freedom of action that this allows us.

Chapter 3. The Root Chakra

One of the very first major chakras found within the body is the root chakra.

This chakra is also known as Muladhara, 'Mula' signifying root and 'Dhara' meaning support or base.

Together, they make up the importance behind the root chakra which is to provide balance or support.

The root chakra is responsible for a sense of emotional safety and security when it comes to ones day to day activities.

It is all about survival and grounding oneself.

The root chakra makes sure that you feel at ease when it comes to things such as love, goals, money, and security.

This chakra represents the color red that is associated with love, strength, security, energy, desire, and power.

It can be found in the lower abdomen, where the tailbone of the spine is located.

It makes you feel alive and brings awareness that you are being on this planet living your own life with nothing controlling you.

An imbalanced root chakra can not only damage the mind but the body too.

Physically, this chakra is associated with problems and diseases inside the spine, nerve system, the lower abdomen, kidney, hemorrhoids, and sleep disorders.

One may also suffer from pain, bladder issues, digestion problems, ovarian cysts, and lower back pains.

When emotionally imbalanced, one will live their life worrying about almost anything every single day.

Negative feelings like anxiety, insecurity, impatience,

and stress will resurface causing other mental illnesses such as depression.

Since the flow of energy is blocked, that energy will not properly reach the legs causing one to always feel exhausted after walking.

When your root chakra is balanced, you will live a life free of worries, situations that refer to your survival requirements won't stress you, and you will be able to react to different circumstances with a calm mindset.

The trust is found within yourself, you believe that you can get through any obstacles without it interfering with your mental health.

Physically, when this chakra is balanced, the body is healthy and energized.

There are no difficulties relating to the lower abdomen.

Emotionally, this chakra deals with anxiety and stress so when it is in balance, those feelings simply fade away.

With a positive mindset, no negative thoughts, and the root chakra can help achieve a mental balance as well as balancing other chakras such as the sacral and the heart by getting rid of negative emotions.

The reaction to obstacles and problems will improve without a panic state of mind state.

Chakras can also be either overactive or underactive, meaning that its either too open which can affect one not in a good way or it's not open enough.

When the root chakra is overactive, the root chakra can also create 'threats' inside your mind, making you believe in it when in reality there is nothing that can harm you.

These threats will cause paranoia, leading to jittery and anxious.

You will also find yourself getting aggressive, annoyed, and angry all the time.

The slightest provocation will tick you off. This type of person always tries to control others for their greedy deeds.

They often resist higher authority, change, and are known to obsess over feeling secure.

When the root chakra is underactive, then it means that one has taken care of the survival needs but not in a healthy manner.

It is not 'open enough' meaning that one still feels disconnected or insecure when it comes to the outside world.

They easily feel nervous, anxious, afraid, and find it hard to finish daily tasks on time.

In order to balance this chakra, one must also consider changing daily habits to help assist in the opening of this chakra.

A change in diet can strongly influence the mind, body, and root chakra.

A healthy and well-balanced diet can help achieve mental clarity, provide health for the body, and even help balance the root chakra.

Try to consume healthy foods and drink a lot of water, it is not only beneficial for the root chakra but can even help to prevent any unwanted diseases within the body.

Especially eating red foods such as tomatoes, strawberries, red peppers, and many others can help assist in the opening of the root chakra.

Exercising like jogging, hiking, or yoga can help the body's health and the root chakra.

An open root chakra will make you feel grounded and more confident in yourself.

Meditation is known to be one of the best ways to awaken and open the root chakra, but before beginning with this meditation, one should ground themselves first.

Grounding can help the person connect to the earth more which is what this chakra is all about.

A perfect way to ground oneself is by walking barefooted in nature, the beach, or the forest.

Walking barefooted at home can also help.

Another popular way is to use the power of visualization by imagining yourself as an energy tree by extending your arms upwards.

Visualize roots below you, sinking deeper into the ground, and the branches above you, extending from your hands.

This is a brief visualization exercise and it can help ground you.

It shouldn't take longer than two to three minutes, it can also help calm the mind before you get into the meditation state.

Meditation For The Root Chakra

Begin by getting comfortable in the meditation sacred place of your choosing.

This time, instead of laying down, you will be sitting with

your legs crossed.

Make sure that your spine and shoulders are straight and tall which will be more effective when healing the lower abdomen and the root chakra.

Allow for your hands to rest on your knees, with the palms facing up.

Form your hands into the mudra hand position by forming a circle using your thumb and your index finger, it can also be interpreted as an okay hand gesture.

Begin to breathe deeply, inhale and hold the breath for three seconds before exhaling it and dragging it out for another three seconds.

Make sure that when you are breathing in and out that you use your chest, rather than breathing in through your stomach.

When you are using the chest, the spine extends and moves along with the breathing, this will enable the relaxation of the body even when you are sitting up.

Take a few minutes to simply relax your muscles and the body as you breathe in.

Bring your attention to your breathing as you inhale and exhale to help calm the mind.

Try your best to not listen to your thoughts and the mental clutter that is going on inside your head.

Instead, bring your focus to yourself as a being in this big universe.

Don't think about anything else that you have to do or things that might be bothering, instead focus on breathing through your chest, making the lungs expand as you breathe in.

Take some time to bring your attention to different parts of your body, relaxing them in the process.

Think of your face muscles, relaxing as they tingle with your life force energy that you always have within you.

Then bring your attention to your arms, legs, belly, and

other parts of your body that you might feel some tension in.

Allow yourself to feel the different tingling sensations all throughout as you let your body go numb and relax.

Gradually bring your attention back to your breathing, notice how your chest rises and falls every time you inhale or exhale.

Allow your eyes to lightly close, as if you are slowly falling into a deep slumber.

Create a breathing pattern, it is often related to how you would breathe normally.

Slow down your breathing by holding it in and extending it one or two seconds longer when you breathe out.

When you take a deep breath in, notice how the air travels down into your lower belly and then back up through your nose as you exhale.

Deeply breathe in and out a few times before bringing your awareness to the location of the root chakra, the base of your spine where your tailbone is.

Focus on your breathing and don't let your mind slip away as you allow for your energy to awaken.

Begin to resurface the energy within you by visualizing your body glowing white, the white that represents your pure energy that is deeply in connection with your soul.

The white begins to surround your body, circulating and connecting with your aura.

Rest in that sensation for another minute or two before concentrating and directing that energy into the palms of your hands.

Center the flow of energy into your palms, by imagining it all flowing to your hands as it travels from different parts of your body, like arms and legs.

Let yourself feel any tingling sensations or warmth.

Allow it to rest there, forming a white ball of light in each of your hands.

Lift your hands up and place them down on your lower abdomen.

Imagine the light and energy that you have gathered begin to change color, from a pure white into a red while allowing it to enter through the lower abdomen and into the root chakra.

Red is associated with the root chakra and using this color can help not only open the chakra but also direct the energy into that specific area.

Visualize that red light enters your chakra point and the healing energy that is being sent with it.

Inhale and contract the muscles between the pubic bone and the tailbone as the light enters, engaging the Mula Bandha that can help to further activate your energy and release the root chakra energy.

You are drawing the perineum towards the root chakra.

Bring your attention to how the Mula Bandha feels as you breathe flows in and your muscles contract.

Hold your breath for one to two seconds before releasing the Mula Bandha and relaxing your muscles.

Repeat again by tightening and contracting the muscles once again, feel how your spine becomes taller, pulling you up while pushing your legs and feet down.

Let go after one or two seconds and let your muscles relax again.

Repeat for at least two to three minutes or however long you seem it fit.

As you release the contract, the root chakra energy increases.

Visualize the energy intercepting with that of the root chakra, connecting and expanding further.

Allow for your body to fall into a state of relaxation, you might find it even more relaxing than when you started your meditation.

Let that energy simply travel around the lower abdomen.

You might feel some tingling sensations or warmth down your spine or throughout your body, this indicates that your chakra is being opened and the body is experiencing high energies.

Let that red light circulate in the lower abdomen, cleansing out all of the negative energy within that area.

Then, continue the healing process by imagining that red light traveling down your crossed legs as you are sitting up, connecting with the muscles and relaxing any tensions that you might have.

Allow for it to travel back up into the lower abdomen, resting there and releasing all the tensions before allowing it to travel back down again.

This time, as it makes its way all the way down to the

souls of your feet, imagine that energy leaving your body through the bottom of where you are located.

If you are sitting on a bed, or on the floor, imagine that energy reaching out into the ground, as if you are a tree and the red energy is your roots.

Let it rest in that sensation, grounding you and connecting with the energy from the earth's element.

Feel the earth's energy connect with your own, intercepting and becoming one before allowing your red root energies to return back to your through the souls of your feet.

Let that magnified energy to travel back up to your lower abdomen, letting it rest there as you take notice of any tensions within your lower abdomen or your legs.

If you feel any tensions or tingling, then allow for that energy to go there.

Let the energy rest in that area while you imagine healing and banishment of any tensions or negativity.

If there are any other tensions within the root chakra area, then allow for the energy to travel there.

The glow is expanding, making you feel warm and relaxed.

Feel the root chakra, feel any sensations, warmth, or tingling in the tailbone area.

Gently rest in the sensations for a few minutes as you breathe in deeply.

Once you feel relaxed and good about your healing, return the energy to the lower abdomen.

Bring your attention back to your breathing as you bring your awareness back into your body.

Take a minute to simply breathe and stay present at this moment.

Allow for your eyes to slowly open, adjusting them to the light and the physical world around you.

Consider laying down somewhere or continue sitting up if you wish, but take some time to reflect and think back to your meditation before proceeding with your day.

When you are done, thank the universe for guiding you and for helping you heal yourself.

Take some time to relax after the healing process, don't push yourself to do anything.

Stay at home, relax, take a hot bath, and let your body heal itself while the energy within your body is still present.

Chapter 4. A Positive Improvement

Most of us are concerned with only what we can see in front of us. Seeing is believing, as the saying goes, and many of us are so fixated on that mindset that we forget there is a whole other spiritual world out there we are completely overlooking. The spiritual side you are not paying attention to right now is affecting your overall state of being, even if you may not be paying attention to it. That constant body aches you feel or the throbbing headache that just will not go away could have more to do with your spiritual imbalance than you think. Maybe you are "not feeling well" because your chakras have not been tended to in a while.

Chakras And Positive Energy

You can never say you completely accept and embrace who you are if you are neglecting your emotional and spiritual side. These are just as important as our physical beings. Just because you cannot see them, it does not mean they do not need to be taken care of. You may not be able to physically see the colors of your chakra glowing in front of your eyes each time you look at yourself in the mirror, but they are there, and they are affecting the way that you feel.

The worse you feel the duller the colors become. Chakras work in the same context. When you are feeling poorly, the colors that represent your chakra centers may not be glowing as bright as they should be, and that is going to affect the flow of positive energy through your body. When you are struggling to maintain a positive, optimistic attitude, your chakra energy needs restoration.

Have you ever wondered how some people are just capable of handling all the challenges that life throws their way while still maintaining an upbeat and positive attitude? Maybe it has less to do with them being "born that way" or being "just lucky I guess" and more about the fact that their chakras are helping them generate those positive vibrations. Where a weaker person would probably be tempted to give up in the face of difficulty, a person with strong and positive chakra energy will keep moving forward until they have overcome the challenge that they are faced with.

Life can be challenging enough as it is, but when staying

positive becomes a struggle, it can seem much harder. Depression, anxiety and chronic worry are just some of the many illnesses that manifest within us when we lack positive energy in our lives, and you must maintain a balance in your chakras if you want to keep this from happening. How do you feel after a good meditation or yoga session? Much better, right? That is because the calm, breathing exercises helped to soothe and relax you again. Yoga and meditation restore your sense of inner balance once more. Maintaining good chakra energy flow will reap those same benefits. You know you need exercise to maintain good physical health. Now, you need to exercise that same care towards your spiritual side.

What Positive Chakra Energy Can Do For You

There's so much to be gained if only we invested the time and effort needed to take care of our chakras and keep them balanced. When there is a good flow of positive energy circulating every fiber of your being, this is what happens:

- You're less stressed
- Your sleep improves

- It becomes easier to cultivate positive habits

- Health and happiness are easier to attain

- You're more attuned to the world around you

- You're better connected with yourself and the people

around you

- You enjoy a better quality of life

- You've got a basis for healing physically, spiritually and mentally

- You feel grounded

- You experience increased feelings of vitality and joy

- Improve mental clarity

Can I Strengthen My Positive Chakra Energy?

Absolutely. If you can shift your state of mind from being negative to positive, you are able to strengthen, build and improve on your chakra energy until it is as the positive state that you want it to be. Having strong and centered chakras can truly be a life-changing and magical experience. It is what those who seem to radiate with positive energy do. They have an uncanny ability to attract all the good things life has to offer and use that ability to draw in all the blessings from the universe – because they have strong, positive chakra energy.

The spiritual world is all interconnected with one another – thinking positive, feeling positive, having strong and positive energy - all of it is connected to each other. It draws on universal energy, and it shows us that even what we cannot see without a trained eye can affect our lives in such a tremendous way. Maintaining positive chakra energy can leave a vast improvement in your life, and bring with it a multitude of benefits you never even would have thought possible.

It is no accident that there is the expression we have heard often enough – that some people have a good "aura" or "presence" about them. You have definitely heard of it before, at least at some point in your life. You might even know of such people, or at least met them once or twice before. The people who can walk into any room and exude nothing but confidence, charm, enthusiasm and positive. They turn heads, grab attention everywhere they go, and the rest of us are inexplicably drawn to them and we have no idea why. You have probably even thought to yourself

"There's something about them", but you cannot quite figure out what it is. That' their chakra at work. You cannot see it of course, but evidently, it is working well.

To strengthen your chakra's positive energy, there is only one thing you need to do first. Keep as far away as you can from negativity. At all times. The minute you feel your thoughts drifting towards the negative, immediately make a conscious effort to put a stop to it and pull them back towards more thoughts that are positive. Focusing on the negative, being worried and stressed out will do nothing except anchor your energy in a negative cycle, and leave you feeling miserable. So, watch your thought process throughout the day. Think about anything that brings you joy several times a day until it becomes a habit. As your emotional state of improving, so too does the energy that surrounds you.

Other Measures You Can Take To Keep Your Positive Energy Going Strong Include:

• Caring for Your Physical State - Your chakras are a part of you. This means every single part, including the physical aspect, even though your chakras are located within. Our physical bodies need to be well cared for too if you hope to strengthen your chakra energy flow in the long run.

Strengthening your chakras physically is probably one of the easier aspects to tackle, as this can easily be done by getting in enough exercise and looking after your body. Something as simple as brisk walking daily and getting in some fresh air can do wonders for your physical state of being. When you are exercising, focus on the exercise alone and forget all the extra baggage and problems that are weighing you down. Focus all your energy on the exercises you are working on. Remember to steer your thoughts away from its negative cycle as much as you can, although admittedly, this could require some effort before it starts to get easier.

- Don't Neglect Your Nutrition - The last thing we would associate maintaining positive energy with us good nutrition. But apart from exercising, you must look after your physical state of being by getting in the right amount of nutrition so your body is not deprived of anything. When we think of physical care, nutrition is rarely at the forefront of our thoughts. But what we put into our bodies is going to affect your system too, and with it, the strength of your chakras. Healthier food choices, lots of fruits and vegetables, less sugar, fast food, and highly processed food would be a good start. Get enough sleep and once a week immerses yourself in an activity that induces pure relaxation, like a round of yoga or perhaps booking yourself a massage appointment. Our bodies need to recharge after a long, stressful and busy week, and when you look after yourself on the outside, your insides start to gradually feel better too.

• Maintaining A Positive Mindset - If there is one thing your chakras are a clear reflection of more than anything else, it is your emotional state. Feelings of stress, anxiety, depression, misery or suffering from some form of emotional pain are all factors which will inevitably contribute to weakening your chakra energy if you let them go on for a long time. It may be almost impossible to feel happy 100% of the time, 24-hours a day. But what you can do is to train yourself to be truly happy and develop a better mindset and outlook on life, no matter you may be faced with. The first step begins by letting go of all the emotional baggage you may have been carrying around with you, and tell yourself that you are starting anew. At least emotionally you are.

• Do Things That Make You Feel Happy - It's as simple as that. When you do the things that make you happy, it's harder to dwell on being negative. The happier you are, the stronger your positive energy becomes, because it's feeding off that state of happiness you're in. Think of happiness as the food or fuel that your energy needs. If a walk in the park on a sunny day does the trick, go for it. If binge- watching your favorite shows for an hour or two gives your endorphins a quick boost, go on and treat yourself a little. Curling up with a good book and a delicious cup of coffee does the trick for you? Do it. Life is too short to stay miserable for long. Do what makes you happy.

• Surround Yourself with Positive People - Feed off the positive energy that radiates from those with strong chakra to fuel your own. Being around people who radiate positivity and make you laugh is another great way to boost your emotional levels. Make it a point to be around people you love or people who make you feel good a couple of times a week. We tend to get so busy and wrapped up in our daily lives that are easy to forget that we need to take some time to breathe, relax and focus on something other than our hectic routines. When you surround yourself with love, it's easy to remind yourself that you've got a lot to be grateful for after all.

How to Keep Your Positive Energy Flowing

Protecting Your Chakras With Visualization

Emotions. They can be both a blessing and a curse, our

strength and our weakness at the same time. Protecting your chakras starts with becoming aware of the energy that surrounds you. Although we cannot run away from negativity completely, what we can do is try our best to keep it out of our lives whenever possible. You need to be able to develop a sort of shield around yourself and your aura and use this shield to repel any negativity that you see heading in your direction.

Protecting your chakras is going to involve you tapping into your visualization powers. Imagine a force field that you have drawn around yourself and your chakras, and practice drawing this shield in place whenever something negative threatens to break through its boundaries. Over time and with practice, you will soon learn how to automatically shift your thoughts and energy towards more positive elements and this, in turn, will slowly strengthen and build your chakras' positive energy over time until it starts to grow stronger, and stronger with each positive experience you undergo that enhances your life.

Protect your chakras by staying on your guard whenever you feel that you are about to cross paths with someone or something that could potentially pollute you with negativity. Whenever you feel a change in your energy, it is time to change your direction and head somewhere else because the negativity has time to really make an impact on you. A regular chakra cleansing will help in strengthening and protecting your chakra over a period of time. Sometimes we may not even be aware that certain energies may be blocking us and is impacting us in a way we may not even be aware of. Signs of this happening could include mood swings, anger, emotionally erratic behavior and even not being able to feel connected to the people around you. Whenever you feel that way, perform a chakra cleansing as soon as possible to help bring some balance into your life.

Chakras And The Endocrine And Immune System

Chakras are aspects of our consciousness, just like auras are. Except that chakras are a much denser element compared to auras, but still not as dense as our physical bodies. It is, however, still dense enough to interact with our bodies, and the interaction takes place primarily through two main vehicles. The first is the endocrine system, and the second is through the nervous system. Each of our seven major chakras interacts with the major endocrine glands in our bodies, which are the:

- Pancreas

- Hypothalamus

- Adrenal

- Pineal gland

- Pituitary gland

- Thymus

- Thyroid

- Parathyroid

Additionally, our chakras also interact with a certain nerve group called the plexus. Thus, the chakras in our bodies are associated with certain body parts or functions, which are either controlled, by the plexus, or one of the endocrine glands. Our chakras (or energy centers) govern a certain area of our body. Like the root, chakra governs the base of the spine, or the throat chakra governing the area around our throat.

The endocrine system part of your body's primary control mechanism. The endocrine system is made up of several ductless, hormone-producing glands, which act as chemical messengers. These hormones get secreted into our body's bloodstream, and the endocrine system works hard every day to maintain our body's optimal health state.

Chakras are connected to the glands, which are responsible for creating these hormones, with each chakra corresponding to where the glands in our endocrine system are positioned. This means that the chakras on some level, affect the way that these glands function.

The chakra's connection to the endocrine glands however, places emphasis towards the holistic side of health. Chakras advocate that a healthy balance in our mental, emotional and physical state is deeply interrelated. This explains why certain health problems, which occur around the area where the endocrine glands are located, are connected to imbalances in the chakra. Let us look at some of the health symptoms associated with the endocrine glands and imbalances in the chakra:

The Root Chakra

This chakra is linked to the adrenal cortex gland, governing the health of our spine, hips, back, feet and legs. The root chakra focuses on feeling stable, secure and grounded, being present in the here and the now, and being connected to your body.

Common ailments experienced when this chakra is out of balance to include kidney issues, autoimmune disease, obesity, anorexia, osteoarthritis, fatigue, cancer, and spinal column issues.

The Sacral Chakra

The sacral chakra encompasses the endocrine glands located around the area our sexual organs reside, including the ovaries, bladder, testicles, lower intestine, and bowel. Which is why this chakra is connected to your sexuality and the ability to intimate and passionate in your relationships with others.

Common ailments experienced with an imbalance of this chakra include prostate cancer, kidney, and gallstones, frigidity, vaginal cancer, reproductive organ issues, pelvic disease.

The Solar Plexus Chakra

Because of its location in the body, the solar plexus chakra governs the endocrine glands associated with the upper intestines, stomach, upper spine and back area of the body. This chakra dictates the level of confidence we feel, and where our self-esteem levels reside.

Common ailments experienced with an imbalance of this chakra include hypoglycemia, digestive issues, adrenal organ ailments, and diabetes.

The Heart Chakra

This chakra is connected to the thymus gland and the body's circulatory system. Spiritually, the love chakra governs your compassion, love, and consciousness for others. Physically, this chakra controls the area where our heart and lungs are located and have a hand in our blood and circulatory system.

Common ailments experienced with an imbalance of this chakra include heart-related diseases, high blood pressure, involuntary muscle issues, thymus, blood-related ailments, and circulatory system problems.

The Throat Chakra

The throat chakra is located at the same point the body's thyroid gland and respiratory system is. This is where communication, sound, speech, thought and even communication through writing is facilitated. Because of its location, this chakra has a hand in how healthy your mouth, teeth, thyroid, jaw and tongue area are. When any one of these is compromised, communication breaks down and you struggle to express yourself as effectively as you should. Difficulties with communication might not just be because you are shy or introverted after all, as many introverts are still capable of keeping a conversation going. When they are chakras are healthy, that is.

Common ailments experienced with an imbalance of this chakra include neck issues, hyperactive thyroid problems, asthma, lung issues, and general throat related problems, which include sore throat, vocal cord, jaw, and alimentary canal ailments. These throats related conditions are one of the reasons why communication becomes a problem when the health of this chakra is compromised.

Chapter 5. Chakra Clearing: The Natural Way To Heal

Would you like your life to have more balance? Are you trapped in your circumstances? Are you looking for a safe way to heal your body and mind? Chakra balancing by meditation is the best instrument because it deals with the strength of your body.

The Chakra system consists of seven stages, which correspond to different bodies and structures of your body. The word Chakra comes from the Sanskrit word Wheel in ancient times. The chakras are in your energy body, not in your physical body.

We each have seven main chakras in our bodies, shaped like a flower or a roll, with petals or spokes detailing their composition. The energy in each Chakra can affect different circumstances in your life. Chakras contain and process energy in your body and can also block you just as power can drive you.

Sometimes we all experience a kind of chakra imbalance, but the goal of chakra curing is to get all chakras to function and spin smoothly and evenly, helping you balance your energy.

The Root Chakra· The Sacro Chakra· The Solar Plexus Chakra, · The Throat Chakra· The Brow or Third Eye Chakra, · The Crown Chakra a musical note and other items such as crystals,

Every Chakra is associated with a color, or signs. The seven main chakras are as follows. Chakra meditation is designed to heal your body's energy and balance it.

It's a beautiful way to balance your strength when you feel stressed and anxious because it revitalizes you from the inside out.

Understanding and balance this energy will help you regain strength and stability and enable you to live a happier, healthier life. Taking the time to balance your energy helps dissipate the heat of negativity and attract these things into your life and your magnetic field.

Chakras are the center of your energy or prana life force, also called chi. Visualize them as rods or circles that run up and down your backbone and refresh your strength continuously is the best way to think of your chakras. In a well-balanced and healthy person, the chakras are light and bright ad move in a clockwise direction.

That Chakra governs various aspects of your body. The root chakra at the base of your spinal cord is associated with the

color red and regulates your sense of security. The root chakra forms your basis and link with the earth. It is also equated with your instinct for survival. A blocked root chakra can cause financial uncertainty, anxiety, a lack of trust, and even basic food and shelter problems.

The 2Nd Chakra, known as the Sacral Chakra, stands in the abdomen and is linked to the orange color. It governs relationships, sexuality, imagination, creativity, and fertility. You might find that clearing this Chakra can work miracles if you have relationship problems.

The 3rd Chakra, the Solar Plexus chakra, is situated at the base of the rib cage and is painted in green. This Chakra is often called the Chakra of power, as it is linked to self-worth, intelligence, confidence, and strength. If blocked, this Chakra can frustrate you with the absence of energy and can even make you feel cynical, or control negative or unnecessarily analytical.

The 4th Chakra, the Chakra of the soul, is the core of the energy body and regulates the emotion of love. Blocks can make one feel insecure, unbelieved, and even bitter or jealous in this Chakra. The heart chakra, because it links the lower chakras to the upper chakras, is essential. The Chakra of the heart is depicted in the green color and lies in front of the chest.

The blue color indicates the 5th Chakra, the throat chakra, which rests on the throat. This Chakra gives us excellent

communication skills and allows us to express ourselves. Individuals with blockages in this Chakra may have communication difficulties or even recurrent colds.

The 6th Chakra, the third-eye or brow chakra is found just above the eyes in the middle of the forehead. This Chakra is the Indigo color and link to the spiritual world and represents our intuitive vision. It visualizes our intuition and develops it with Chakra's helps. Blockage can lead to confusion, poor concentration, and even headaches in this Chakra.

On the top of the head is the seventh Chakra, the crown chakra, and is represented by violet or white. The Chakra of the crown leads us to higher guidance and gives us spiritual awareness, and it is our link to a superior power.

Cleaning the chakras can relieve blockages, and many techniques can be used; meditation is only one of these. You can clear the Chakras by visualizing the color of each Chakra, which spins clockwise in front of your body. It takes time to imagine emotional problems when the colors rotate.

Meditation is an incredible way to heal your mind and body, and taking time to work with every Chakra can help you overcome problems that you have fought for all your lives.

Meditations are potent and can support you in every way to transform your life. There's a lot more to meditation than to the eye, and there are many psychological advantages to meditation.

Meditation provides you with an escape from reality, and may also help you live longer, improve the neuroplasticity of your brain and help you think more clearly.

Meditation also enables you to release endorphins that are good chemicals for your body and make meditation nearly as powerful or even more potent than common drugs.

Kundalini: A Spiritual Awakening

There are many different opinions about the process of Kundalini awakening and many different experiences. Many claim Kundalini's awakening will lead to madness, others to illumination, our birthright, and the next step of human evolution. I think it is the latter, but both are right in some ways. When Kundalini is awoken, it leads to some madness, loss of one's mind, and ego. As all of our lives are coming back to us, and our consciousness expands beyond what we could imagine.

All things considered, we are getting increasingly straightforward, break free of our modified, direct perspectives, it might feel that we are going insane and losing our psyches, allowed to recognize the truth about and experience the world. A huge change is taking place in our view, and we can see the

relation of all things and understand our true nature and full potential.

As the cycle continues, our outer layers are slowly pulled away before our true self emerge, free of all history and emotional blockages. A metamorphosis is occurring from within remove and repair traumas that linger within the body and consciousness.

The reason many people are labeled as insane and have psychological problems is that they try to stop or hinder the cycle through traditional methods without a clear understanding of what is happening. Kundalini purifies the soul, the mind, and the physical body. If necessary, there is a psychological disorder and a physical disease.

However, you have to let Kundalini do not resist, do what he has to do, as that only makes the experience worse and more traumatic. Don't be afraid, welcome, and nurture it, and the process will be much more harmonious. Read about Kundalini, all you can. Look at different views and think, find your reality. None can tell you what's right and what's wrong, the truth is in you, there is already wisdom, remember.

Some methods and techniques, including certain types of meditation, you can use to wake up Kundalini. However, know that when you start on this path, there is no way back, because

those who awaken Kundalini and then try to suppress it will have problems.

Some advice that a "Master" or "Guru" is needed to awaken Kundalini and it depends totally on your level of spiritual development, it is your choice, personal knowledge, understanding, and belief system. You have to prepare mind and body for what is in store if you choose to try to waken it yourself, try to clear the body's limit of contaminants, eat correctly, and avoid alcohol and recreational drugs, all of which can interfere with the system and lead to problems.

Keep active, and you need to find ways to release excess energy; otherwise, it will stagnate and can cause problems. Kundalini Yoga, which is specially designed to bring Kundalini to light and is reported to be one of the earliest forms of yoga, is an excellent way to combine physical activity with the process.

It's like Hatha Yoga but more oriented on Kundalini awakening. Hatha means Sun-moon, and yoga means union, and that's what happens during the Kundalini awakening process.

It is essential to read as much of the process as possible, but do not rely on anyone else to find your truth and say what is right and what is not. Kundalini's approach with the right attitude and the correct training is an unforgettable, joyful experience. If we go through this cycle of devotion, compassion,

and forgiveness in our hearts and fully embrace it, then it is the goal, the correct road to enlightenment and the progression of consciousness, of spiritual development.

Signs Of Spiritual Awakening

It recently discovered on the Internet many signs of spiritual awakening (also known as symptoms of spiritual awakening). For example, aches and headaches feeling for no reason in an emotional rollercoaster, shifts in energy levels and relationships, sleep patterns, jobs and gaining and losing weight, and even a scalp, all of which seem to be an itchy one for no reason).

In the process of awakening, a list of nine things is experienced: synchronicities that make sense to you. (This helps you in the right direction or contributes to significant new insights.) Intense painful "changes" to life that you can't explain or know how to get through. (This ensures that you search for the answers within.

Note that "change" is often a cute way of calling "loss") An omnipresent inner reflection followed by a possible reassessment of beliefs, particularly at 3 or 4 a.m. (usually due to events or stuff that you cannot explain with your current system.

To accept "secret messages" from people who do not know they are sending unique messages to you. You have the same (especially something unusual) that happens to you two or three times over a relatively short period, say, like, 24 hours. (you may have hesitated, If you knew, and sometimes spirit does not want to take chances.) (This ensures you notice what your higher self wants you to see.)

Wake up in the center of the night and feel intense confusion. (It means that your convictions are being reassessed, secure, and before your new awakened state is clear and you are mocked through a time of profound confusion.) (You may expect them to occur after you follow your inner guidance regularly.) Dreams that seem to focus you in a specific direction Intense, vivid. (The more you go, the more clearly your goals are, and the more your dreams help guide you in your everyday life.

Ideas are metaphorically shaped, often in metaphors

that make sense of you.) (Sometimes wake up at midnight and think of something profound that is funny and then laugh out of the head. This is not a joke. Your superior self is playful, and you want to have fun while you're awakened.)

Experiencing any of these signs means that the mind (your excellent self) tries to attract your attention! The spirit is funny and encourages you to enjoy the awakening process. You will also be shocked at your higher self's ingenuity.

Remember, the rapid path of spiritual awakening did not depend on how well-known (or currently possessed) you are or how many advanced degrees you are, but how much you are willing (temporarily) to forgive your comfort zones for the noble purpose of personal and spiritual growth. This is important because, at this juncture in the joint development of humanity, it is your individual growth that is extremely important. Also, remember that the signs and symptoms you experience are not just symptoms or signs; they are designed to help you in the process of spiritual awakening.

Mind Study Healing In New Directions

Mind wellbeing Mind their effect on wellbeing has become a fascinating endeavor, as the mental age of the last century unites with today's information age. With the aid of technology, knowledge about mind experiments has increased, and data is processed in support of a link between mind and body. Admittedly, data meanings are multifaceted and disturbing in terms of their health effects.

The power of the Mind to cure the body is surrounded by divisive vagueness. The collective human consciousness, however, becomes an acceptance of a connection between Mind and wellbeing. Mind and body are redefined to fit the new awareness.

Thousands of years of mental activity have been observed. The mind usually involves studying functions that are not apparent to the physical senses, such as consciousness, perception, intelligence, reasoning, and other intellectual capabilities. Nevertheless, technology has allowed mainstream science to demonstrate the synergism between biology and culture.

The subject of Mind, therefore, now also includes the

examination of functions that are obvious to the physical senses, such as physiological reactions, nervous systems, microtubules, and mirror neurons.

In brain imaging data, such as fMRI readings, in turn, an unbreakable relation between the Mind and the body was interpreted to confirm that the Mind can be reduced to chemical and electrical activity in the brain. Not unexpectedly, cognitive healing strategies can also be diminished or damaged in the sense of a reducible mind by the ever-evolving brain risk worldwide.

Aside from the way that there is no standard chemical and electrical brain activity, there is a detail that reductions in mental healing techniques are short-lived, sometimes dying before the brain or vice versa.

Besides, cognitive research data is also used to promote the long-standing concept of Cartesian dualism, which specifically

distinguishes between Mind and body, but can evolve to regulate the organization and its wellbeing better. But a human mind's idea of manipulating a body or bodies is troubling. The dualistic hypothesis leaves the door to coercion, the loss of self- control, accessible not only as existing and undeveloped mind healing techniques as human minds participate.

The common assumption that the Mind is irreducible is an interesting side note to the dualistic theory. A mind-independent from the body is possible. However, it can be diminished if the Mind is reduced to a human personality.

These analyzes should not say that the popular theories of mental research today are wrong; this is not a point. Arguments are forgivable and will continue to be modified with the emergence of new evidence and observations. Human knowledge evolves and adapts to less restrictive methods of mental healing, as the classical worldview of both Mind and health adapts to a paradigm shift away. Ultimately, it is critical to understand the importance of abstract analysis in rethinking cognitive studies and their impact on health.

For example, reducing Mind to the brain, or even to quantum physics, is as untrustworthy as reducing rhythm to a great piano player. The excellent piano player reflects rhythm, but the rhythm does not have to be the piano player.

Similarly, for the life of consciousness, the human mind, or even the human being (personality), is not required. Furthermore, human beings are not yet necessary to prove to heal. Caution is apparent in Mount Saint Helens, Washington, which is recovering beautifully after a volcanic eruption 30 years ago.

Such examples, of course, do not, clarify Mind or healing, as a result, but reflect a revolutionary break from human consciousness which, may establish a robust conceptual understanding even for the sake of the claim of the mind healer of the 19th century, the poet, Mary Baker Eddy.

Are body and Mind connected? Indeed, if the brain is the human Mind, its interconnection is such that the Mind is the same as the body that it occupies. Evidence shows that the body always improves as the human Mind progresses. But not always. Not always. Because it has also been demonstrated that humanity wanders through a complex, confusing network of mutating and ephemeral connections and experiences, the question is, therefore, posed again.

Are body and Mind connected? Indeed, when the Mind is understood, it is the infinite Mind. The human body/mind is not even an endless mind material, as we know today or manifestation.

And, where does the human mind/body leave this? Just where it is found, it grows from itself. The human mind/body needs to improve, but not because it eventually evolves into an infinite mind or a divine mind manifestation. That's not going to happen. The improvement is the reality of our existence, not the human mind/body. Expanded awareness symbolizes Mind and health.

This reality can influence the human condition or cognitive perception. For example, there are second-degree burns on half of the face after a terrible accident. Don't use the limited human brain to repair the body. There was no manipulation of the brain or skin. Even pain relievers are not needed.

The human nurses cleanse the gravel so gently as physically possible from the burnt skin. It was my understanding that I loved it. New skin began to grow within two days, and my face was regular, not a single scar, within three weeks. The human Mind represented damaged skin and was forced into non- existence, while the brain and wellbeing of endlessness remained intact.

The study of the Mind and its healing effect is essential since the human Mind recognizes that its only purpose is to consider the divine Mind and its health effect. There is no question that a mind beyond the human Mind is hard to perceive. But then we do not know that the Earth revolves around the Sun at a speed of 67, 000 miles per hour.

Mind science, not the study of the human mind, but the education of the universal brain, gives the central universe a compelling counter cosmology. The perception of the divine Mind and its effect on health anticipates an existence without a finite, incomplete, rehabilitating, disintegrating, ill, limited, observable mind, person, categorized as useful, animal, and quanta. Mental healing techniques are no longer the effects of manipulation or dualist conflict, but are practiced based on the infinite Mind and its wholesome manifestation.

Chapter 6. Chakras, Endocrine System And The Immune System

In addition to the benefits mentioned earlier, there are many things that chakras control including the efficient functioning of our endocrine system and our emotions. Let us look at each in a bit of detail:

Let us start by recalling the 7 primary chakras and their locations:

Root Chakra – situated at the base of the spine Sacral Chakra – situated below the navel

Solar Plexus Chakra – situated above the navel Heart Chakra – situated in the middle of the chest Throat Chakra – situated in the throat

Third Eye Chakra – situated at the center of the forehead Crown Chakra – situated at the top of the head

The Endocrine System

Next, let us look at the Endocrine System in our body. The Endocrine System is our body's central mechanism of control. It consists of many ductless glands that are responsible for secreting, producing, and distributing different kinds of hormones required for various physiological functions of our body.

These hormones are directly sent through the bloodstream to the places that need them. Effective functioning of the Endocrine System is essential for overall good physical and mental health. The Endocrine System consists of the following elements:

The Pineal Gland – The most important hormone secreted by this gland is melatonin that is responsible for maintaining and regulating your body's circadian rhythm or the internal biological clock. This cone-shaped gland along with the pituitary gland regulates and balances the entire biological and glandular functioning in our body. The third eye chakra can be activated optimally when the pineal and the pituitary glands work perfectly in tandem.

The Pituitary Gland – Also referred to as the 'master gland,' the pituitary gland controls the activities and functioning of most other glands. Attached to the hypothalamus (between the eyes), the pituitary gland regulates the functioning

of other organs and other glands. It communicates via signals in different forms.

This pea-shaped gland works in tandem with the pineal gland controls and balances the overall smooth functioning of our body's physiological and biological activities. The energy of the third eye chakra can be released when these two glands are well synchronized with each other.

Pancreas – The two kinds of hormones produced by the pancreas are needed for two basic functions; one to aid in digestion and the other to control energy levels in our body.

Ovaries – These glands produce the female hormones namely progesterone and estrogen and also produce and release eggs for reproduction

Testes – These glands come in pairs and are responsible for the production and release of the male hormone, testosterone. They also produce and release sperms.

Thyroid – A very important gland, the thyroid is responsible for regulating the heart rate, the metabolic rate and also controls a few digestive functions along with bone maintenance, muscle control, and brain development. The thyroxin produced by the thyroid controls the rate at which our body converts stored food into energy for use. A malfunctioning

thyroid can be quite a debilitating factor that comes in the way of a leading a happy life for anyone.

Parathyroid – This gland controls calcium levels in the bloodstream so that the muscles and the nerves function smoothly. The parathyroid also helps in keeping bones healthy and strong.

Hypothalamus – This gland responds to multiple external and internal factors and triggers various reactions to enable stability and a consistent state in our body. The hypothalamus triggers various physiological reactions in response to feelings of hunger, the temperature of your body, feelings of excessive eating, blood pressure, and others. Based on these conditions, it sends signals to other glands and organs to respond appropriately to these triggers to enable a stable and consistent condition of your body.

Adrenal Glands – These glands secrete different kinds of hormones referred to as 'chemical messengers' which travel through the bloodstream to triggers physiological and chemical reactions in various organs.

The Immune System

Millions and millions of cells come together and waltz together in perfect harmony exchanging critical information thereby triggering appropriate and important physiological, biological, and chemical reactions in our body. The cells of the immune system help organs and organ systems in our body to function smoothly helping us live a happy and peaceful life.

Moreover, those cells that are not performing optimally are retired and new ones are automatically generated to take their place thereby enhancing our health and our longevity. If these weak cells are not correctly replaced in the immune system, they end up sending erroneous signals to all parts of the body resulting in disorders and discomforts such as weak digestion, general body weakness and delayed recovery from even simple illnesses.

The way modern medicines work to set this right is by suppressing the action of the well-functioning cells too until such time all the cells do not achieve the same level of functioning. The medication is continued until all the cells in the immune system get back into the synchronized dancing pattern. This is where chakra healing can help in getting our immune system in order.

The Thymus Gland – It plays an important role in the production of T-cells which form an essential part of the white blood cells that form the core of our immune system. In fact, if you speak to any chakra healer, he or she will tell you the dance of the immune system is the most beautiful and well- coordinated dance in our body.

Chakras And Glands

If you notice the locations of the glands, you will see that they are more or less placed close to different chakras. Although the traditional systems do not speak about the connection between chakras and glands, the modern followers and experts started outlining clear connections between the various chakras, glands, organs and the immune system of the body.

Each chakra is connected to different glands of the endocrine system and facilitates the smooth functioning of that particular gland. Here is a list of the various chakras, the glands they regulate, their functions and the signs of warnings associated with an inefficiently functioning gland/chakra:

Root Chakra – This is connected to the adrenal glands and stands for self-preservation and physical energy. The issues that the root chakra and the adrenal glands handle are associated with survival and security. In the males, the sacral chakra is closely linked to the gonads. The fight/flight response of the adrenal glands located at the top of the kidneys is directly connected to the survival drive of the root chakra.

A weak root chakra could result in a weakened metabolism and immune system resulting from a compromised working of the adrenal glands which are responsible for releasing and producing chemical messengers needed for all the physiological, chemical and biological functions of your body.

A not-so-strong root chakra results in nervousness and a sense of insecurity whereas an overly working root chakra could result in greed and a sense of excessive materialism.

Sacral Chakra – Governs the reproductive glands which are the ovaries (for the females) and the testes (for the males. The well-balanced and healthy root chakra facilitates the uninterrupted functioning of these glands ensuring well- developed sexuality in the person.

The root chakra also regulates the production and secretion of the sex hormones. The potential for life formation in the ovaries is reflected in the sacral chakra as these two energies are connected.

When this chakra is open and free, you are able to express your sexuality well without being overly emotional. You feel a comforting sense of intimacy with your partner. A healthy sacral chakra enhances your passion and liveliness and helps you manage your sexuality without feeling burdened with undue emotions.

A sacral chakra that is not functioning at its peak efficiency is bound to leave you frigid, very close to people and relationships, and poker-faced. On the contrary, a weak sacral chakra will make you feel overly and unnecessarily, emotionally compelling you to attach yourself to people for a sense of security and belonging. Your feelings could be overly sexual towards one and all.

Solar Plexus Chakra – This controls the pancreas, which is directly connected to the sugar (through the control of insulin secretion) and, therefore, energy levels in your body. Thus, if this chakra is not working properly you could potentially have a weak pancreas, resulting in a compromised metabolic state. Compromised pancreas could lead to digestive problems, lowered blood sugar levels, ulcers, poor memory, etc. which are all connected with a bad metabolism.

Heart Chakra – Regulates the thymus gland and through it, the entire immune system. Being the center of love, compassion, spirituality, and group consciousness, a malfunctioning heart chakra will result in the malfunctioning of the thymus gland leaving you prone to low immunity.

Our feelings and thoughts towards ourselves play a crucial role in keeping our immune system working well. When we love ourselves our immune system is powerful and strong. When we are uncertain of ourselves and our strengths and our capabilities, we feel disappointed which drives us to react wrongly to negative things.

All these negativities leave our immune system weak and we end up holding on to toxins. It is imperative to keep our heart chakra healthy by investing time and energy in self-love so that our immune system is strengthened. An underactive heart chakra makes you feel distant and cold and an overactive one could result in selfish love in your heart. Be wary of both states and work at keeping your chakra balanced.

Throat Chakra – controls and regulates the thyroid gland and hence is directly responsible for a healthy metabolism and to regulate body temperature. This is the center of communication and plays a vital role in the way you speak, write, or think. An unbalanced throat chakra results in a malfunctioning thyroid resulting in an overall poor physical, mental, and emotional health.

Third Eye Chakra – directly controls the functioning

of the pituitary gland or the master gland which controls and regulates other organs and glands in the human body. The Pineal gland is many times associated with this chakra too, as we already know that a well-coordinated, combined working of the pineal and the pituitary glands is responsible to keep our entire body, mind, and spirit well-oiled and working well.

Crown Chakra – This regulates the functioning of the pineal gland, which controls our biological cycle and our circadian rhythm.

Connection Between Glands And Chakras

Even the slightest disturbances in the chakras or our energy centers can result in physical manifestations of issues and problems. When the chakras don't function efficiently the corresponding glands and organs they are associated with are also affected.

Chakras as you already know are the energy centers in our body and have no physiological or physical shape or form. These energy centers influence the way we live in different layers of our lives, including the biological, the physical, the emotional, and the psychic layers.

When any of the energy centers malfunction or become imbalanced, the problems are manifested in a physical, mental, or spiritual form. An underactive or an overactive chakra can cause problems for you. Keeping them balanced is critical for your overall health.

Any disturbance even in one energy center could result in problems in any other chakra and/or related glands and organs. For example, if there is a blockage in the heart chakra, you are going to feel unloved or listless or could have high blood pressure etc. All these problems could affect other organs which, in turn, can potentially harm associated chakras.

Therefore, it is imperative to keep all chakras in perfect balance to achieve overall physical, emotional, and spiritual health for yourself. Let us look at some examples of how a malfunctioning of chakras can affect the associated gland.

The Third Eye Chakra And The Pituitary And The Pineal Glands

When the third eye chakra is imbalanced or not working at its peak of efficiency, the functioning of both the pineal and pituitary glands will be affected leading to associated problems. For example, the pituitary is the master gland that regulates the functioning of other glands. So, when the third eye chakra is inefficient, other glands can also be affected negatively resulting in an overall breakdown of your systems.

The pituitary gland regulates intellect and emotion and working in conjunction with the pineal gland helps achieve overall balance in your body. The pineal gland will either resonate or counter the effects of pituitary gland for optimum benefit to our body and mind. Therefore, the third eye chakra is required to be given a lot of importance during your chakra healing and maintenance process.

The Heart Chakra And The Thymus Gland

Located in the middle of your chest, the heart chakra or the anahata controls and regulates the working of the thymus gland which is an important aspect of our immune system. A calm and balanced heart chakra results in an effectively-working nervous system and prevents undue agitation of your mind.

Here is a simple technique to help connect and activate

your thymus gland. Tap gently in the middle of your chest at the collarbone level with your fingers. This helps in calming down agitated nerves. When you gently tap at the collar level about 3- 4 inches away on each side helps to increase your energy levels.

Glands And Chakra Healing

Chakra healing will lead to improved functioning of the endocrine system which is great for physical healing of your body. The connection between glands and chakras represent a link between the energy points in your body to the physiological and physical functions.

Another useful entry point for chakra healing is the nervous system which is connected to glands and organs in multiple ways and at multiple points. A chakra healing session is ideally begun by calming the nerves and then targeting a particular gland and/or chakra.

By understanding the connection between chakras and the glands, you can use healing in different ways that will help you overcome physical, emotional, mental, and spiritual issues in your body and mind. Connecting the chakras and the glands will help in your overall well-being.

Chapter 7. Crystals And Chakras

Crystal Healing And Chakra Healing

Crystal healing is undoubtedly an enchanted and old practice that is alive to date as there are bunches of individuals who practice this structure to treat individuals and fix various illnesses that others might not have been restored. There are a considerable number of individuals around the globe who feel that this structure is particularly useful, particularly while treating diseases like ceaseless torment, sadness, addictions, vision issues, or even diabetes.

They are commonly put on your body part or even in your drinking water or bath, or in some uncommon cases, they are likewise utilized as a type of back rub gadgets that are accepted to inspire the healing reaction and help in restoring the sickness from profound inside.

You surely can utilize these crystals alongside charkas,

and the outcome is frequently extremely adjusted fix and is especially advantageous to people. There are various charkas like the 'base or Muladhara, ' which is commonly spoken to by the red shading regularly animated with tigers eye to invigorate past diseases. If there should be an occurrence of

imperativeness, sex, and feelings, second charka or 'Swadhistana' can be worked via Carnelian stone.

There are various charkas like 'Manipura, Anahata and Vishuddhi,' which are administered by multiple hues and stones or crystals for healing various diseases. The two diamonds and charkas are utilized together for treating reason, yet you unquestionably need to have the correct information on the shading and how to use it well. The entire treatment technique is finished with the complete centralization of both specialist and tolerant and unquestionably requires more than one session as the procedure is tedious, yet particularly successful without taking any drugs.

Crystals For Chakra Balancing

Just like you convey a couple of regular things in your

handbag, pocket or vehicle, similar to hack drops to calm your throat, lip gleam to secure and light up your lips or exercise center shoes for your noon walk, having a lot of crystals can help clear energy blockages and opening chakras.

They need not be extravagant or flashy and appear to work best when they are permitted to pick you. As verification that "everything" in this life is alive, mindful and responsive, hold your hand over a couple of crystals and hold up until at least one of the signals you that they are prepared to turn into yours, to go with you and to work with you by both retaining and emitting energy. Presently, as the new watchman of your crystals and the beneficiary of their incredible power, you have a duty to keep them clean and stimulated. First, steep your new crystals medium-term in an answer of ocean salt and water and dry them thoroughly before you start to utilize them.

Occasionally, re-wash your crystals in the salt arrangement or water and afterward re-stimulate them by presenting them to the moon or daylight for a few hours. Exploit the healing energy of each full moon by leaving your crystals outside the medium-term. Crystals can be basic yet amazing assets when you're looking for balance and a feeling of prosperity in your physical, mental, passionate, and spiritual self. To help as a rule pressure alleviation, have a go at putting three clear quartz crystals, focuses confronting outward, in a triangle just underneath your navel. Next, place three rose quartz stones in a circular segment over your pubic bone and unwind for 4-5 minutes. Rehash as frequently as is required for the ideal energy stream.

For a total Chakra Balance, attempt this straightforward crystal format to strengthen your chakra energies and guarantee they are working admirably. Pick an establishing stone (dark, brown, or dull red) to put between your feet. At that point pick a stone or crystal comparing to the various shades of the chakras, putting the red one between your knees, the orange right over your pelvic bone, the yellow right over your navel, the green over your heart focus, the light blue on your throat, indigo or dull blue on your brow and a violet or clear stone on the floor directly over the highest point of your head. Rests with these stones set up for a time of around 5 minutes or until you feel total. At that point, evacuate the stones beginning with the one over your head. Unwind for a couple of more minutes, as yet resting, at that point, appreciate sense prosperity and equalization, prepared to confront the worries of the day ahead.

A Quick Guide To Using Healing Crystals And Gemstones

Crystal healing has been famous in numerous societies around the globe since the beginning and remains so today. The intensity of healing crystals and gemstones is an intriguing one and stays to be clarified entirely. Notwithstanding, there's nothing to prevent you from attempting crystals for yourself, and encountering their belongings firsthand. How about we investigate what's associated with utilizing crystals for healing and other life-improvement purposes.

The utilization of crystals for healing is based on the idea of the body as an enthusiastic system. Blockages can happen in the order, at last prompting physical disease or different issues. Crystals have their trademark energies, which might be utilized to help break down blockages in the energy body, or to upgrade

their working. Correctly, diamonds are frequently used related to the chakra system. Chakras are energy vortices that are found in numerous spots in the unpretentious body, albeit most healers center around the seven principle essential chakras, which are situated in an unpleasant line between the crown of the head and the base of the spine. Chakra lopsided characteristics can prompt physical and mental issues, and crystals might be utilized to help 'tune' the chakras and reestablish them to typical working.

How Is It Done?

It isn't unexpected to put crystals straightforwardly on the influenced regions of the body during a healing session. On account of utilizing crystals for chakra work, they're ordinarily set in the territory of the chakra(s) being referred to. A healer may likewise use instruments, for example, a crystal wand to coordinate the energy in a progressively explicit manner, or utilize a crystal pendulum to acquire data about the area of energy blockages or different issues.

A few people additionally prefer to wear crystal adornments, or convey little stones, (for example, tumble stones or thumbstones) around with them, to profit by the stone's properties for the day. When utilizing healing stones and crystals routinely, it's vital to wash down and revive the rocks. This can be practiced by holding them under running water for somewhat, at that point, putting them in a bright spot.

Which Stones Are Best?

Various gemstones have various properties. Thus specific stones might be fit for explicit purposes. Rose quartz, for instance, has an extremely alleviating, quieting energy, which makes it useful for managing enthusiastic bombshells, though the carnelian is particularly prized for maintaining issues in the lower stomach area, (for example, stomach related or conceptive problems).

Clear Quartz (rock crystal), then again, is considered the 'general healer,' as this ground-breaking stone can be valuable in a broad scope of conditions. In case you're keen on crystal work, there are numerous great aides accessible that give itemized arrangements of the properties of different stones - 'The Crystal Healing Bible' by Judy Hall is a decent spot to begin.

Does Crystal Healing Work?

Numerous individuals have had excellent outcomes from the utilization of crystals, which is the reason it keeps on being an extremely significant part of the necessary prescription. Standard science is less persuaded, and qualities a considerable number of victories to the misleading impact or unrealistic reasoning concerning the patient. Likewise, with other 'elective' interests where discussion exists, it's typically worth testing for yourself. It arrives at your very own decisions, as opposed to just taking the expression of others, as inclinations exist on the two sides.

On the off chance that you have a physical or mental issue and are trusting that crystals can help, your best game-plan is to visit a trustworthy crystal healer for appeal, yet to proceed with whatever course of treatment your primary care physician has endorsed meanwhile.

Chakra Therapy And The Healing Powers Of Stones

Crystal therapy is considered as an all-encompassing system or an elective technique for healing that can be utilized to fortify the psyche and body. Crystal healers have been around since the antiquated occasions, to our days. It is a kind of treatment that is built up and demonstrated to be protected and gainful to the body.

Crystal Therapy and Chakras

Essentially, crystal healers give healing to the body and psyche by putting the gemstones on zones of the body alluded to as "chakras." It is the term used to depict the spiritual energy focuses, which can be found in everybody. There are seven primary chakras all through the body, and each chakra works related to others to frame a person's energy. When the chakras

are not adjusted, it can realize negative or terrible energy that can be coordinated to the body and brain.

What the crystals do is to divert all the negative energies and take them back to positive energies, which can bring the characteristic equalization of the body, including the chakras. In this manner, Crystal therapy is broadly utilized by healers to give a fix to different ailments, just as spiritual misguidance and enthusiastic errors.

Crystal Therapy Benefits

Gemstone therapy offers enormous amounts of advantages on the physical viewpoint, however, on the psychological and enthusiastic perspective too. A portion of the benefits incorporate the accompanying:

- It works incredibly to advance self-awareness, imperativeness, and wellbeing.

- It can give healing to an assortment of physical conditions that even contemporary drugs can't fix. It can likewise be adequately utilized related to the current medication.

- It gives alleviation to uneasiness, stress, and gloom just as advance relaxation.

- It can aid conditions like cerebral pains, torment, menstrual issues, weariness, and even focus and learning challenges.

- It can likewise work with riches building, individual satisfaction, and social connections.

- It balances the spirit, body, and brain to accomplish the ordinary parity of energies in the body.

Regardless of all these healing advantages, it is exceptionally advised that Crystal therapy ought not to be utilized in trade for treatment. This can be used as a helpful therapy as it is useful in upgrading your all-out prosperity.

Chakra Opening With Crystals And Brainwave Entrainment

In the advanced world, we will see in general disregard our energy systems, which all the time become over-burden and pushed, and thus, we become exhausted and begin to fail to meet expectations in our work. The body's energy system is upheld by a network of hubs, which are known as the chakras, and it is the point at which they become hindered that you will feel sickly. By unblocking and opening up your chakras, you will feel re-empowered and ready to last during that time without your energy getting drained. With the present riotous ways of life, this is a higher priority than ever. Working on your chakras can likewise build up your inert psychic energy.

There are seven major chakra focuses, which you can take a shot at and they are related with specific hues:

1.   The base chakra is arranged at the base of the spine and is related to red and for adjusting physical energy. This chakra will likewise ground you and help with inspiration.

2.   The sacral chakra is arranged in the lower midriff

beneath the navel and is related to the shading orange. This is to discharge squares and create innovativeness.

3. The sun based plexus chakra is arranged around the lower ribcage and is related to the shading yellow. Taking a shot at this chakra will create certainty and unwavering discernment.

4. The heart chakra is related to shading green. The heart chakra will build up a feeling of direction throughout everyday life and improve associations with others.

5. The throat chakra is related to the shading blue. This chakra is connected to correspondence and serenity and how you convey what needs to be to the world.

6. The temples chakra in the brow is related to the shading indigo. This is the chakra related to mental and intuitive exercises, and chipping away at this chakra will encourage the opening of the third eye.

7. The crown chakra is related to purple. This is the chakra identified with the entire being and equalizations the entirety of the faculties of self, spiritual, physical,

enthusiastic, and mental.

Chipping away at this chakra will build up an association with your higher self and lead to a higher religious association.

Each of these chakras is vortices of energy which can be animated by utilizing crystals and mental representation. Crystals can be used to open up chakras by resting serenely on the floor and setting a diamond-related with the shade of each of the chakras on the suitable situation of the body. Inhale gradually and unwind while picturing the shading about each chakra.

There are different guided chakra purifying activities and contents which can be utilized for chakra opening, yet the ideal approach to check out the energy designs is to join the chakra working with brainwave entrainment. Working with your chakras along these lines will give your entire body a revitalizing energy lift and make you all the more rationally alert, just as honing your natural detects.

Crystal Healing Bringing A Metaphysical Subject Down To Earth

More than five billion years back, a star detonated in a blazing supernova. More than a considerable number of years, the whirling, impacting vast flotsam and jetsam delivered bigger and bigger spatial bodies. Our close planetary system came to fruition, and as the intensely hot liquid stone cooled,

water fume dense in the world's air. Mists framed. A storm of downpour made the early stage seas, and crystals shaped.

Crystals are profoundly organized units of energy in steady movement:

• They gestate profound inside the earth and, allegorically, help with revealing individual covered stores of intensity and quality

• They are organized by exact scientific standards and cling to characterized geometric examples.

- They are compelled to transmute under exceptional weight and are made dazzling by boundaries of time and temperature

Each crystal is one of a kind, with properties and attributes as shifted as their individual qualities. The investigation of crystals would expend years, yet an astonishing number of advantages can be ascribed to all crystals. Every single crystal can be customized to get, store, discharge, reflect, refract, amplify, change, adjust and fit, compose, intensify, center, and divert energy. Therefore, the comprehension of their unlimited applications generally reported in all societies. Old Egypt's Pharaohs were buried with vast amounts of valuable gems, gemstones, and resplendent brilliant statues to guarantee their delight in life following death. These gold encrusted metals were ornamented with:

- Carnelian - accepted to ensure the spirit's section into the netherworld

- Lapis lazuli - the old chemist's stone of paradise; utilized by the regal undertakers in cosseting and painting

- Turquoise - accepted to avert the "stink eye."

- Quartz - the backbone of the crystal world, and the most adaptable, multipurpose stone

- Amber - accepted to help in finding old insight and information.

- Emeralds - supported by the Pharaohs for their amazing green shading, symbolized life, development, fruitfulness, and innovativeness.

- Ruby - thought about one of the most significant gemstones of our earth; symbolizes power, energy, and want

- Sapphire - the stone of flourishing and the sister of the ruby

- Topaz - when thought to be tinted with the brilliant sparkle of the Egyptian sun god Ra, accepted to increment physical quality.

Chinese jade, since quite a while ago, accepted to be an image of riches and respect, has been loved since 2950 B.C. The old Chinese utilized jade broadly in treating ceaseless disease,reestablishing energy parity, and reinforcing the spiritual healing force. Jade is consolidated in feng shui to assist one with improving life by getting positive qi (energy).

The baffling, cryptic crystal skulls of Mexico, Central, and South America speak to the absolute most intriguing archeological finds of the twentieth century. Inside the most recent ten years or somewhere in the vicinity, there have been as of late found crystal skulls, either revealed or held by private authorities. The secrets of the Mayan Crystal Skulls have suffered for centuries; most strangely, the forecasted, parallel end of our reality as we probably are aware of it, and the extraordinary cycle of the Mayan.

People acquainted with regular healing practices are, for the most part, really well tolerating of the general laws of psyche/body/spirit interface methods of reasoning crucial to Indian Ayurvedic and Native American systems. Crystal healing instructs the essential standards and qualities of the human energy field:

- barite - a sky-blue stone, is supported by numerous Native Americans, who use it to change from physical to spiritual creatures in their formal practices; is likewise said to rouse transparent dreams and dream review

- Emeralds - the old Incas and Aztecs in South America accepted emeralds were blessed; the Vedas, the antiquated consecrated compositions of Hinduism, instruct that emeralds are fortunate stones that upgrade prosperity.

- Nebula stone - dark with cloud-like markings for access to astronomical shrewdness and comprehension

- Pink Mangano calcite - is in some cases called the Reiki stone; healers use it to amplify their healing energies

- Serpentine - accepted to make preparations for the chomps and stings of venomous animals; on a mystical level, it is thought to help with the ascent of kundalini, or "snake fire" energy through the chakras.

- Shiva lingam stones - any Indiana Jones fan knows about Indy's mission for the three hallowed stones symbolizing the Hindu god, Lord Shiva; the markings symbolize yoni or female energy, for the ideal equalization of manly and ladylike richness

- Sugilite - utilized by healers to disperse torment and impart significant serenity

- Sunstone - used to disperse antagonism and dread; emanate wellbeing, joy, and favorable luck.

Specialists of crystal healing create and experience individual energy affectability and healing capacities. By "tuning in" and being "in order" with their crystals, they can divert undesirable, negative energy designs, restore, adjust and adjust their hot bodies.

Acculturated social orders rely upon quartz as the key segment in cutting edge innovations. The revelation of active state silicon radar crystals and transistors switched things around for the Allies in WW II and created new ideas for gadgets in oceanographic and air inquire about. You will never again take a gander at your PC, advanced camera, mobile phone, crystal watch, compact disc or DVD player, or even an x- ray machine; without contemplating the quartz controlling these.

Crystals, all by themselves, don't mind. Instead, they can be utilized as a point of convergence for motivation and improvement; they can provoke specialists to think and live in more beneficial manners, and they can be used as courses of healing energy. This information will stir instincts to control you through science and the superstition.

Chapter 8. Second Degree Reiki (Okuden)

Second Degree Reiki improves your knowledge and healing abilities by teaching you how to live in accordance with the principles you were taught earlier. This is a personal journey in making Reiki part of your essential being. In this journey, you are guided to further your spirituality and your physical reality by achieving a state of oneness. The spiritual teachings at this level are focused on the Buddhist sutras; the Lotus Sutra, the Heart Sutra, and the Diamond Sutra.

At this level, your Reiki healing abilities are much more enhanced and you will be able to send full treatments to anyone as if they were right there with you. You will also be able to heal very serious mental and emotional complexities at this level.

You may have noticed that I did not include treating others at First Degree Reiki. Though you can heal people if you have received your attunement at the First Degree level, I particularly feel it is more effective when you are at the Second Degree level.

As with First Degree Reiki, you need to get an attunement from a Reiki Master. This energy attunement boosts your healing abilities by strengthening your healing channel allowing

far more Reiki to pass through you. At the First Degree, you still get the same Reiki but at Second Degree, the quantity you can let out is sometimes tripled.

Depending on your Reiki master, Reiki Second Degree courses may be put in a slightly different order. Here is what you're most likely to expect when studying the Western approach:

Friday: outlining what Reiki Second Degree is all about which is usually followed by guided meditations and then a question and answer session.

Saturday: a brief discussion on the main elements of Second Degree Reiki (the healing, personal, and spiritual development). Students are also taught the three Reiki

Symbols and their mantras (The power symbol, The Harmony Symbol, and the Distant Symbol). This is usually combined with guided meditations and some free time to connecting with nature.

Sunday: a brief revision of the Reiki symbols and then a practical healing session where student learn Second Degree techniques for treating others, enhancing the sensitivity to scan for energy imbalances, aura cleansing, directing Reiki into the aura, distant healing carrying out full mental and emotional Reiki treatment using the symbols.

Again, this may vary depending on the Reiki master but this is essentially what to expect when practicing Reiki Second Degree.

Second Degree Attunement

The process of a Second Degree attunement is not so different from the First Degree attunement.

During your attunement, your eyes would be shut throughout the process and you will stay calm and silent with your hands in Buddhist Gassho position.

The Reiki Master starts the attunement from behind you, then moves in front of you and finishes the attunement behind you. It is important you stay still as, during the attunement, you will sense blowing on your head and some gentle touch. You will then be asked to raise your hands above your head for a few moments before you place then back down.

Once you have been attuned, I personally recommend you go into meditation, and the whole idea behind that is for you to attain mindfulness. Reaffirm your commitment to living this way and make mindfulness your way of living.

After An Attunement

Just as you went through a 21-day clearing process for Reiki

First Degree, you'll need to go through the same process again. After your attunement, your receptiveness is heightened and you are now able to tap into a higher frequency of Reiki.

For many, they experience the changes immediately. Their senses become heightened and they become aware of everything around them. The most common effect is an increased color consciousness; some even say they smell the mornings and have an intense connection with nature. What is most certain is you would notice profound changes including an increased intuition and heightened sensitivity in the crown chakra area.

Reiki connects you to divinity and I strongly recommend you go into meditation for at least a day. Remember, Reiki is a journey, not a competition. The more you practice it, the more you get better at channeling its energy.

Reiki Second Degree Symbols

A symbol is a mark or character that represents an object, a function or process. A symbol also represents an idea or quality. When you see the $ sign what comes to mind? When you see the O_2 sign what comes to mind? All these are symbols that represent something and you are probably familiar with them.

Contrary to popular belief, the Reiki symbols do not hold any special power themselves. These symbols represent certain metaphysical energies and are represented by four symbols.

They were discovered by Dr. Mikao Usui in a Sanskrit book and he infused them in the Reiki teachings to help make Reiki healing more powerful.

The Power or Focus Symbol (Cho Ku Rei)

This symbol comprises of three strokes. It activates other symbols and can be used alone or in combination with either or both of the other two symbols. Its sole purpose is to increase the power of Reiki in the present bringing the energy of Reiki to the moment. The Japanese tradition refers to this as the Focus Symbol because it is used to invokes Reiki over anything it is called upon.

The main purpose of this symbol is to cleanse, empower and protect. If you are out of balance, the power symbol works with Reiki to restore your balance. It permeates the first and second chakras and revitalizes the whole body. To use this symbol;

Visualize and draw the symbol in mid-air in the way you wish to direct Reiki.

Visualize and draw the symbol on your hand before placing them on anything or anyone.

Visualize the symbol and project it to the back of your hand using your third eye chakra as you heal your client.

The Harmony Symbol (Sei Heiki)

This symbol comprises of nine strokes and also comes from Sanskrit. This symbol does not work on its own and is combined with the power symbol. It helps restore emotional balance, psychological balance and emotional balance bring peace, oneness, and harmony. This symbol works with the second and fourth chakras.

The Distance Symbol (Hon Sha Ze Sho Nen)

This symbol comprises of 22 strokes and just like the second symbol, it also is used in combination with the first symbol and sometimes the second symbol. Time and space become irrelevant as it brings all time into the Now and all space into Here. Your Higher Self connects to divinity and you can send healing back in time or in the future. There is absolutely no barrier at this stage and Reiki that is sent using this symbol would not lose any of its power.

This symbol completely eliminates time and space as we know it as everything is in the now. You can channel Reiki to anything and through anything. To use this symbol;

Visualize and draw the symbol in mid-air in the way you wish to direct Reiki.

Visualize and draw the symbol on your hand before placing them on anything or anyone.

Visualize the symbol and project it to the back of your hand using your third eye chakra as you heal your client.

Treating Others

I'll like to mention that you don't need the Second Degree attunement to heal friends and family, but the Second Degree attunement is necessary if you want to be a Reiki Practitioner. I chose to include it here because I have seen the power of Reiki when you attain your attunement and when you use it in combination with the symbols.

Before you carry out a treatment on others, make sure to cleanse yourself. You should also cleanse the area from any residual negative energy. Use the Power symbol to cleanse the room and the couch. Do this by walking to all corners of the room and drawing a large Power symbol on each corner using the arc of your hand. Also, move to the center of the room and with the same method cleanse the ceilings and the floor.

Before you begin a healing session, you should make sure the person about to be treated is relaxed and calm; explain to the person receiving the treatment what they would experience. It is also vital that you fill your aura with Reiki forming a protective edge against any negative energy that may be expelled during your sessions.

Hands Positions For Treating Others

For the Front of the Body

The back of the Head: Have your client lay down and get relaxed. Remember to tell them what they are likely to experience. Place both hands underneath the head with the heels of your hands pointing upward (do this with one hand as a time raising the client's head gently). The head should rest perfectly over the heals of your palms. Do this for about 3-5 minutes.

The Eyes: With the client laying down flat, place one

hand over each eye (about 2-4 cm away from the eye) in a slightly cupped manner having the heel of each hand resting over the brow without the fingertips touching the face. Do this for about 3-5 minutes.

The Ears: With the client laying down flat and relaxed, stand behind the head and place both hands slightly cupped beside each ear. Let the heels of your palm rest gently on the side of the head. Ensure your fingertips is at least 2 cm away from the face. Do this for about 3-5 minutes.

The Neck: With the client laying down flat on the back and relaxed, place one hand on each side of the neck. Your palm should face the neck and your little fingers should sit gently on the client's shoulder. Keep your fingers distant from the neck as it may make the person feel very uncomfortable. Do this for about 3-5 minutes.

The Chest: With the client laying down flat on the back and relaxed, place both hands flat over the chest forming a V shape. Your hands should rest on the chest and your fingertips should meet. Be mindful when treating a female not to put your hands on her breasts. Do this for about 3-5 minutes.

The solar plexus: With the client laying down flat on the back and relaxed, stand beside the client and place one hand covering the midsection and the other on the covering the navel with both fingertips pointing away from you. Do this for about 3-5 minutes.

The Waist: With the client laying down flat on the back and relaxed, stand beside the client and place one hand covering the hip and the other on the waist just below the navel with both fingertips pointing away from you. Do this for about 3-5 minutes.

The Pelvic Area (Male): With the client laying down flat on the back and relaxed, stand beside the client and place one hand on each hip bone. Both hands should point in opposite directions. Do this for about 3-5 minutes.

The Pelvic Area (Female): With the client laying down flat on the back and relaxed, stand beside the client and place one hand on the hip bone and with the other, form a V shape with the fingertips pointing diagonally towards the pubic region. Do this for about 3-5 minutes.

The Shoulders: With the client laying down flat on the stomach, stand in front of the client's head and place both hands on the shoulder so that the heal of each palm rests gently on the shoulder and your fingertips point down the back. You may also place both hands on each shoulder, with your fingers pointing towards the ribcage to intensify the healing on one shoulder. Do this for about 3-5 minutes.

The Back: With the client laying down flat on the stomach, stand beside the client and place one hand in front of the other but both fingers pointing away from you as you place it on the client's back midway between the shoulder and the waist. Do this for about 3-5 minutes.

The Waist: With the client laying down flat on the stomach, stand beside the client and gently place one hand in front of the other but both fingers pointing away from you as you place it on the client's waist so that each hand covers almost the entire waist. Do this for about 3-5 minutes.

The Waist: With the client laying down flat on the stomach, stand beside the client and gently place one hand on each buttock but both fingers pointing away from you. Do this for about 3-5 minutes.

The Leg and Feet: With the client laying down flat on the stomach, stand beside the client and gently place your hand in a cupped position on the affected area. Start from high up and every 20 seconds, slide down gently till you work your way to the ankle and then the soul of the feet. You can also do this while the client is laying on the back.

Arms: With the client laying down flat on the back, stand beside the client and gently place your hand in a cupped position on the affected area with your fingertips pointing to the client. Start from high up the hand and every 20 seconds, slide down gently till you work your way to the wrists.

Once a healing session is complete, I strongly advise you smoothen the client's aura. What happens in a healing session is the negative energy has been removed from the physical body and moved into the aura. Smoothening the aura creates an energy balance and helps the client come out of that deep relaxation state.

It is also important that you start at the head and work your way down the body as any other way goes against the natural flow of energy (*ki*).

Chapter 9. The Effects Of Various Substances On The Chakras

Alcohol and heavier drugs break the vertical flow of energy between the chakras along the spine. Each addictive substance has an initial affinity with one of the chakras, which is the first one that is affected when the substance is abused. The fears associated with a chakra may have something to do with the choice of your addictions. People with multiple addictions have multiple fears. When dealing with several of the different addictions, we will refer more specifically to the chakras that affect each substance. However, in general, the harder the substance will be, the lower than the center with which it has an affinity. Hard drugs like heroin or the barbiturates sweep with all the centers and with the vertical flow between them. Over time, any addiction can damage all the chakras.

You should also know that the overflow effect is inherent in blocking a particular chakra. It can cause stagnation of energy in the chakras that are on each side such that if the cardiac chakra is injured, either by addiction or by trauma, eventually the energy will also stagnate in the solar plexus, with implications for self-esteem and will result in a self-centered behavior. The thymus, as it is not yet awake, may become even more paralyzed. On the other hand, the throat chakra may also be affected, so that the person stops talking about their feelings.

If the sexual chakra is damaged, either by addiction or by trauma, it can cause effects on the root chakra and on the solar plexus. In general, substances classified as stimulants - from coffee or even cocaine and amphetamines - carry the energy down by force. When the overflow persists for a long time, there may be a search for support in the centers that are above and below the line. It is very similar to what happens when a pipe is clogged or when there is a short circuit in an electric cable.

Many of the common problems among addicts and those who love them are due to this damage. The self-centeredness, the progressive confinement to smaller and smaller worlds away from human contact and sexual problems (either impotence or promiscuity) are understandable in the context of the malfunction of the chakras. Later we will give exercises, floral remedies, and stone and crystal treatments to help repair the chakras. As the person recovers, there are often crises corresponding to the chakra being healed. For example, there are often periods of unreasonable rage, anxiety attacks and others related to one's sexuality

Addictions And The Cardiac Chakra

In people who have not been damaged by drugs or other chemicals, energy flows from lower chakras towards the heart center and from the heart towards others. An exchange is established of loving energy. When the upward flow is interrupted, the person becomes increasingly isolated and self- centered and can drink, get high or overeat to stop the pain caused by the energetic interruption.

Addictions are a growing problem for all of us and a contributing factor is the virtual one. For example, the disappearance of breastfeeding in countries like the United States. The chest is close to the heart and the loving and gentle stimulation of the baby to the mother's breast does much to open the heart of the Mother towards the baby and keep it open. Love and breastfeeding were inseparable, the baby automatically receives a flow of loving energy several times a day every time he ate. That automatic opening does not take place when you are fed with bottles and there is no peace exchange.

As a result, many adults and children of these cultures have suffered from starvation in the chakras, which implies a deficit in machine learning of how energy flows through those chakras. Having not learned, we do not know how to give it or receive it, then all our relationships suffer from depth. We can learn to open the flow using the exercises that we will give later.

A damaged heart center becomes a magnet, instead of being a spout that pours out. So, addicts become leeches for others in desperate and distorted ways. They end up twisting their relationships. On a subliminal level, the addict perceives that trying to win your sympathy will result in more energy as your heart literally "goes to it". For this reason, it can be incredibly draining to work or be close to an addicted person, which predisposes to more losses. When the other person can no longer endure being drained, the relationship can end. The addict, reeling from a new heart wound can deepen further in addiction.

Having the heart center closed is one of the vicious circles of addiction. In fact, a wound in the heart can be one of the ways in which the addiction begins first. Many people begin to abuse substances after the loss of someone they love. Many young people find that drugs become a problem once they have abandoned the nutrition of paternal home, or when the home ceases to be a source of nutrition.

The children and spouses of addicts have a natural predisposition to addiction. One of the reasons is that living with an addict ensures malnutrition of the heart center. Other people growing up in environments where there is no love or suffering losses at an early age, they may also have malnourished the heart center, which predisposes them to addiction. Growing up we learn from those who surround us and in such homes, you cannot learn how to let the energy of the heart flow.

Gay people are another group with a high cup of addictions: one in three is an alcoholic and can abuse drugs. Heart wounds can play a role in it, because often, friends and family reject them when they reveal their homosexuality and also because, in a way, they have to deny or distort their true feelings, which causes them to suffer from isolation. They do relate primarily to other homosexuals who have suffered injuries.

Similar heart conditions may contribute to energy malnutrition. The gay community can reverse this tendency consciously feeding the heart centers of each other, as well as practicing the exercises presented below. People who "pour their hearts into their work" may also suffer from malnutrition of the heart since there is no flow back and forth, work cannot return their love. Therefore, addicts who put all of their time and efforts into work and those who have to live with them, often become alcoholics or addicts. Disconnected from the workaholic, who spends it at the headquarters or in the office, it doesn't matter, the person drains and remains empty, resorting to the substance to withstand pain.

Even when the addiction has stopped, the heart center problem will continue unless there is a conscious effort to re- educate and retrain it. In some there is a spontaneous reopening in the form of a powerful spiritual awakening or a great love relationship. However, too soon, the brightness fades and the heart center may close. However, for many, it won't reopen unless trained. People who have stopped addiction but have not reopened their heart center may feel miserable because they are disconnected from love and have nothing to endure the pain. The temptation to return to addiction can be very strong, causing multiple relapses. The healing exercises that we will do later are designed to restore that flow.

The Navel Block And Addiction

During fetal development and childhood, there is another energy center functioning in the human body, the navel chakra. It is the one that nourishes us on an energetic level, allowing us to grow so quickly. By the second year of life it should already be closed, allowing energy to flow upwards to the upper chakras that begin to function after delivery. That's why the age of two years is particularly crucial and any loss or separation at that age increases the vulnerability of the child. If a loss has occurred or if the navel chakra has been neglected or supercharged, this area may be blocked after the chakra has closed, avoiding that energy flows freely upward, depriving the upper chakras and causing problems later in life.

In the same way, when the navel chakra has not been sufficiently nourished in childhood, this becomes an extra source of stress and the person seeks relationships or substances to fill the emptiness. In such cases, the cardiac chakra has not developed properly, so the person doesn't know how to give or receive love. This often happens with children of addicts, where one or both parents suffer from blockages in the energy flow.

Sometimes, an over fed belly button chakra can produce the same results as the malnourished one. Parents who can only relate to the navel due to their own blockages over stimulate the child's navel chakra at the expense of the development of other centers. According to this, the person grows and becomes an adult but the initial overstimulation of the navel can lead to addiction towards food, drugs or alcohol in order to reproduce that childish state of unconsciousness. The person who is conditioned to relate primarily at the level of the navel may suffer feeling isolated or unloved when confronted with adults who interact through other chakras. Binge eating food or drugs blur the isolation.

It is easy to get caught because of a blockage. The problem is that in our culture, it is not considered appropriate for an adult to be trapped in the navel area. It is assumed that adults are sexual, not dependent in any way a child is. The sexual chakra is conveniently located next to the navel chakra and its energy output can be easily accessed. An exaggerated emphasis on the navel area then is more acceptably transformed into an emphasis exaggerated in sexuality, or in a kind of power relations between the sexes that comes from a bad utilization of the energy of the solar plexus, on the other side of the navel chakra. Both men and women can use sexuality as a costume to try to meet their needs; the promiscuity is often nothing else but an intense need in disguise. The more oral the sexual expression, the more you may be serving the purposes of the navel center. The severe "Oedipal" problems are more related to the navel area than to the sexual chakra.

Blocked Chakras, Sexuality, And Addiction

All chakras are created equal. The sexual chakra is only one of the centers, its expression is not even more important or less important than that of other chakras to be in balance and have a healthy life. However, an external observer of our culture might think that this chakra is the boss if you listen to our conversations, read our books, listen to our music, see our movies and get swallowed by our ads. Why this disproportionate emphasis on the sexual chakra today? What we have mentioned about the navel chakra is one of the causes. There are others related to what is happening in society.

Addictions, which many of us suffer to a lesser or greater extent, clog the energy of Cardiac chakra and progressively distort that of the chakras that are located beneath it. If your heart is frozen, your relationships suffer and when your relationships suffer, your self-esteem (the solar plexus) is damaged. When your self-esteem is low, you seek satisfaction in material goods, the addictive substances or co-dependent relationships to fill the void. At this stage, you probably have problems releasing energy through the sexual chakra, or it may be that this exit area is the only one that is working, so that sex acquires a quantity of disproportionate attention.

This progressive distortion of energy certainly occurs to the addict, but more and more it happens to the society as a whole. In part, this is because almost all people have at least one or two addictions that affect your energy field, coffee, tobacco, television and this continues until you get more severe addictions. In addition, there are other chemical pollutants that hinder free energy flow.

The sexual chakra can be a source of addictive tendencies. The child who is sexually stimulated quite early by adults in your environment (or by the media) can divert too much energy towards this center that should have served to balance or to develop all the chakras. Traumatic events such as sexual harassment, incest or rape can cause severe blockages so that the individual has a deep fear of sexuality. Addiction can develop as a way to cushion fear. A parent's addiction may increase the risk of trauma. For example, some studies show that one incest victim in three has an alcoholic father.

Essences that can help with sexual difficulties include BASIL, FIG, HIBISCUS, and STICKY MONKEYFLOWER.

Manufactured chemicals aggravate the problem of the chakras. In our society, we are constantly exposed to artificial substances, we breathe them, we eat them, drink them, put them on our faces and spread them on our hair. How I know this is mentioned at the beginning, the human body has been exposed to organic substances for millions of years and is composed of similar substances, which is not the case with artificial chemicals. This can be extremely harmful.

Manufactured drugs are much more harmful to those who are addicted to them than organic drugs. In the same way, food additives, cosmetics, and industrial fumes, in the long term they can cause damage to both the physical body and the subtle bodies.

Chemicals found at work, in life or in the diet can aggravate the damage that has occurred in the past and prevent attempts to carry out healing work in the present. Additional cleaning may be necessary if such chemicals have been part of your life for long periods. If your work or other circumstances make your exposure to these chemicals necessary, you may need to continue cleaning and protecting yourself to allow healing to continue. Truck and taxi drivers, for example, have a high rate of alcoholism, and this is partly due to the effects of the constant bombardment of gasoline fumes in the liver.

Conclusion

Thank you for making it through to the end of Chakra Healing for Beginners, let's hope it was informative and able to provide you with all of the tools you need to achieve your goals whatever they may be.

There are five energy centers outside the body that are located in other dimensions of being. Although they exist in the present, they are invisible and inaccessible to our senses. These chakras appear in pairs. The first would be located about 30 cm. over the head and 30 cm under the feet; the second around 90 cm in both directions and the third pair at a meter. The fourth and fifth pairs would exceed our three-dimensional concepts and extend to infinity, both up and down. When we increase our vibration, we can perceive them, feel them and be their partakers.

There is also an eighth, ninth, tenth, eleventh and twelfth chakra that operate with or without our conscious participation. All are located above and below the body. There are several techniques for leveling our centers, including chromotherapy, physical exercises, visualization techniques, etc. The techniques mentioned in this book collaborate so that our centers work correctly. We hope you learned all that you needed to regarding chakras.

BOOK 2

Reiki Healing For Beginners:

The Definitive step-by-step Meditation Guide to Improve Your Health, Energy and Increase Positive Vibrations to Find Balance. Discover Your Spiritual e Physical Wellness

Introduction

Since humanity's commencement of mending treatments, for example, Therapeutic Touch, and their regularly specialist Eastern otherworldly practices, for example, reiki, appealing people have added to the way of healers' advancement.

Mikao Usui composed a manual of his lessons on Reiki in 1920. In April of 1922, he opened his first "Seat of Learning" in Harajuku, Tokyo. His lessons roused the senior populace, who encountered this learning as an arrival to the more seasoned "profound practices."

Reiki is mending craftsmanship advanced from Eastern dreams of what our universe is and how it capacities. Today, in the West, we develop ace educators, who, similar to their patients and understudies, have hurried up the positions through a "moment" reiki arrangement of end of the week classes, offering pretty much nothing, assuming any, establishment in Eastern reasoning, and who are proceeding to stir the ace making hardware.

Is Reiki a legitimate integral mending methodology? Truly. Are there fair, genuine ace instructors? Truly. Nonetheless, qualified reiki experts are uncommon, and the obligation of

figuring out how to explore the excellent reiki way has a place with the understudy.

I trust that foundation information in Eastern orders and ideas is essential for both an authentic ace instructor and for genuine understudies who wish to accomplish a profound, submitted reiki practice. The qualified ace instructors have achieved an adjustment in their reality see that is comprehensive, and an understudy utilizing a strong foundation in Eastern philosophical and profound perspectives is bound to perceive this quality in a planned ace educator.

Achieving a phase of bona fide individual change in any Eastern control along The Path requests that a searcher plan for a five to multi-year adventure of scholarly severe examination, and another five to ten years of real practice: taking all things together, around twenty years of mental, enthusiastic, and profound practice goes before a genuine change in mindfulness and changing one's mindfulness, the points of view that direct one's life, is the initial step along The Path.

The Art of Reiki

Reiki implies Universal Life Force Energy. We are made of energy, and science has as of late demonstrated this reality. The littlest issue that has been estimated to date is vibrating energy. The body comprises of a few noteworthy and minor fiery pathways (or meridians) which associate every organ and

license the progression of power all through the body. These energy pathways have been known for a considerable length of time by different old Chinese practitioners. Needle therapy, for instance, is a technique for discharging blocked energy by embeddings fine needles in the body's meridians to animate explicit power focuses.

Reiki and needle therapy have similar goals. However, the methods are extraordinary. In Reiki, the practitioner will utilize either a hands-on methodology or hands off (contingent upon the practitioner). The customer will stay in a casual position for the length of the session while the Reiki Master realigns the body's energy through non-moving touch. Reiki practitioners frequently have an endowment of sense, either through the capacity to feel the heat, or see power (or both). There are numerous advantages to Reiki, for example, expanded imperativeness, expanded unwinding and center, the decline in pressure and uneasiness, diminished torment, and accelerating recuperating/recuperation time. Everybody unexpectedly encounters Reiki, which is one reason it is so one of a kind and extraordinary.

A standout amongst the most significant things to recollect about Reiki is simply the angle obligation. No practitioner on the planet can mend an individual who isn't eager to recuperate themselves. The customer must assume liability for their very own wellbeing and health when they wish to see the full advantages that Reiki can bring into their life. It is likewise essential to recall that Reiki influences both the brain and body (as they are interconnected). Ongoing examples or uneven characters in our mind will change our everyday life, just as our physical body. Reiki will address both the physical and mental energy levels, yet it is dependent upon the customer to roll out relating improvements in their life. The body and brain can be realigned through Reiki, yet if a similar issue that made the irregularity continues, at that point the advantages of Reiki may be brief.

Eastern customs:

Since a robust and valid case can be made that cutting-edge reiki is a rediscovery by Mikao Usui Sensei of an antiquated Tibetan practice known as Medicine Buddha, I will draw a couple of Medicine Buddha nuts and bolts, looking for a valid establishment, from an Eastern perspective, addressing contemporary Reiki practice.

Tibetan drug is established in India's Buddhist framework, taught as ahead of schedule as the 6th century BCE. From the Buddhist attitude, physical malady is a dynamic, energetic manifestation of the mental, social, and otherworldly issue.

Buddhism is a coordinated, contemplative or reflection practice on the all-inclusive dimension of "right living" and includes taking advantage of mental, social, and profound

mending vitality as it strips away layers made cover behind the unhealthy physical manifestation. These are the same attitudes taught in the present real reiki practice.

Inside this Indian Buddhist establishment, the Tibetans widened their recuperating works on including different medicines and drugs. The Tibetan Buddhists made amending framework, called Medicine Buddha: regarding otherworldly thought, contemplation, instinctive enchanted recuperating techniques - including hands-on vitality control - all mixing as amending structure dependent on the Buddhist statutes of "right discernment" and "right activity", and of wellbeing being an amicable harmony between mankind's vital relationship interfacing our physical, mental, profound, and regular universes as different manifestations of one vitality or life power. The purpose of Medicine Buddha practice is to show one's periodic energetic potential.

Recuperating through the Medicine Buddha happens using a progression of strengthening influences intended to stir the natural mending vitality that exists in. Rehearsing the Medicine Buddha reflection, and getting increasing controls from a certified Buddhist contemplation ace, go hand in hand for both the healer and patient. In present-day reiki, the reiki ace gives enhancing to the patient or understudy or individual healer in levels called "attunements." Attunements open the subject to their natural vitality potential in stages.

Scarcely touching the most superficial layer at that point, we have portrayed a case for the authentic improvement of the present reiki by visiting the 6th-century Buddhist lessons of the Tibetan Medicine Buddha:

1.   Drug Buddha includes a laying-on of hands like Reiki.

2.   The capacity to perform Medicine Buddha recuperating is transmitted to the understudy through a strengthening given by the instructor, like a Reiki attunement.

3.   The perspectives and attitudes of Medicine Buddha practice firmly parallel the framework presently known as Reiki.

A Twenty-year, three-day class:

Reiki is made out of two Japanese characters. The top style, "rei," is characterized as "soul." The base character "ki," is characterized as "vitality." It is reasonable for the state that the expression "reiki" signifies "soul vitality" or "life power." However, If I ponder these words in the Western sense, I can't get a handle on their actual implications. It is necessary for the Western understudy of reiki to comprehend that they are setting out on a voyage to a spot in our understanding where we come into direct contact with and are changed by, the dynamics of language.

Figuring out how to utilize regular Western terms in an Eastern sense, to conceptualize in a "Reiki" style, is vital to seeing how reiki recuperating succeeds. Without this learning of the contrast among Eastern and Western ideas of vitality or life power, we can be given the apparatuses of the spirit recovering calling yet won't have the capacity to take guidance on using them; the terminology, obscure images, reflection guidance, and data coming to us through contemplation practice will be confounded.

After our three-day reiki course, we will outline our endorsements and open our note pads. In any case, we will experience images and contemplation directions through our Western originations of what the Eastern photos and guidelines are putting forth us. The images, mantras, and courses are intended to communicate aspects of life power vitality in the reiki sense, in the Eastern mind - however, we have no clue what that implies!

A Beginner's Guide to Reiki

Inspired by Reiki, yet don't have the foggiest idea where to begin? Does the universal life energy confound you? Reiki is a necessary procedure, made in the twentieth century; however dependent on old Eastern principals in regards to ki or chi.

Reiki (articulated beam key) is a Japanese word that implies universal life energy. Rei signifies the universal soul or soul,

and ki means life power energy. Ki is equivalent to chi, which you find in the word kendo. Our bodies and everything around us is comprised of energy. When we are receptive to this energy everything streams in a reasonable way. Reiki focuses on evacuating energy blockages and doing this is a proposed treatment for physical, mental, and other worldly issues.

In a Reiki session, a customer rests on a table while the Reiki practitioner moves her hands over the body. She channels the Reiki energy and guides it to the customer. There is an assortment of hand positions that are educated as a premise to Reiki recuperating, and a practitioner utilizes these alongside their very own involvement and instinct as a guide.

When an individual is keen on turning into a Reiki practitioner, there are three dimensions that he should think about. In the first aspect, the understudy is sensitive to the Reiki energy with the goal that they may start to mend themselves. With the second dimension, the understudy learns images and reflection so they can turn out to be progressively engaged and take their investigations to the following size. This dimension likewise presents remove mending. The third dimension is the Master Teacher level. Notwithstanding adapting more images and reflections, he is instructed the attunement processes of every one of the three sizes and is currently ready to teach Reiki to other people.

The Secrets of Reiki Healing

The supernatural power that Reiki was recuperating has have gotten on pretty much every grown-up who is into the Japanese mending work of art. Who wouldn't be with the moving tributes that Reiki practitioners and educators keep on regurgitating in Reiki-facilitated sites and in books specifically on the recuperating power that Reiki has brought into these individuals' lives?

In any case, precisely what are these individuals affirming about? What are these mysteries of reiki recuperating that have improved them and have persuaded their loved ones to take up a Reiki class or two?

The insider facts aren't a "major mystery." Truth be told recuperating in Reiki is showed quickly the minute a patient is contacted with the hands of a practitioner. It is affirmed in the way a practitioner carries on with his life when Reiki contacted him. It is standing out he speaks with you. How delicately and gradually he talks, breathing life to each word, each expression his mouth relinquishes. It is in the life reason he pronounces, that is, harmony and harmony especially harmonious relations with relatives, companions, collaborators, and the neighbors. It is in how healthy and accommodated his body is currently. It is in how dynamic and more youthful looking he has moved toward becoming. It is by the way he appears to repulse sicknesses and misfortune.

These and more can transpire, as well. You can have the healthiest, fittest, and hottest body you had always wanted.

You can have all the good karma on the planet, repulse maladies, and live harmoniously with your mate and kids, with your in- laws, with your companions, and with your neighbors.

Reiki recuperating can make these occur. Reiki will get these going for you. This is the "huge mystery" that Reiki professes to have and which it can share to the individuals who acknowledge the fine art into their lives with all truthfulness, who resolutely and calmly learns the methods for Reiki, and who remember to share these "privileged insights" of Reiki to those needing recuperating.

Begin with a genuine converse with a Reiki practitioner to promise you that Reiki isn't some clique yet a lifestyle and of mending. At that point, try out an essential Reiki class. Consequently, gain proficiency with the methods for this old Japanese work of art. Inundate yourself in the mending that learning Reiki ought to convey to your life. Relish each experience you are in a class and practice attunement on yourself and others once you've turned out to be sure of your abilities.

In a matter of moments and without you seeing it, you'll be an alternate individual. You'll be conveying reiki recuperating to each you go over within your business dealings, in the work environment, and at home. The "mysteries" are at long last in your grasp, showed in your lifestyle.

Chapter 1. What Is Reiki For? Understanding The Uses Of Reiki

Reiki comes from a long history of spiritual practices and beliefs that are part of a massive cultural identity. Buddhism has millions of followers, dedicated to and affiliated with practicing the concepts of Universal love, enlightenment, and growth. You don't have to be a Buddhist to practice Reiki at all, and learning about some of the origins, history and structure of Reiki has shown you that this simple healing tool may come from the ideas of Buddhism, but that it is a Universal healing technique that crosses culture, continent, religion, belief, and race.

All over the world, people of all ages, backgrounds, and values are using Reiki to heal and help each other. It is still gaining popularity and momentum as an available resource for healing a variety of severe issues including serious and chronic illness, disease, mental health issues, emotional and physical trauma, and so much more. You are also going to discover some of the ways that Reiki can be a benefit to your overall practice of self-worth, personal abundance, and feelings of joy and happiness. Reiki has the ability to change your vibrational frequency to a higher, brighter, lighter level.

So, with all of your understanding of medical science, prescription drugs, over the counter medications and various other types of healing that can be done, how often have you heard about Reiki being used in mainstream medicine? Probably not as often as you hear about people choosing surgery over other therapies, or an easy to use pill that you pop in your mouth for a few years that won't resolve the problem, only quiet it down.

Reiki has been healing and helping many people in so many different ways since it was born into being in the early twentieth century and here are just some of the powerful ways that Reiki has healed, cured, or inspired people from all over the world:

Reiki...

- Calms the nerves, relieves tension in the body and

reduces stress on all levels

- Acts as a practice to help you ascend in your spiritual

  growth and reach enlightenment

- Forces negative energy to the surface of the auras to be

  purified, cleansed, balanced, or released

- Shifts your emotional state from negative to positive through a series of actions and routines

- Brings balance to the body through the various systems, including the glands and hormones, organs, circulation, respiration, reproduction, brain function, and more

- Changes your blood pressure to a normal function

- Alleviates the symptoms of many diseases and can

even

reverse them in the tracks

• Helps cancer patients during remission and can even be useful in reducing the size of some tumors and growths as an alternative to chemotherapy

• Works well with people who suffer from dementia, Alzheimer's and Parkinson's disease, as well as other neurodegenerative disorders to create more balance with the body and the mind

• Has various uses in the field of psychotherapy as it energetically heals past wounds and traumas by lifting them to the surface and removing them (trauma and wounds are stored in our bodies in the form of energy)

• Alters your consciousness to be more open and accepting of all races, religions, and beliefs

• Alleviates arthritis and arthritic symptoms, sometimes fully curing it

• Takes you away from thought patterns and destructive behaviors so you can build newer, better, healthier habits for yourself

• Helps relieve and heal addictions, including addictions to substances

• Benefits your whole being, not just one part of you (physical, mental, emotional, spiritual)

• Manages your levels of stress so that you are able to function more flexibly in a chaotic and intense world

• Helps you to find a positive footing in any new path you are choosing

• Deals with a variety of problems relating to the immune system include autoimmune disease and chronic issues

• Treats the past with the same amount of healing ability as the present, or the future

- Welcomes an entirely new level of self-esteem and self-love

- Opens your heart to love, joy, and happiness

- Can be a very positive outlet for anyone who is asking for a more spiritual life journey and awakening to psychic potential

- And more!

The applications are endless and you are only limited by any lack of imagination. Your ability to understand how it really works, but for now, let's look at the various parts of the self and body that are influenced by Reiki, one at a time:

Physical Uses

Your physical body is made of blood, tissues, bones, cartilage, ligaments, organs, and many pumping, flowing, excreting, and surging actions. It is very visceral, complicated and senses all kinds of different things, like pain, pleasure, hot, cold, loud, soft, and ticklish. The body is one of our most reliable informants for telling us how we feel and what we need, but sometimes we are not able to fully understand the source of any of these feelings and why they are showing up.

A doctor will give you the scientific reason and will give you a prescription or a remedy to cure the problem or tell you to go home, rest for a week, and push fluids. Reiki would look for the source of the problem and use energy to eradicate the blockages, negative vibrations, and tune it to a new frequency to heal it in another way.

Let's use the example of arthritis: Arthritis is an inflammatory condition that can be caused by a lot of factors. It can be related to a genetic predisposition, a particular diet, a lack of healthy movement and exercise, certain medications, and other causes. Reiki doesn't ask why you have arthritis. The energy of Reiki simply looks for the reality of arthritis and finds a way to shift the energy of it into something better, less painful, and more comfortable.

If your arthritis is caused by a poor diet or medications,

you may have to either change your diet and drop the meds or perform Reiki on yourself every day. A genetic predisposition could actually be completely healed through Reiki so that you would not experience it again, perhaps until you are much older in your life.

This information may come as a shock to you, but the medical industry actually knows very little about healing the frequencies of human beings and will actually only suppress, dilate, repress, side-step, and put a band-aid on many health problems. There are of course plenty of situations in which modern medicine will cure you, but it isn't always about looking at the whole person; only the physical part.

In reality, there are some medical conditions that need medical attention and should be looked at by a medical professional, but in addition to those medical treatments, Reiki can actually attack the source of the problem while your doctor's prescription can attack the issue from another angle.

A lot of people are looking for alternatives to drugs, surgery, and the medical racket that will charge you an arm and a leg for one visit to hear that all you need is a little rest and some vitamins. Reiki is a wonderful example of ways that you can avoid over the counter medications for common colds and sicknesses, regular prescriptions for ongoing issues, pain medication, and more.

The physical body is a complex machine and should be looked at from every angle. Talk to your doctor about any serious concerns, but also consider Reiki for additional healing aid, repair, and recovery.

Chapter 2. Reiki And The Science Behind It

Research and Findings to Support the Science of Reiki's Benefits

In recent decades, Reiki has grown in popularity as a form of therapy and treatment that helps many people with a wide range of health and medical conditions.

While it is considered an alternative therapy, it has been used with positive results that complement and improve the effectiveness of conventional Western medicine.

There are some studies that indicate a positive effect on cancer patients who receive Reiki treatments, including pain relief, reduced anxiety and less stress overall.

Reduced pain and tension, in general, are also benefits that have been reported by people who have experienced the powerful therapeutic effects of Reiki.

In the United States, Reiki has grown significantly in the 1990s, evolving from a historical discovery and concept to a new, modern way to heal with universal energy.

Due to the positive feedback from people using and practicing Reiki, it has increased in popularity and now widely offered in hospitals across the U.S. and in other countries as well.

Reiki provides a gentle, relaxing therapy that gives relief during difficult experiences patients may undergo in hospitals and clinics, such as cancer treatment (radiation, chemotherapy), surgery as well as other procedures (CAT scans, MRIs) and medications.

There are other benefits that support the use and practice of Reiki, either in a hospital, clinical setting, or a less formal space:

- Reiki is completely risk-free and does not cause any harm nor side effects to the person receiving treatment. In other words, even people who may be skeptical at first will give it a try, because there is nothing to risk or lose.

Most, if not all people, have a pleasant experience during their first treatment.

- There is always a benefit from Reiki, whether it's relaxation and stress reduction or a reduction in pain.

Some people have reported the remission of disease or reduction of certain ailments, as a result of Reiki, though results can vary from one individual to the next.

- Reiki is not used to substitute conventional therapy, but rather, as a support for the body's natural ability to heal and improve your health overall.

This is another reason why it is strongly supported by the medical community and hospital network in the U.S., as it can alleviate the stress and negative symptoms often associated with some treatments.

It gives patients something to enjoy and look forward to, after a difficult day of treatment.

- Some people report feeling more energetic and less

fatigued after a session of Reiki. Chronic fatigue is a condition that affects a significant number of people, and many will take prescription medication or other forms of therapy to cope.

Reiki can also provide additional support and energy while delivering this healing effect with a calm, peacefulness, opening, and increasing the flow of energy without added tension.

- Reiki can be used on everyone of all ages, backgrounds, and abilities.

Since there is no risk of harm or side effects at all, anyone from a newborn baby, someone who is pregnant, to someone of advanced age can benefit from Reiki.

Pets are also great candidates for treatment, as well.

Reiki is also beneficial for people who may not have a specific condition or medical issue but would like to experience a general sense of relaxation and peace.

Most people experience stress on a regular basis, and this often becomes chronic, even when we are unaware of it.

We may hold onto tension and worry too often, or find it difficult to unwind and relax, even when there is an opportunity to do so.

Reading and learning about Reiki is a good start, and speaking with friends, colleagues or acquaintances who may have experienced a Reiki therapy session, or took a class themselves, will give you a better idea of what to expect before you begin.

Chapter 3. Benefits Of Reiki

Reiki has many benefits, including healing the body, mind, and spirit but it also helps promote balance and harmony both within the body and our environment. Reiki is a non-invasive healing energy that helps enhance and promote the body's natural healing abilities while encouraging the flow of Ki which overall enhances the body's wellbeing. Reiki can restore balance on all levels within the body and it can directly heal the problem instead of just taking away the pain or relieving some symptoms.

In terms of balance, Reiki can create an emotional and mental balance between the good and the bad. When healing the body from its problem, you are putting less stress on the mind, which affects the mental and emotional state of the human brain. Balance comes from when a person is able to live free from any worries about their own bodies. When there is no stress, there is no anger meaning many negative feelings simply fade away, leaving the body with a balanced and harmonized mindset. Reiki has also the power to heal depression, anxiety, negative emotions, and many other mental illnesses.

Reiki can also relieve any tension within the body and stress itself. When the treatment is in process, Reiki doesn't just go through a particular part of the body that has a problem, it might start with that part, but it makes itself flow all throughout the body, relaxing it and releasing of any stress and tension. Many practitioners reported feeling relaxed, clear- minded, lighter, and peaceful after performing Reiki on themselves or after Reiki has been done on them. This is because the energy flows everywhere, releasing tension that has been put on any parts within your body.

Many of today's known diseases are linked to a stress factor such as work stress, environmental stress, or even emotional stress. This leads to irregular heart rhythms that can cause a stroke, angina, gastrointestinal problems, eating disorders, mood disorders, sexual problems, and many psychological problems. Reiki can help you regulate this stress to avoid any problems within the mind and body.

You are able to achieve natural balance with the body, mind, and spirit due to Reiki dissolving any chakra or energy blocks. These energy blocks can also affect the body physically or mentally. When Reiki is done regularly, it can bring a more peaceful and calmer state to the body and person who is dealing with stress in their everyday lives. The mental balance can also enhance mental clarity, memory, and learning, as well as heal emotional or mental wounds, frustrations, anger, mood swings, fear, and even personal relationships. In general, Reiki enhances your ability to give love and receive love, making you more open to any people and relationships around you.

Reiki is able to give one space where they are able to become more aware of what is happening within their bodies, causing them to make decisions that change the way they live their lives in terms of diet, habits, etc. Many practitioners even report changing their habits or abandoning them. When you become more present of what is happening within your body, you start to access inner wisdom or knowledge. It changes your point of view on certain things in your environment or life.

We are so easily affected by the stress we experience every day in our lives that sometimes it even becomes our 'normal,' and our bodies completely forget what it's like to be in balance once again. Many practitioners can tell you that Reiki is a wonderful and gentle healing practice that makes their body and mind feel amazing, that is the body's true, normal, and balanced nature. It can be rather difficult to maintain this balance but that is why Reiki can be practiced regularly to ensure the body is able to return to its balanced state. Reiki is able to remind our body how to shift into its own self-healing mode even when Reiki is not being practiced. This parasympathetic nervous system state allows you to digest and sleep better, which is very important when it comes to the body's health and vitality. The more often you are able to achieve this state, the more you can become productive and active without the feelings of exhaustion, stress, or burnout floating inside you.

Reiki improves your connection to the Universe and nature. It also has the power to ground and center you by improving focus within the mind. With the help of this energy and your mind, you will be able to stay centered in this present moment instead of living in the past and always being stopped by guilt and regrets from moving on and living your best life. Reiki can help strengthen the ability that revolves around accepting yourself and any events that happen around you, even if they are not aligned with your desires or goals. Instead of acting out of habit, you are able to be more supportive of yourself and others around you; Reiki can help you look at the brighter things when life throws you challenges.

As mentioned above, Reiki can promote better relaxation, which aids in better sleep. With sleep and relaxed bodies, the healing process can go by more smoothly and at a faster rate. You are also able to think more clearly, become focused, and move forward on your spiritual path. This deep relaxation releases many tensions within the body, making it finally function smoothly which is different from your old toxic and tense body. Many practitioners who practice Reiki on themselves or during their attunement, report falling into a deep sleep due to the deep relaxation they experience.

After Reiki has been performed, your body goes to your natural state, accelerating the self-healing ability drastically. During this period, your heart rate, blood pressure, and breathing improve. You will be able to inhale and exhale more deeply and easier than before, this is usually one of the first things that show improvement after performing Reiki on yourself or when someone does Reiki on you. Deep breathing naturally settles our minds, and oxygen also helps fight cancer!

A Reiki treatment is able to restore balance on a very deep level, encouraging the system to improve the body's vital functions such as sleeping, breathing, and digesting.

On a more physical level, Reiki is able to relieve the pain and symptoms of sciatica, migraines, arthritis, asthma, menopausal symptoms, chronic fatigue, insomnia, and many other illnesses. Reiki can also help stimulate and increase mobility in many cases of lower back pain, wrist pain, and shoulder pain. It also has the power to heal inflammations and infections within the body. Reiki, done on yourself or sent to someone over distance healing, has proven to work efficiently as told by many of those who received Reiki and perform Reiki on others. It can also improve indices of the metabolic syndrome which is associated with a risk of type two diabetes, many chronic conditions, and even heart disease.

Not only does Reiki cleanse the body physically, but spiritually too. Cleansing both the mind and body helps promote spiritual growth and personal development. Although you do not need to be spiritual to receive Reiki, it does help in your spiritual path. Instead of targeting individual symptoms, Reiki goes through the entire body. Often a practitioner receives messages, change of attitude, visions, or see things from a different point of view. It makes you see your condition in a new light and makes you deal with it in another and more positive way.

When one is relaxed, the healing process is accelerated. Reiki is a very gentle treatment that can be used on medical conditions such as diabetes, heart conditions, epilepsy, and many others. Reiki also supports chemotherapy. Reiki can also support women on any stage during their pregnancy and gives them the energy to carry on their day-to-day activities.

Many people often replace therapy with a Reiki practice, which is able to give you more self-love, enable you to connect with people on a more emotional level, strengthen your relationships, and solve problems that occur outside of your body. The way we think and what intentions we set for ourselves affect the environment around us; for example, when someone is always angry, their environment will be full of negative energy which can attract many problems and disappointment instead of desires and goals. Having clean thoughts and mindset can help you achieve your goals, Reiki can do that and so much more!

Reiki heals very fast, sometimes even way too quickly. Especially when it comes to healing emotional traumas or mental disorders, there are always negative feelings that occupy our thoughts. Many people go through something called the 'healing crisis,' which is a phase of the body in which the self- healing process started to work by vanishing any negativity and stress out of the system. In order for anyone to move on from something that is bothering them, either mentally or physically, one must first accept and acknowledge the situation. This is what happens in the 'healing crisis,' the energy acknowledges what the issue is and started to remove it from your system. Sometimes this healing process works way too fast, releasing emotions that you've been holding on for quite some time in order to heal yourself on a deeper level.

It's the same concept as fevers. When the body senses a virus from the outside of the body, it raises the temperature drastically, giving one fever and killing that virus in the process. The body just releases all that energy and emotions all at once, and for those who suffered very painful past traumas, it can be a very poor experience having all those emotions back up and running through your head. Many practitioners or clients report crying or yelling a lot during this time, but one shouldn't let these emotions get the better of them. It's simply the final step to releasing the negativity and moving on. Don't get too attached to that moment in your past but think of it as a challenge in life that you have overcome.

It is also not recommended to use Reiki for healing broken bones. Since Reiki is fast healing energy, broken bones might heal the wrong way and will require breaking them again for them to heal in the right direction. Reiki is a pure form of healing energy unless the practitioner or Reiki master uses the energy in the wrong way; there are no serious side effects.

On a more mental level, Reiki can help reduce anxiety and depression by changing your mood. When you feel more relaxed and less stressed, you feel more calm and happy about yourself and your environment, but when you are angry, you often take this feeling out on yourself and others around you. Changes in mood are associated with depression and anxiety. Many studies have proven that there is an overall improvement to one's mood after Reiki, these improvements lead to a reduction of confusion, fear, doubt, depression, anger, and anxiety in many practitioners. Loss of vigor, which is one of the symptoms of depression, returns to its original state once depression dissolves, which then improves the body's mental state.

Overcoming anxiety and reducing negative thoughts is the goal of a healthy body. A research study published in 2006 had a goal determining if Reiki can actually reduce anxiety in women who were experiencing hysterectomies. Those who received the Reiki treatments experienced having a drastic reduction in anxiety than those who were in the control groups. This study, however, only applied to women who were undergoing surgery. Another research carried in Turkey wanted to determine whether Reiki treatment can reduce pain, fatigue, and anxiety among cancer patients. The study found that those who had a Reiki treatment done on them had experienced a reduction and improvement in all these variables. Another different study aimed to discover where treating older adults would improve their anxiety, depression, and some other issues. Yet again, the results didn't disappoint. Many participants of that study reported that not only did their symptoms fade away, but they experienced complete relaxation during a Reiki treatment.

It is safe to say that you, too, can heal your anxiety and many other issues with the help of Universal life energy. But first things first, you must learn a bit more about this amazing and pure energy before jumping into the healing process. Reiki isn't just done on oneself but it can be performed on others too, such as people, animals, events, and plants.

Self-healing is the most popular practice. There are many different ways and techniques of one performing Reiki on themselves. This works by using your hands and placing them in a certain position above countless parts of your body, from top to bottom to ensure that the energy travels everywhere.

Hands-on-healing is the most basic form of healing that revolves around giving the healing energy to someone who is physically present with you. You ask the person to lie down in order for them to relax completely, with their eyes closed and in a comfortable position. The healing begins with the practitioner's hands hovering above the crown chakra and making their way throughout the other chakras in the patient's body.

Distant healing involves a practitioner performing Reiki on another that is not physically present in the moment. When performing distant healing, you must ask the person to have some time to themselves to relax, sit down with their eyes closed and legs crossed for a couple of minutes while you perform the Reiki healing. Reiki can also be done on those who don't believe in the process or those who never had Reiki done on them before. Reiki can also be done to those who are unaware that this process is happening to them. Distant healing energy can also be sent using object forms, such as a photograph or an image of them, an intention slip, or an object that belongs to them.

Distant healing can also be used for occasions or events such as healing broken relationships or sending love and healing to families who are going through tough times. Reiki can be used on past events such as heartbreak or childhood traumas. Reiki doesn't have the power to change the past, but it can help you move on and change the way you feel about that event. Such as changing fear into strength.

Reiki can also be used on other living things such as plants and animals. Applying the same hands-on-healing but slightly changing your intentions can help. For an animal or pet that requires healing, simply focus and hover your hands around the animal. It can be difficult for them to stay still, which is why it is best given when the animal is asleep. For plants, sending Reiki through roots to promote faster and stronger growth, it can also be used on soil, water, seeds.

Reiki helps the body in self-purification, thus promoting immunity. There are much energy and time needed to fight stress and its causes that dictate the nature of lives. At long last, we forget to balance our lives. Our bodies are tuned to the game of stress management naturally until there is no room for relaxation. When Reiki comes in, it acts as a sympathizer that brings us to rest so that we can experience a moment of healing. At this stage, you will still remain active as usual and much productive. The difference will be that your body will be given more room to rest and meditate which is essential for body health and strength. When you allow Reiki in your life, it makes life more productive and active, free from stress and exhaustion or depletion.

Frees Up the Mindset, Makes You More Focused, Rooted, and Stable. You will remain composed and in a steadier condition as opposed to, overthinking over the past events, or even worrying for the future unknowns. Reiki lets you live today as a day and not live in the past or the future. At the end of the day, you will feel sober even when the conditions are not favorable to you, especially in your work environment. Instead of allowing the situations to control you, you will be in a position to challenge them and stand out as strong as if there was no challenge at all. You will end up being of great help to others who feel low or weak as a result of stress or de- motivation.

Chapter 4. Symbols Of Reiki

You might be aware of a Reiki session from a self-practiced session, or you might just hear about it. Reiki is an ancient healing method based on the energy transformation in the body. It is a great mental, physical, and emotional healing process, which has an amazing amount of health benefits.

The most amazing and significant features of Reiki are its symbols. These symbols allow people to continue their healing sessions and experience the energy of the universe. In most of the cases, the symbols only affect the involuntary actions of the body. However, the Reiki symbols work in a different method. These symbols change and modify the functioning of mind and body. The Reiki practitioners envision of Reiki's symbols and loudly say their names draw them in the healing process. If you are utilizing your intentions in the initiation process, then you will experience success for your efforts.

Therefore, it is significant to know about the symbols of

Reiki and their actual meaning. These symbols have always been kept in secret; however, the research and exposure in the past few years influenced the symbols, and we have collected quite a lot of information. Here is the most important information regarding Reiki's symbols.

1.   The Power Symbol: Cho Ku Rei

The powerful symbol of Cho Ku Rei is utilized to boost or reduce the power depending on the specific direction. The purpose of this symbol is to illuminate the light switch, which represents its capability to brighten up our spirituality. It is quite similar to the coil, which is believed by Reiki practitioners to increase and limit the energy flow in the human body. The power could be in different forms in Cho Ku Rei. This symbol is highly effective in the physical healing and purification of the soul. It can also be utilized in drawing attention and the focus of an individual.

If you are thinking to enhance or decrease your power, then Cho Ku Rei is the perfect symbol for you. It can be recognized by portraying a coil, which can be in clockwise or counterclockwise, representing chi that is the movement of energy from the body. You can think about a switch for imagining the power symbol. When this switch is activated or on, then a Reiki practitioner has a higher capability to brighten up the energy channel in your body.

Effectively Utilization of Cho Ku Rei

Cho Ku Rei is normally utilized at the beginning of a Reiki session. It assists in enhancing energy and power at any point in the ongoing session. One of the most common ways of utilizing Cho Ku Rei is while healing a wound or injury. It can be highly effective in dealing with common to severe pains or injuries.

In theoretical terms, Cho Ku Rei can be great in clearing out negative thoughts, energy, and feelings from your body that could be an obstacle in your Reiki session. If you are dealing with negative energy in your body, then Cho Ku Rei is the solution to your problems. It helps in taking the symbols out of your body and assist in filling it with light and positivity.

Cho Ku rei can be highly beneficial in improving the strength of your relationships. Moreover, Cho Ku Rei can be effective in getting a job or working on getting a job or relationship with your loved ones. It can also provide protection against different misfortunes, which happens because of having unclean energy in the body. Therefore, utilizing Cho Ku Rei could be a great boost in improving your energy system. On the other hand, if you are thinking to give a natural advancement in your nutrition, then Cho Ku Rei is the solution for removing negativity from your food and system.

2.   The Harmony Symbol: Sei he ki

This symbol represents harmony. The primary purpose of this symbol is purification for improving the mental and emotional healing process. This symbol is identical to the beach wave, which has the natural capability of washing and sweeping negative feelings. Different Reiki practitioners utilize this symbol while treating patients of depression and addiction. It helps in improving the natural balanced state of the body. It can also help treat the patients to recover from the emotional or physical state of disturbance. The symbol of Sei he ki is highly important in unblocking the creative energies of our system.

If you have been looking to purify and balance your

emotional and mental health, then sei he ki is the perfect solution for you. The symbol of sei he ki is quite similar to a wave getting ready to crash the bird's wing or the beach. The symbol is extremely beneficial in establishing a balanced state between right and left-brain. It also serves as the protection symbol. You need to establish a healthy balance in your brain to perform your daily tasks in a perfect manner.

Effective Utilization of sei he ki

Have you been looking to remember new information for taking a test or improving your memory? Then sei he ki is the perfect solution for you. You can draw a symbol of sei he ki on your book during reading or studying for improving your memorizing power. You will remember the information for years. If you just utilize this symbol of Reiki during visualization, you will experience a boost in your information.

Moreover, if you have been struggling to quit some habits like drinking or smoking, then turning to see he ki could be highly beneficial for you. Remember, people adopt bad habits after experiencing some bad energy. If you utilize the symbol of sei he ki around you, then you can reduce negativity and spread positivity to get rid of bad habits.

Having headaches could be another form of dealing with depression or poor mental and emotional health. You can consult sei he ki for getting rid of your headaches as well. You can eliminate your headaches and the habit of consuming different unnecessary medications. Sei he ki also helps in giving you protection from negativity. This symbol removes negative from your body. Even better, it can enhance your positive affirmations. If you write affirmations daily, then try drawing sei he ki next to them. You will experience great positive and motivational energy within your body.

3.   The Distance Symbol: Hon sha ze sho nen

This symbol is highly effective in sending qi over large distance locations. The intention of this symbol is timelessness. It contains a tower-like appearance, which provides the basis of its second name as a pagoda. The primary function of this symbol is to bring people together over different time or space. Hon sha ze sho nen can change itself for unchaining the Akashic records, which is believed to be the fundamental source of human awareness. Reiki practitioners consider this an ideal tool in dealing with previous life issues and inner-child state of customers.

The idea of hon sha ze sho nen is a little difficult to understand as compared to other symbols of Reiki. The primary meaning of hon sha ze sho nen is having no present, past, or future. This symbol is utilized for sending energy and power of Reiki in different space and time. Moreover, this symbol cannot change your past; however, it provides healing to deal with past traumatic situations.

It can help in the identification of actual life experiences and getting over old wounds and injuries. The symbol of hon sha ze sho nen can help to turn an awful incident into a learning experience. The symbol helps Reiki practitioners to send the energy in the future that could result in some bad news of exams, jobs, or tough communication with our special loved ones.

Effective utilization of hon sha ze sho nen

Hon sha ze sho nen is a little different than utilizing the other symbols of Reiki. Hon sha ze sho nen is one of the most powerful symbols of Reiki; however, correct implementation is required for getting results. This symbol works effectively on the subtle body than that of a physical body. Therefore, Reiki practitioners recommend utilizing this symbol regularly for successful healing of past, present, and future.

4. The Master Symbol: Dai ko myo

This symbol represents the whole concept of Reiki. The primary purpose of this symbol is to bring enlightenment to the body. Reiki masters only use this symbol while initiating the attunement. This symbol allows healing by bringing the power of healing. It is one of the most complicated forms of symbols to be drawn with hands during a Reiki session.

All power to the wonderful symbol of daily ko myo, which is also the master symbol. This is responsible for bringing nourishment and enlightenment to the body. Therefore, this is also known as the holiest symbol of Reiki. It brings the great forces of vibration and provides the awesome transformational power than all the other five symbols of Reiki. The healing powers of dai ko myo consist of the upper chakra by involving the soul in general. Dai ko myo is the representation of empowerment and represents the meaning of 'bringing shining light' in the body. This process of spiritual empowerment through dai ko myo helps in getting closer to God with the help of Reiki practitioners.

Utilization of Dai ko myo

You can utilize different methods to visualize, think, and draw the symbol of dai ko myo for getting it to your third eye. You can meditate with dai ko myo for receiving and nourishing your soul or body. It releases amazing power to help yourself and the world.

On the other hand, if you are thinking to improve your relationship and establish awareness to get better spiritual insight, then dai ko myo is the most significant symbol for you. Utilizing this symbol along with other symbols of Reiki can do wonders for you. Dai ko myo is an excellent way of improving the health of your immune system. Dai ko myo helps in improving the energy flow in your body. It helps in removing blocked particles that could be affecting your immune system. If you are taking any homeopathic medications to improve your health, then considering dai ko myo could enhance your capability to avail from the benefits and improving your well- being.

5.   The Completion Symbol: Raku

This symbol is utilized during the last stages of the Reiki session. Grounding is the primary purpose of this symbol. The Reiki practitioners turn to this symbol during the end of a Reiki session. They utilize this symbol for closing, settling, and sealing the qi within the human body. The outstanding lightning bolt is the ideal symbol, which is drawn by the hand movement during the completion of the Reiki session.

Raku is an ideal symbol of Reiki, which can be utilized at the master level. Raku symbol is also known as fire serpent; however, just having a look at its shape will tell you the reason for its name. It contains a zigzag bolt-like shape that is greatly utilized for grounding a Reiki session. It is similar to the utilization of savasana at the end of a yoga session, which helps the body to absorb and get all the advantages of Reiki. This symbol is effective in clearing and removing any negative energy from the body during the practice.

It is highly effective to utilize the symbol of Reku at the end of the Reiki session for getting all the energy and benefits of the process. You can draw the symbol for experiencing the grounding benefits in daily life.

Utilizing Multiple Reiki Symbols at the Same Time

You do not need to utilize these symbols individually; however, they can be utilized in combination with other symbols at the same time. One of the significant ways of doing this is by sending Reiki's energy for treating a sick child. You can hold the picture of the child and start visualizing Cho Ku Rei, sei her ki, hon sha ze sho nen, and Cho Ku Rei with three repetitions per symbol. You can call recipient name three times by holding his or her picture in your hand; this could be a great way of sending healing energies to them.

You can utilize these symbols for curing a future event with the help of Reiki. It could be bad news, a job interview, a marriage proposal, or a doctor's appointment. You can simply repeat Cho Ku Rei, sei he ki, hon sha ze sho nen, and Cho Ku Rei with three repetitions. This will bring you peace, relaxation, and positive energy to help you deal with that day. You will lose feelings of depression, anxiety, and stress with the help of Reiki. You will focus on building positivity around you.

These symbols are an amazing way of enhancing your mental, spiritual, emotional, and physical health. If you have never received a Reiki session, then you should give one try to it. Reiki will assist you in understanding these symbols and signs more effectively to improve your daily life.

Chapter 5. How Reiki Works

Everyone is born with a force that is specifically given to them by the breather life. This force connects all living things because they can transfer the energies from one person to another in the healing process. The human body has millions of cells, and each cell in the human body is filled with wisdom and the energy that is everywhere at the same time that they can use to heal themselves and others. The omnipresent wisdom composition in the cells of the living things provides high connectivity between them. It is part of our genetics. It runs in all our cells and cannot be separated from them, but it can only be weakened by various things.

Reiki works harmoniously. For it to work, the entire mind, the body, and the soul should be at peace. They should be balanced in that they can correspond with each other. When one's mind, body, and soul are at peace with each other, the functioning of the body and its healing are enhanced. The body will be in a position to heal itself because of biological intelligence. The cells of the body notice the balance initiated by the harmony of the mind and spirit and they can function very well and heal the body.

The flow of the life force in the body is controlled by different points. These points channel the force that the practitioner is

using to the respective desired place. If it is channeled to heal the physical part of a human being, then the point's main work is to ensure that those physical parts of the human body receive this force to be healed. If the force is aimed at emotional healing, theses controlling points make sure that the force exerted is taken to the aimed place. These controlling points are called the chakras.

The chakras are like the wheels that spin the energy in the body. The primary chakras are seven, but they have others so many smaller ones that are attached to specific parts of the human body. Each chakra has its specific job of supplying energy to different specific parts of the body. They work as the energy conductors with their specific frequency attached to them. They cannot confuse and take this energy elsewhere. Just like in the case of blood vessels. Each blood vessel has its specific job that must be delivered, but the whole blood vessel's ultimate goal is to ensure that all the blood in the body is flowing well and the body is strong and healthy. Failure to which, the body system will weaken. This is the same as the chakras. Every chakra must perform its duty, and it should be delivered to the specific place, but the ultimate goal of all the chakras is to make sure there is energy flow in the whole body for it to be healed or to heal someone.

Just the same way when the blood vessels blockage causes health problems to the body, chakras do the same too. When the chakras are blocked, the body becomes weak and sick. The flow of energy in the body is reduced and at times, diluted. Due to the lack of the positive charge of the energy in the body, the energy cannot flow to the desired places because the functionality of the body is disturbed. The cells that host the energy are weak, and therefore, they cannot function properly. The energy within them is diluted. When energy flows too fast or too slow through the chakra, this means this chakra is unbalanced, and something is causing its blockage that needs to be attended to.

Reiki treatment must be full so that it can open the blockages caused by various things and rebalance the flow of the universal force within the body. The body's immune system will be fully stimulated, and the energy flow will be boosted if a person finishes a full dosage of Reiki treatment.

The body will clean all the poisonous properties in it to allow the flow of the universal force. The poisons from drugs, tobacco, lack of sleep, stress, alcohol, negative habits, and so many other things will be cleaned during the Reiki treatment to make sure that the natural healing abilities are boosted to allow the energy into the body and to allow the flow to be smooth which allows the healing process to begin. A full dosage of Reiki is four days for energy flow boosting.

Different things cause blockage of chakras. It can be due to the physical body's exposure to stress or other emotional stresses and imbalances. Understanding the function of each chakra and its location can help open and energize each of the chakras to work well and be able to control the flow of energy without any problem. Different cultures around the globe have come up with ways that can be used in the stimulation of ki energy. There are ways like Tai Chi, Yoga, Meditation, but Reiki is very simple to learn and to use in the healing practice. It is not complicated.

Reiki's techniques are very simple to understand, and the results of knowing and mastering Reiki are so good and amazing. Everyone has Reiki in their bodies, and anyone can use this non-physical healing energy, however, if one is not committed to this universal life force, he may not be able to use it wholly but may only use 10% or 20% of its healing quantity. Reiki is used when hands are placed on your body or the other person's body. The energy is transferred from the hands to the hurting place because of the connection with the universal life force. The gift of Reiki has a lot of wisdom in it and unconditional love that if Reiki is used in a negative way to bring harm to yourself or others or to serve any destructive agenda, one can be able to lose it otherwise if used for the right purpose; Reiki will leave the human body when one dies. Because of its purity in love and wisdom, it likes being treated with the respect it deserves for it not to leave. The seven chakra points transmit the energy to the specific requirements a place, and these are;

The Crown Chakra

This chakra is always on top of the head. Like a crown on a queen's head, the chakra is a crown on a patient's head. This chakra is full of consciousness. The chakra is in violet or white. This chakra moves downwards up to the eyes then goes upwards again. This energy moves from the pineal glands to the upper brains, and then it continues up to the right eye. It has three main aims. It gives spiritual vision.

This chakra is a dream of so many spiritual warriors. The spiritual warriors need visions to be able to know where they are moving to. This chakra also enlightens you. It opens your eyes to things you did not know. It opens your eyes and feelings to the power within you that you did not know it resides there. The intuition of things in you is all the work of this chakra. It makes sure that you understand the things that are within you and things about others.

The Third Eye Chakra

This chakra is marked by an indigo color. The position of the chakra, unlike the crown it is in the middle of your eyebrows or the forehead, and then it moves to your nose and then slightly above the eyebrows. This chakra opens up your mind and allows it to see beyond the material world. Your perception of things changes because of this chakra. How your thoughts function changes. The force in your changes and is channeled to the direct direction because this chakra makes sure of the direction — your sense of perception of things changes. How you perceive the force within you changes positively. You can tell me what to do and at what time. The energy in this chakra is sent to the spine which has very high sensitivity and then it is sent to the left eye, the lower brain, from here the energy flows to the ears and the eyes then it lastly goes up to the nervous system of the body.

The Throat Chakra

The light blue color is an accompaniment to this chakra. The throat chakra is located in the middle of the neck. Right at the center. It moves down to the center of your heart, and then it goes up again up to the center of your eyes. This chakra makes all the personal truths are heard and attended to. This chakra gives a representation of the self-expression. One is able and should express themselves differently. When they are angry, they should express themselves, and when they are sad and devastated, they should their expressions should be known. Their emotions should be well seen and attended to. All their feelings should be attended to and the only chakra to represent all this is the throat chakra. It is like a voice to expressions and the emotions of the humans.

People can communicate how they feel or what they want to do because of this chakra. The energy in this chakra allows one be able to communicate to others around him and the world at large how they feel, what their ideas are, their problems, the solutions if they have found any and they are also able to communicate to others about the progress of their healing or how to treat them. The creativity of what to be done in case of problems is handled by the throat chakra. How one creates solutions or ideas are all the energies from the throat chakra. The throat chakra is very important because it gives voice to the deepest feelings of a person.

The Heart Chakra

This chakra is represented by the rose and green colors. This chakra is located in the middle of the chest. Here all your compassion, love, and kindness come into being. The love for yourself and love for others are empowered by this chakra. The universal force in this chakra targets to bringing out the compassion for you and others. How you are devoted to the people you love or care about is brought to life by this chakra. This chakra also shows how far you have come in your spirituality. It shows the progress of your spirituality if it has gone up or reduced. The kindness you show to others is also represented by this chakra. How kind you are to people is the force channeled by this chakra to you. The energy in this chakra travels to the heart because that is where the compassion and love come from then it takes its course to the thymus gland. From this gland, this energy goes up to the lungs and the liver and finally, it rests in the circulation system.

The Solar Plexus Chakra

It has a yellow color. This chakra starts just in your belly button then it moves up to your breast bone. It is a representation of the center of the body. This chakra gives birth to all the personal powers. The identity of different things is revealed, and self-confidence is gained. The foods taken in by the body are digested, and the energies from the food are channeled to different parts of the body like the liver, stomach, gall bladder, pancreas, and the emotions.

The Sacral Chakra

The orange color is its representative color. This chakra is located below the belly button. These chakras are the master of creativity that enriches human life. It gives you the creative life that makes your; life on earthy worthy and better to live. Your chakra allows you to engage in activities that give you a lot of pleasure like good food, sex, swimming, intimacy, and so many other things that make your life enjoyable on this earth. The energy in this chakra is sent to the legs, the reproductive system, and the sensory glands.

The Root Chakra

This chakras color is red. The chakra is in the middle of your genitalia. This chakra gives all your energy a connection with earth then this energy gives you the things you need for your stay on this earth. The chakra is a great representative of life itself. The birth of all living things and how they were created are all the representations of these chakras. The energy in this chakra goes to the spine; then it moves to the kidneys, the bladder and lastly, it settles to the glands.

Chapter 6. The Five Reiki Principles

When Dr Usui taught Reiki, he took a holistic view and taught not only Reiki healing but also Reiki as an opportunity for spiritual development and personal growth. Coming from a Buddhist background and perspective, Dr Usui believed that constant progress towards enlightenment was just as important as - or perhaps even more important than - purely physical healing.

As well as the essential Reiki hand positions, symbols and techniques, he would teach his students a range of spiritual practices and philosophies, with the aim of helping them to develop themselves as well-rounded individuals, and to subsequently become better healers.

Among the philosophies, spiritual practices and ideologies shared and taught along with the Reiki healing system, were the following five Reiki principles:

Just for today, I will not worry Just for today, I will not

be angry Just for today, I will be grateful

Just for today, I will work hard on myself

Just for today, I will be kind to every living thing Dr Usui told his students that these were principles for Reiki practitioners to live by, in order to live happy and fulfilled lives. Over the years, there has been a great deal of debate about their correct translation and meaning, and you will find a bewildering number of slight modifications and variations online. Meditate on them and see which ones feel useful and resonant for you, and feel free to choose your own version from the ones available. There is no dogma in Reiki, just trust what you feel.

Here are some of the things I understand from the version I have chosen to share with you here. Please do your own research and check in with your heart in order to understand their meaning personally, and on a deeper level.

Each of the principles begins with the words, "Just for today..." I remember years ago posting the Reiki principles on Facebook, in order to share them with others. The responses that came back were incredibly judgemental about the words "Just for today". People wanted to know why just for today, why not every day. They filled up that comment feed with a whole load of shoulds, shoulding all over what I consider to be the real beauty and wisdom of these principles.

I find the "Just for today.." affirmation to be one of the wisest and most profound aspects of the Reiki principles, because it allows for human frailty, and is therefore based in reality and compassionate understanding of the human condition, rather than piety and pretence. In these days of instant gratification and misrepresentation, it's all too easy for any one of us to post a pretty picture quote on social media about being good, patient and kind, when that's what we're feeling in that brief moment. But if, five minutes later, we're getting annoyed with someone for not doing their washing up or for playing their music too loudly, or jumping the queue in the supermarket, the wisdom of our post will have expired within minutes.

Dr Usui recognised and acknowledged that the journey towards enlightenment and a peaceful spirit was a human journey, and that, as human beings, we were bound to fail or be utterly miserably if we constantly set ourselves unrealistic goals for self-development. He knew that the journey to Nirvana was a one day at a time thing! So, he gave us freedom to take it one day at a time. Just for today, I will not anger... is, for most of us at least, an achievable goal. When we reach it, we feel a great sense of achievement; while striving towards it we are able to remain mindful of it, minute by minute; and when we fail, we can try again tomorrow... and the next day.

Just for today, I will not worry

How many times has worrying robbed you of your peace in the moment, only to be exposed as fruitless when things turn out to be okay after all?! Worrying solves nothing and always robs us of our peace. If we are natural and compulsive worriers, worrying can take days, or even weeks away from us and in the end, when we look back, we often discover that it was all for nothing. When we let go of worry, we are more connected to higher consciousness because we are demonstrating trust in the divine plan, and this in turn inspires us with more confidence. When we worry, we are essentially saying that we don't trust the divine Power that runs through everything. This world- shaping Power is the exact same force that runs through us when we activate our Reiki channels. Worrying things will always happen, but if we are working with Reiki energy daily and making it an integral part of our spiritual work, why would we ever need to worry?!

Just for today, I will not be angry

Although anger is a very natural response in many situations, as Reiki practitioners and spiritual seekers, it's important for us to be able to notice our anger and set daily intentions to refrain from reacting angrily. Just as worrying things will always happen, so too will things that make us angry. There are times when the world seems to be a very fraught and angry place, however, it's important for us to remember that we also have access to the energy that created the universe. The Divine Reiki energy that flows through us can be called upon throughout the day, when we feel in need of comfort, understanding and emotional balance. Getting angry disrupts our emotional balance and, as healers, we can maintain a stronger connection to that divine presence when we refuse to react to incendiary situations and learn to reflect, re-connect and respond instead. And even if we find it impossible to remain calm every single day of our lives, with the energy of Reiki to sooth us and calm our nerves and tempers, most of us can honestly say, just for today, I will not get angry.

Just for today, I will be grateful

Gratitude is essential for opening our hearts. When we feel unhappy, it is often because we are focusing on all the negative things in our lives, and feeling unable to appreciate the good. When this lack of gratitude continues over time, we may become depressed and depleted. A lack of gratitude lowers our vibration, and in order to become consistently happy and remain clear channels for Reiki, it's important for us to find, on a daily basis, several reasons to be grateful. "Just for today, I will be grateful" could be adhered to simply by keeping a gratitude journal and writing down five things each day for which we are truly grateful.

Just for today, I will work hard on myself

There is often a variation on this particular principle, which I have also seen translated and interpreted as: Just for today, I will earn an honest living. However, there are many Reiki masters who believe that the translation is much closer to, Just for today, I will work hard, and that the 'work' to which Dr.

Usui was referring was the work we do on ourselves to

achieve spiritual progression and eventually enlightenment.

Both translations are important. Obviously, as spiritual beings and practitioners of a spiritual modality, we want to also live with a high degree of integrity and live in an honest way that feels good to us within our hearts. This also keeps our energy vibration high and clear. But, once again, it's important to remember that Dr Usui was a devoutly spiritual man and would always encourage his students to not only work on others but to also commit daily time and effort to the pursuit of spiritual development.

I have seen from personal experience that daily spiritual practice can yield innumerable rewards and benefits, but it's not always possible to maintain a rigorous daily scheduled of personal development, meditation, yoga, chanting, self- examination and any number of the wide variety of tools available to us. However, right now, in this moment - Just for today - we can all commit to doing one thing that enhances our spiritual progression or keeps us mindful of our evolutionary path. Dr Usui believed that working hard on ourselves should always be a priority, and that if we all worked hard on ourselves and allowed Reiki to transform us, the world would eventually also be transformed and become a much better place.

Just for today, I will be kind to every living thing

As healers and spiritual seekers, it's important for us to expand our desire to do good, by attempting to bring healing into all of our encounters with others in the wider world. There's no point connecting with this beautiful energy for the purpose of improving the life conditions of a handful of people, when we treat the rest of the world unkindly. Reiki is not only a practice, it is also a consciousness, and a pledge to move through the world seeking to do only good, and to share the healing vibration of this beautiful energy and practice. And, of course, the best teacher is the example we set in the world.

Being kind to every living thing doesn't mean allowing ourselves to be taken advantage of. Being kind can mean seeing things from a higher perspective and trying to understand why certain people behave the way they do, rather than becoming angry or defensive. The more we connect with the Reiki energy, the more we become able to see the higher perspective. We may even receive psychic insights about others which allow us to become even more compassionate towards them. We might see glimpses of their past lives or even lives we have shared with them, and often when we gain these higher perspectives, we begin to see others much more through the eyes of love, or through Reiki-eyes, always attempting to develop a Reiki spirit that permeates everything we do.

In other words, giving someone a Reiki treatment and then kicking the cat is not consistent energy. It's like becoming a vegan to save the animals and the planet, and then making endless angry videos about meat-eaters ..and other vegans who are not strict enough. At some point the loving-kindness needs to penetrate into our souls. Being kind means trying to find the balance and compassion in our hearts that allows us to love others unconditionally, and to be channels of Reiki all day, every day, flooding the world with this wonderful heart-centred awareness. This way, we always leave people and situations in a much better state than when we first found them, and increase our own capacity to remain in a happier state.

Being kind to every living thing and seeing the higher perspective doesn't mean, however, that we should remain in abusive situations or tolerate abuse in any form. Sometimes we learn a very hard lesson this way. Being a healer doesn't mean we can fix everyone, in fact, it's not our job to fix everyone... Always be humble enough to remember that there is a higher plan for every one of us. Being kind also means being kind to ourselves, and being wise enough to step aside and allow divine love to do the work when we are not able to.

There may be times when we don't feel like being kind, for example, when circumstances force us to live with unpleasant or unreasonable people, but it's important to remember, even in the midst of these difficult times that everything teaches us something and, in each moment, even if we know with all our hearts that we are in the presence of people we cannot possibly tolerate for a lifetime, we can certainly awaken each day with the resolute intention that, Just for today, we will be as kind as humanly possible, and endeavour to bring peace and happiness to ourselves, to others and to the wider world, no matter what. Even when you're packing your bags in secret and arranging therapy to heal your addiction to abusive partners, you can smile inwardly as you dream of your new life, and say quietly within your heart, "Just for today, I will be kind to every living thing."

Chapter 7. Is Reiki Worth It?

The benefits of Reiki

Reiki works on different levels: the physical, emotional, mental, and spiritual to enhance every aspect of life. Reiki is not just one of the oldest healing techniques; it is also one of the most versatile. This ancient Japanese healing method utilizes energy to balance the body and mind. Its effects are experienced by both Reiki healers and their patients.

In fact, it is believed that Reiki can enrich just about any aspect of life, from an individual's physical health to their emotional well-being, to reducing stress and boosting mental clarity. It has been proven that Reiki can provide healing for various major as well as minor illnesses.

It is also use it as a complementary treatment in a number of health facilities. It enhances the healthcare the patient is receiving both in hospital as well as from outpatient care providers. Reiki can help patients with physical ailments as well as those with psychological and emotional problems as well.

Major health benefits of Reiki:

1.   Relief from pain, fatigue, and anxiety

Reiki has been found to be effective in providing relief from pain and anxiety. It is also effective in reducing fatigue.

A 2015 study found that people being treated for cancer had lower pain, fatigue, and anxiety levels when their therapy was combined with Reiki. These levels were significantly lower than those who only received the conventional cancer treatment. These patients received 30-minutes of Reiki treatment 5 days a week.

Another 2015 study focused on the effects of Reiki on women who had undergone cesarean delivery. The study showed that Reiki significantly reduced the anxiety, pain, and breathing rates in women one to two days after the procedure. There was a reduced need for and the number of analgesic medications. However, the study did not find any Reiki effect on pulse rate or blood pressure.

A 2018 study compared the use of Reiki to physiotherapy for treating lower back pain in people with herniated disks. Both Reiki and physiotherapy were found to be equally effective in providing relief from pain. However, it was found that Reiki was more cost-effective and provided faster relief from lower back pain.

2.   Treating depression

Reiki may be combined with other treatments to help relieve depression. In a 2010 study, researchers studied the effects of Reiki treatment on older adults with depression, anxiety, or physical pain. Participants reported that there was an improvement in their physical symptoms, moods, and overall well-being. They also reported feeling more relaxed, more curiosity and improved levels of self-awareness.

3. Enhancing quality of life

The positive benefits of Reiki can greatly improve an individual's overall health and well-being. A 2016 study found out that Reiki was helpful in enhancing the quality of life among cancer patients. Patients who had Reiki had healthy sleep patterns, were self-confident, and were less depressed. There was a noticeable sense of calm, relaxation, and inner peace among cancer patients who received Reiki.

4.   Boost the mood

By providing relief from depression and anxiety, Reiki can help improve an individual's mood. According to a 2010 study, Reiki recipients reported feeling greater mood benefits compared to those who did not receive Reiki. Participants in this study received 30 minutes of Reiki daily for two weeks. At the end, they showed greater improvement in their moods.

5.   Improvement from certain symptoms and conditions Reiki has proved effective in treating these symptoms:

- Tension
- Headache
- Nausea

- Insomnia

The relaxation response that happens after Reiki symptoms may benefit these symptoms.

6.   Improved balance and harmony

Reiki can be an effective tool for restoring the body's balance on various levels like physical, mental, emotional, and spiritual, so that the entire body can function in total harmony. By operating harmoniously, your body is capable of augmenting its natural healing abilities to improve your overall health and wellness.

Thus, Reiki can be extremely beneficial for infants. It can contribute to the baby's sound growth and development. It can directly target potential health problems and rectify them before they can escalate into serious illness.

7.   Helps one relax

Reiki can provide can incredible peace and relaxation to

leave its recipient completely rejuvenated. Individuals who are suffering from stress can consider for relief from anxiety as it inspires recipients to expel stress, anxiety, tension, and any negative energies from their bodies in favor of health, peace, and well-being.

8. Dissolve energy blocks

Reiki treatment activates an awareness that makes you become more conscious about the problems and challenges that are working against your peace of mind. It can help you get rid of the negative energies that cause negative thoughts and self- deprecating feelings.

During your Reiki treatment, you will be trained to listen to your mind and body and take appropriate and conscious decisions for better health. Self-awareness can help you access inner wisdom and knowledge, which is key when dealing with every days stresses in a healthier way.

9. Boost immunity

Regular Reiki sessions can help your body eliminate all

forms of toxins to boost your immune system. Most people tend to be in a constant stress-responsive fight mode that interferes with their body's natural balance and immunity.

In turn, this leaves them vulnerable to different kinds of diseases. The body practically forgets how to reinstate its balance. Reiki plays a crucial role in "reminding" to shift to self- healing mode which is crucial for intensifying its natural healing process.

10.   Help sleep better

Reiki stimulates the body to achieve its natural balance, that improving the recipient's quality of sleep. With your mind relaxed and at peace with nothing to fear, you are bound to enjoy your sleep. The more relaxed you are in your space, the more you will be productive and active without feeling exhausted or burnt out.

11.   Healing infections and inflammations

A Reiki charged water can be an effective natural remedy for infections as well as inflammations. Stress is the root cause of most ailments. Reiki will not only help overcome stress but also strengthen your body to fight infections. Reiki has been found to be very valuable for expectant mothers. A pregnant woman can sign up for Reiki therapies to overcome joint pains, pregnancy related stress, and common infections.

12.   Refining personal relationships

Reiki can help restore and strengthen personal relationships by rebuilding your emotions. It can enhance your ability to connect with people in a more profound way thus boosting your relationships. It can help you get rid of negative thought and feeling, allowing you to realize inner peace which is crucial for fostering healthy relationships.

You will start responding to life issues and people in a more respectful, loving, and supportive way. Most important, it will help you identify the right relations while avoiding toxic ones.

13.   Promote spiritual growth

Reiki treatments can take you through a self-healing journey through personal development. This way, it can help you create a connection with the soul. The result is love, understanding and personal acceptance. Personal acceptance is key to spiritual growth.

Reiki limitations

Reiki is a non-invasive treatment. It does not come with any known side effects. However, for patients who have experienced trauma in the past, lying in a dimly lit room with someone close by can be a little bit uncomfortable.

It is important to understand that Reiki is not intended to replace a doctor-approved treatment.

That said, here are some of the shortcoming associated with Reiki

1.   Lack of formal regulation

Since Reiki largely works outside the concept of western science and medicine, its practice is not regulated in the United States and most western governments. Reiki practitioners do not receive any official certification or license to practice. However, according to the principles of Reiki, a practitioner must learn from a Master and receive direct Attunement from the Master.

One drawback of seeking Reiki treatment, thus, is the varied skill levels among its practitioners. If you do seek Reiki treatment, be sure to choose your therapist carefully. Find out how long they have been in practice as well as the level of training they have completed. Every practitioner should undergo at least three training levels that culminates in a master-level attunement.

2.   Limited science backing

If you prefer seeking treatment based on western medicine and scientific facts, then Reiki will definitely offer you very limited assurance on its effectiveness. Most major hospitals and medical facilities like the Columbia University Medical Center have Reiki practitioners as complementary care providers.

However, there is not much scientific explanation on this healing technique. For instance, a 2008 trial as published in the Journal of Alternative and Complementary Medicine could not explain the connection between Reiki therapy and relief from fibromyalgia.

3.   Limited insurance coverage

Just to be sure, find out if your insurance carrier is covering alternative and complementary medicine before signing up for Reiki treatment. If you are interested in Reiki but unable to meet the costs, then shop around for an insurance provider that offers extensive coverage for alternative and complementary treatments. Some carriers cover treatment for subscribers who seek Reiki treatment for relief from pain and some serious illnesses.

4.   Individual variation

Even with a reliable, first-hand testimonial to Reiki's effectiveness in providing relief for an ailment similar to yours, the effects of Reiki therapy may vary from one patient to the other. According to a University of Texas Health Science Center's study, the results of touch therapies like Reiki are not measurable within the confines of the scientific method. While this should not be reason to give up Reiki treatment, you should not expect specific results with any statistical accuracy.

What happens during a Reiki session

A typical Reiki treatment session lasts between 30 and 90 minutes. During your first appointment, you will meet and interact with your practitioner. This is the time for a brief introduction or chat about Reiki, your expectations and intentions when seeking it.

It is important that you let your practitioner know about the symptoms you wish to heal or if there are specific parts of your body you would like them to focus Reiki on. Also, this is the time to let your therapist know if you have any injuries or spots in your body that are sensitive to touch.

Preparing for your Reiki appointment

Put on loose-fitting but comfortable clothing. You may want to wear natural fabrics like linen, cotton, or silk. Take off your shoes, glasses, and jewelry before the treatment session. Also, switch off your phone and leave it behind.

After the session, drink plenty of water. Some people feel calm and energized after a Reiki session. Others may feel a little bit tired.

Chapter 8. Reiki For Self-Healing

Reiki for self-treatments is highly beneficial and important for a Reiki practitioner. Once you have received your attunements, your connection to Reiki and the universe will be stronger. One of the best ways to foster that connection is practice. You are your best practice subject. Also as a practitioner, you will be working closely with others, and while you cannot take on their energetic burdens, working with clients who are injured or have emotional traumas can be heavy work. Using Reiki on yourself will help keep your energy and body in the best condition.

There is always more to learn when it comes to Reiki and energy. After completing your course, keep yourself open to learning more and trying new things. Using yourself for practice allows you to try out new things if you aren't yet comfortable with trying them on a client. Keep practicing on yourself to build your confidence.

When you first receive your attunements and are starting on your healing journey with Reiki, it is best to focus on yourself. Healing your own imbalances with Reiki will better prepare you for working with clients. It could also very well change your entire life and help you discover more about yourself and your own path.

Many of the greatest healers have struggled with emotional, physical, or spiritual traumas or burdens. Reiki is almost unique in the sense that you can use it on yourself. It isn't selfish to take the time and focus to work on what you need before taking Reiki to the next step of working with others.

Every session will feel different, this includes sessions you perform on yourself. Give yourself some realistic expectations about your own comfort and practice with Reiki energy. It will get stronger and feel more natural the more you practice.

In some instances where practitioners focus only on healing others and not using Reiki on themselves, they may be quite effective in the healing room, but their lives outside of their healing space are quite different. In their personal lives, they might struggle with low vibrations, not live by the five Reiki principles, or struggle in other areas of their lives.

To be the highest version of yourself and the best Reiki practitioner, Reiki should be a lifestyle. It should be a part of you and your every day's tasks and actions. Not just a service you provide for others.

The greatest benefit you can provide others is by healing and balancing yourself. That energy will them affect them even if they are in close proximity to you, not just from receiving a Reiki session. The world can benefit simply from your presence when you reach that naturally balanced state.

The more your energy changes and balances, the more your vibration and frequency change, the greater you can affect your environment, draw to you what you most want in life, and impact the people that are closest to you. With Reiki, sometimes balance and peace are the greatest rewards, because once you are balanced and at peace, you can truly accomplish anything.

Self-imposed barriers are removed, limitations get lifted, you can see the bigger picture and have a clarity of mind that allows you to progress how and where you want to. Releasing the belief that we aren't good enough, or that we can't make money following our passions, or that we have to work hard for what we want is entirely liberating. Reiki can provide that liberation and allow you to actually start living how you want!

With Reiki, you can also learn a lot about yourself and come to terms with a lot of things you deal with day to day. Reiki is there for you and can be a huge support. If you're tired, give yourself a boost with Reiki. If you feel down or sad, lift your spirits with a little Reiki. The uses are infinite, especially for yourself.

Reiki will help your body-mind get to the source of any imbalance in your body and that will only benefit you and your life. Performing Reiki on yourself every day will help you recharge your body and your own energy. The body is a machine. Like all machines, it requires maintenance, care, and alterations. Reiki is a natural source of energy to provide the body with all the maintenance and care it needs!

A poorly maintained car gets rust, parts break, it starts to make strange sounds, doesn't drive straight, and little things start to pile up until it is no longer usable. Your body and energy are the same! Every day actions such as driving, sitting at a desk all day, running, construction work, yard work, things that seem mundane cause wear and tear. So does fatigue, emotional stress, domestic tension, anger outbursts, and other emotional build-ups.

Rather than the body starting to make strange sounds and no longer being able to drive straight, we develop injuries, illnesses, even diseases. Some are physical, some are emotional, and some are mental. Daily Reiki treatments for yourself are the maintenance to keep these at bay. Reiki is your daily oil change, alignment, filled gas tank, filled washer fluid, brake line check, light check, and full-body car wash in one!

Benefits of Daily Self-Treatments

Reiki self-treatments provide you with more than just a way to practice and hone your skills as a practitioner. There are physical, mental, and spiritual benefits of Reiki that you can provide yourself with every day!

Benefits of Reiki:

- Reiki will provide you with relaxation
- Reiki brings you mental clarity
- Reiki can give you an energy boost
- Reiki calms you
- Reiki gives you insight into solving problems
- Reiki relieves physical and emotional pain
- Reiki promotes and accelerates the natural healing process
- Reiki prevents and slows the progress of disease and illness
- Reiki purifies and detoxifies the physical and energetic body

- Reiki fixes energy blocks

- Reiki releases emotional blocks

- Reiki changes the vibrational frequency of the body

- Reiki helps promote positivity and break negative habits and behaviors

These are just a few of the benefits that practitioners feel daily when they give themselves treatments. Reiki benefits don't have to be huge an immediately noticeable. Sometimes, they are more subtle. While it is great to set some time aside every day to perform a full Reiki session for yourself, sometimes life gets in the way and you have to improvise.

Maybe you are getting a headache at work, place your hand on your head and do a quick five-minute session for yourself. Maybe you need a little extra boost to get yourself out of bed in the morning, place your hands on your stomach and give yourself a little Reiki to help get up and get moving.

Self-Treatment can be used for more targeted benefits, like a headache or energy boost. The Bodymind knows what needs to be addressed with Reiki if you are experiencing a specific symptom, but that five or ten-minute quick session can target your symptom quickly and allow you to get on with your day.

How to Perform a Self-Treatment

Many new Reiki practitioners have this concern that they aren't 'doing it right.' Energy work is subjective, much like art. There isn't necessarily a right or wrong way to perform a session on yourself. Most likely, you will start with a routine in the beginning and then as you get more comfortable, start to modify or change that routine as needed.

Even though as a Reiki practitioner, you don't target a specific symptom, sometimes starting a session with your hands over a painful or afflicted area can benefit the session. Some practitioners will start on a painful area of themselves and then continue with the remaining hand positions as normal.

A common question with new students is 'If Reiki goes where it is needed, why are there hand positions?' Generally, the hand positions are an effort to limit conscious resistance on the practitioner or client's part. This is especially true when working with clients as they often like to feel the whole body being worked on with physical touch. However, when working on yourself, you don't have to use hand positions if you feel comfortable enough performing Reiki without them.

Even in personal use though, placing the hands over a specifically painful area can create a conscious feeling of relief just by having a physical focus on the painful area.

Hand positions can also be a part of the treatment process and determining where there are energy blocks or areas that need attention. You may sometimes notice yourself avoiding certain hand positions or positioning your hands over certain areas of your body.

If this is the case, going back to performing a full-body self- treatment or adding additional hand positions might be beneficial. You may avoid an area subconsciously for many reasons, and if you find that to be the case, understanding why you are avoiding that area may help you in your self-healing.

In the beginning, it is especially helpful to follow a routine and the suggested hand positions. This will also help you to learn what positions are used during treatment on a client as many are similar, or placed similarly on the body. However, once you are familiar with the recommended positions, your intuition can guide you as to what positions work best for you.

During a self-treatment, get comfortable. Play some relaxing music, light a few candles and dim the lights. Burn some incense or diffuse and essential oil. Try to pick a place that won't be disturbed during your self-treatment. This will ensure the highest vibration of work.

Try to set aside between 30 and 45 minutes a day to perform a self-treatment of Reiki on yourself. This should become part of your daily routine and lifestyle. To really live the Reiki life and be a strong, practiced practitioner, giving yourself the proper time to heal and soak up Reiki energy is important.

There is no right or wrong time to perform a session. If you'd rather wake up and do a session that is great. If you'd prefer to perform a session at night or take a break in the middle of the day, any option works. You will need to decide which time is best for you and your lifestyle and schedule. That being said, a self-treatment doesn't have to be performed at the same time every day. Work it in where you can.

As you perform the hand positions on yourself, each position should be held between 3 and 5 minutes. You may find yourself needing to spend more or less time on specific areas. Allow your intuition to guide you.

Generally speaking, a little Reiki is better than no Reiki. If there are days that you don't have time for a 30 or 45-minute self-treatment, do what you can. It is said that shortening the time you hold hand positions is better than skipping hand positions all together if you are strapped for time.

Another option if you don't have a lot of time is doing smaller sessions on yourself when you can, 5 to 15 minutes throughout the day. It is worth noting, that these should be balanced out with full-body self-treatments when you can do them, but it is still better to perform a smaller session on yourself than none at all.

At the beginning of every self-Reiki session, try setting an intention for yourself. Your intention should be to heal yourself on all levels and balance yourself on all levels. Use your breath in your self-treatments. With every inhale, visualize yourself drawing Reiki into your body-mind. As you exhale, imagine yourself releasing energy that no longer serves your highest health and good.

Be present in your sessions. Teach yourself how to focus on the Reiki and not have your mind wandering. This is important for self-sessions but also sessions with clients. There is nothing more disheartening for a client to be on the table and feel like their practitioner is thinking about anything but them!

Being present is incredibly important during a Reiki session. This is called conscious touch, thinking of your client, even if that client is you during a self-treatment. If your mind is wandering to what you are going to be making for dinner later that night, or who you are hanging out with this weekend, that can impede the energy flow.

It may seem unrealistic, but clients can and do feel and pick up on those absent-minded feelings from their practitioner. Working on yourself is a great way to practice presence and mindfulness while treating yourself and others. Meditation is another great method for practicing mindfulness.

After your self-treatment is completed, make sure to drink a glass of cold water. Keep yourself hydrated in between Reiki sessions. Make sure to properly close your session and the energetic flow with a deep breath and intend that the Reiki session is complete. Make sure to thank your own body, Reiki energies, and any other forces you give thanks to at the end of a session.

At the end of your session, you can say an affirmation to affirm that you have received the healing and balance you need from your Reiki session. Many Reiki practitioners also like to touch each other their seven main chakras at the end of a Reiki session.

Some common feelings that arise after a session can include lightheadedness, fatigue, or just lethargy. Give yourself a little time to recover if you need to. Practicing a grounding exercise, or just slowly ease back into activity.

If you fall asleep during a self-treatment, the next treatment you perform on yourself, pick up at the last hand position you remember leaving off at before falling asleep.

It is not uncommon to see visions, colors, or get specific feelings or ideas while you are giving yourself a Reiki session. If you'd like, keep a journal or notebook nearby to record what you see and feel. Then you can take the time to understand what they meant to you.

Self-Treatment Hand Positions

The following self-treatment hand positions are a guideline for how to perform the treatment. Not every self-treatment has to be long or ceremonious. You can also use whatever hand positions feel right for yourself.

The self-treatment hand positions are designed for ease and comfort while performing a session on yourself. Generally sitting down is the best way to go. However, lying down is sometimes more comfortable. Lying down does run the risk of you falling asleep in some instances. If you are not ready to go to bed, sitting might be the best option for performing self- treatments.

Many practitioners will wait until they are going to bed to perform a self-treatment though because it assists in their ability to get to sleep. If you are lying down, some of the hand positions may need to be modified.

Consistent Self-Treatments

Over time, you might come to find that your commitment to performing Reiki treatments on yourself begins to dwindle. This is common with practitioners, but also unfortunate. In order to provide an effective healing service to others, or to the entire world, you need to be balanced in yourself. Reiki isn't just a tool for healing and balancing. Reiki has the amazing ability to increase awareness and clarity. These benefits are highly important when practicing Reiki as a service for clients.

Throughout our lives we grow, we change, and we heal our past, present, and future. Without properly balancing ourselves we can shift back into unhealthy habits, negative thinking, and lost sight of what it is that we wanted to accomplish by starting down the Reiki path.

It is possible for healing and change to occur spontaneously, however, it is more likely that it needs to be stimulated or encouraged. Using Reiki every day to treat yourself will continue to encourage growth and change in your life rather than regression.

Our current society idealizes immediate gratification. People don't want something if they can't see immediate results or feel better immediately, pain-free instantly. This mentality has contributed to many issues including obesity and opioid addiction. There is no magic fix or cure-all that will instantly take the pain away and make the world better. It is unfortunate, but true healing and balance and growth take time!

If you feel like you are wasting your time by performing self- treatments, or like too much time has passed without benefit, remember that it does take time. Brushing your teeth and flossing is to maintain dental health and prevent cavities. You still do it every day, even though you don't see that plaque being scrubbed from your teeth.

In the same way, Reiki should be worked into your daily routine. Even if you don't feel or see immediate results, it is the long term benefit and the continued care and balance that you want to maintain.

Saying you don't have time or energy to perform a daily Reiki session is just another way to limit and restrict yourself with society imposed beliefs. Your time is your own. Your health is your priority, and Reiki is a tool that can momentously change your health.

If Reiki is an interest of yours and you want to study it and learn how to use it and heal others, remember that the most important starting point is in healing yourself. Choose to follow a more positive, balanced, aware lifestyle that will benefit yourself, your environment, and those around you by treating yourself with Reiki daily.

Chapter 9. Advancing Your Reiki Practice

You should always begin your Reiki practice by doing sessions on yourself. Once you are confident in healing yourself, if you have the desire to, you can also learn to heal the flow of energies through other people. It is generally advised once you are ready to advance your practice that you learn from a professional.

The Three Degrees of Reiki

Reiki practice is something that has different levels, with the lowest level being reserved for people who want to practice Reiki on themselves and the highest level being reserved for people who learn from and become Reiki masters.

First Degree Reiki

First Degree Reiki is the main focus of this book. This involves self-care and is training that allows you to practice Reiki in daily life. Many people trained in First Degree Reiki can also place their hands-on family and friends to promote Reiki healing. It is not uncommon for people in the healthcare field to learn First Degree Reiki, as it can be used as a complementary medicine. Usually, massage therapists, nurses, and other people who are in a profession where it is appropriate to touch patients will study First Degree Reiki.

Second Degree Reiki

Second Degree Reiki is practiced across a distance. It is ideal for situations where touch might not be possible or when it is inappropriate, such as in the case of psychotherapists who may want to learn Reiki to help patients to process emotional trauma. Second Degree Reiki relies on creating a mental connection, rather than a hands-on approach. In other situations, the mental connection may be established to enhance the effects of the Reiki session and promote a greater flow of energy.

Third Degree Reiki

Third Degree Reiki is the highest level, being achieved only by Reiki masters. To officially earn certification as a Reiki master, it is generally accepted that you must receive an invitation from an existing Reiki master. The people who are extended this invitation are those who have devoted their lives to the practice of Reiki and teaching it to others. Since it requires an invitation from a Reiki master, Third Degree Reiki is generally learned through a long apprenticeship.

Reiki Attunement

A major component of practicing Reiki is the vibrational frequencies. You can only channel the healing energies of the Universe that you have been attuned to. It is not uncommon for a Reiki attunement to be performed before someone moves up to the next degree of Reiki since increasing your vibrational frequency will give you the opportunity to increase your healing potential.

A Reiki attunement can be done by a Reiki teacher who possesses the ability to open your chakras in a way that allows a higher state of consciousness to flow through you. To have the ability to make your energy flow through someone else, these chakras must be able to put forth and absorb energy, connecting you to the flow of life energy in the universe and allowing you to channel it through someone else's body. The process of Reiki attunement may also be called expanding your energy channels. If you do not want to work with a Reiki teacher, then you may also be able to raise your vibrational frequency by doing Chi exercises.

Alternatively, you can work on balancing and then energizing each of your chakras on your own. While this may take longer and require a greater deal of focus than when working with a Reiki master, it is a great alternative if you do not have access to a Reiki instructor. Below, you'll find guidelines for opening each of the chakras. As you read the chants, keep in mind that 'A' is pronounced 'ah' when chanting and 'M' is pronounced like 'mng,' as if it has an 'ng' like the word thing.

• Crown Chakra- To open the crown chakra, place your hands in front of your stomach. Allow the ring fingers to point upward and touch at the tips before crossing the other fingers, ending with the left thumb being positioned under the right. Once your hands are in position, begin to focus on the crown chakra. You may visualize this as a white or purple light above the head if you would like. Then, chant the sound NG. As a note, you should not use this to open the crown chakra unless you have a solid foundation upon the root chakra.

- Third Eye Chakra- Sit somewhere you are comfortable and bring your hands to the lower part of your chest. Place your hands so the middle fingers are straightened, with each touching at the tip and pointing forward. Then, bend the other fingers so that they touch near the top at the second joint. Allow the thumbs to touch as well, pointing toward your body. Now, focus on the third eye where it is located above the eyebrows. As you visualize its indigo energy, chant the sound AUM.

- Throat Chakra- To open the throat chakra, position your hands so your fingers overlap each other on the inside. Allow the thumbs to touch near the top, then pull them up slightly so they stick out. You may position your hands near your chest. Focus on the blue energy of the throat chakra, which is located at the base of the throat. While you do this, chant the sound associated with this chakra—HAM.

- Heart Chakra- You should begin opening the heart chakra by sitting in a cross-legged position. Bring your index finger and thumb together to form a circle. Then, place your right hand just above your solar plexus and place the left hand on the left knee. Focus on the green, glowing energy of the heart chakra, right near your chest. The sound associated with this chakra is YAM.

- Navel Chakra- To open the navel chakra, position your hands on the area just below your ribcage and above your stomach. Let your fingers join together, palms against each other with the fingers pointing directly outward. Let the thumbs cross and be sure the fingers are straight. Now, focus on the area above the navel and see it as a ball of glowing yellow energy. As you visualize this energy and feel it course through you, chant the sound RAM.

- Sacral Chakra- You should open the sacral chakra while in a sitting position. Place your hands in your lap with the palms facing skyward. Let them overlap, with the left hand on the bottom and its palm touching the back of your fingers on your right hand.

Once your hands are in position, allow the tips of the thumbs to come together. Now, focus on the energy in your lower back and navel, imagining it as a glowing orange ball of energy. When you are ready, begin chanting VAM.

- Root Chakra- Open the root chakra by bringing

your thumb and index finger together at the tip, so they form a circle. Focus on the root chakra, imagining a glowing red ball of energy if you would like. As you feel the power of the root chakra, chant the sound LAM.

Before you settle into a chant to open one of your chakras, be sure that you are relaxed. It is best to fall into a meditative state of mind beforehand. This will give you the focus and attention that you need to bring about change with your chanting.

Chapter 10. Developing Your Intuitive And Empathic Skills

If you want to become an effective Reiki practitioner, it is best that you develop your intuitive and empathic skills first. These two skills will be very useful for your future Reiki practice.

Why is Intuition Important in Reiki?

Being intuitive will allow you to provide specialized individual care for your patients. Intuition is your "gut feeling", it is that feeling that you get in the pit of your stomach that is telling you to do something that you would not normally think of doing, but you feel is the right thing to do.

Intuition is important in Reiki because it actually makes you more in tune with the energy involved in the practice. When you are intuitive, you pick signals that others do not or cannot. When you are a Reiki practitioner, your intuition will let you better read your patients' energies, which means you will be able to provide personalized and more effective treatment. If you are highly intuitive, it will be as if your hands already know which part of the body needs more healing, and they will seem to automatically place themselves over there.

Why is Empathy Important in Reiki?

Empathy is the ability of a person to sense another person's emotions, almost to the point that he/she can actually feel, or at the very least, relate to what the other person is experiencing.

An empath can be a great Reiki healer because he/she is highly sensitive to what the other person is feeling. Even if the patient is not being truthful about his/her condition, the empath healer can find out the truth through his or her own feelings.

Both of these skills are important for the Reiki practitioner. In fact, there are Reiki healers who market themselves as Intuitive Empath healers. These are highly effective Reiki practitioners who, aside from their Reiki attunement and training, also use their heightened intuition and empathy to provide the best care for their patients.

If you are planning on becoming a Reiki practitioner yourself, you should develop your intuitive and empathic skills so you can be a lot more effective at healing.

How to Develop Your Intuition

Some people say that you are either born naturally intuitive or you are not, which is not the truth. Everyone of us are born with an innate ability of intuition, it's just that some people are more intuitive than others. The good news is that you can develop and improve upon your intuition, if you work on it hard enough, your intuition would become so accurate that it is almost borderline clairvoyance.

So, what are the things that you need to do to improve your intuition?

1.   Practice Meditation

The messages that come from your intuition are like whispers, if you are not aware of them then you might not get them at all. Hearing what your intuition is saying gets a lot harder when there is a lot of noise and chatter in your mind. Meditating regularly will help you quiet your mind, or at least make it less noisy, so you can hear the messages from your intuition clearly.

2.   Use All Five of Your Senses to Notice Everything That You Can

You might think that you are already using all of your senses properly, but that is not the case. For instance, as you are reading this book, are you aware of the smells around you? Are you aware of how comfortable your chair is right now? Human beings tend to shut off the senses that they do not need to use. There are times when this ability comes in handy, especially when you have to work in a place where there are so many stimuli around you that concentrating on just one is very difficult.

When you learn how to use all five of your senses, it will be easier to unlock your sixth.

3.   Pay More Attention on Your Dreams

When the cognitive part of the brain is too busy, all that noise and activity tend to block the subconscious mind, which is the source of your intuition. Things flip around when you are asleep; this is when your cognitive mind is resting, and your subconscious is more active. Often, your subconscious will give you intuitive messages in the form of dreams, so if you are suddenly jostled out of your dream, try your best to recall what you dreamt of and write them down on a piece of paper.

4.   Get Your Creative Juices Flowing

When you partake in activities that engage your creativity, like painting, scrapbooking, journaling, and others, they relax your cognitive mind enough that it allows your intuitive side to get its message out loud and clear.

5.   Gather Advice from Oracle Cards

One good practice that will heighten your intuitiveness is to learn how to use and read Tarot cards, or you can use other oracle cards that you fancy. Using oracle cards help by giving a physical form to your intuitions, making them easier for you to pick up on.

6.   Test Your Gut Feeling

Do you have a hunch about who will win tonight's basketball game? Do you have a sick feeling in your gut about the new guy that one of your friends is dating? Do you strongly believe that it will be raining tomorrow? Whenever you get gut feelings like the ones mentioned, write them down in a small notebook, or use an app on your phone. Check them later to find out how many times your hunches were spot on, and how many times you actually came close. Do this religiously, after some time, you will find that the number of times your hunches were correct.

7.   Follow Your Body Compass

Your intuition communicates using your entire body, and the more often you cultivate awareness, the more intuitive you become. Whenever you get sick feeling in your stomach when you are trying to make a choice between two things, pay attention to what your body is saying. There is a chance that what you are feeling may be due to the stress that you are experiencing, but then again, it could also be your intuition tugging at your gut to reconsider your choice.

8.   Break Free from Your Usual Routine

Is your work starting to bog you down? Ask human resources if you can cash in all of those "leave credits" and go on a sabbatical from work. When you are too preoccupied by work, it can be quite difficult to listen to the quiet voices of your intuition. Take a break from work sometimes and see if your intuition tells you something.

9.   Be More Attuned with Nature

The prehistoric ancestors of human beings lived in the wild, and they had to heavily rely on their intuition in order to survive, and that innate instinct is still inside modern man today. When you spend time out in nature, far away from modern technology and the stresses of work, your cognitive mind starts to relax, thus causing your intuition to spike up in strength.

10.   Learn from Your Past Experiences

Try to remember a time in the past when things didn't turn out the way you wanted them to; something that happened fairly recently is best. Before things went wrong, did you feel an urge to do things differently, like something in your gut that told you that things are not right? Perhaps you had a dream or a vision that foreshadowed what was about to happen, but you opted to ignore them as just your imagination going wild.

Remember what you felt like back then, try to recall as much of the details as possible. Now, the next time that you feel that way, instead of dismissing it, try to get more attuned with your intuition, and learn to trust it more.

11.   Don't Think, Feel

The human mind is always thinking, it is always coming up with different ideas and pitting them against each other; to put it bluntly, it is like a crazy person who is constantly arguing with himself. On the other hand, intuition feels. Learn how to differentiate when you're feeling or thinking, and then do the former more often. Do what you FEEL is right, not what your THINK is right.

12.   Do Tasks That Require Repetitive Movement

Go jogging, dance, chop vegetables, anything that requires you to do repetitive movements without the need to think will do. These activities will not engage your cognitive mind, thus quieting it enough so that your intuition has space to grow.

13. Do Not Stray Away from Your Values

There are times when your mind steers you away from your integrity, however, your intuition will not. Feel at ease with what you are feeling when you are betraying your values, this is the opposite of what your intuition feels like. Instead of feeling discomfort from the pit of your stomach, you actually feel like your hunch is the right thing that you need to do. You need to learn how to live more aligned with your values, this way you will be able to sense your intuition much easier.

14.   Practice by Observing Strangers

When you are out in public, say in the supermarket or on

the train to work, discreetly observe the people who are around you. Normally, you would just ignore other people and just go ahead with your tasks at hand, but now, consciously take notice of other individuals around you. Try to glean as much information about the person just by what you can observe about them, you will realize that you can actually know things that you would not have known if you only use your cognitive mind alone.

15.   Constantly Train Your Intuition

The only way to improve your intuition is through constant practice. It will be hard at the start to find out what your intuition is trying to tell you, but with constant practice, in time, it would become second nature to you. You will get so good at it that you can sense trouble even before it can even get a chance to get near.

16.   Release Your Inhibitions

Do not be ashamed of your intuitions; many people call themselves crazy whenever they get a hunch about something.

This is the result of the cognitive mind arguing with your intuition, and it is winning the battle. Do not try to rationalize your intuition, it is almost impossible to do anyways, just trust that your hunches will never lead you astray. Think about this, what if you were to rationalize yourself out of a decision that would have changed your life for the better, you will never forgive yourself for not trusting your gut instinct.

How to Develop Your Empathy?

Just like intuition, everybody has at least a trace amount of empathy in their bodies, and just like intuition, you can cultivate empathy. Even if you are not planning on becoming a Reiki practitioner in the future, you should learn to become more empathic with people as it makes you a better and more likeable person overall.

Here are some tips on how you can become a more empathic person:

1.   Challenge Yourself Constantly

Try new things that you have not done before; constantly push yourself out of your comfort zone. This does not have to be anything extreme, you can start by learning new skills, like learning to play a musical instrument, learn how to write computer code, any skill that you have always wanted to learn but for some reason have not yet. Not only will this make you improve as a person, constantly starting from the bottom will teach you how to be humble; and humility is one of the key enablers of empathy.

2.   Get a Change of Environment

Have you been living in the same small town for the most part of your life? If yes, then maybe it is time for you to have a change of scenery. A bit of travel will do you good, especially if you have not even gone out of state even once. Take the dive, pack your bags and go to a place that you have always wanted to go to; it does not have to be so far, it just has to be somewhere that you not been to. However, it is advisable that you get out of the country and travel somewhere where the culture and the people are vastly different from those of your hometown.

3.   Ask for Feedback

Ask your friends and family what they think of your relationship skills, and then ask again later to see if you have any improvement, or if you need to work on things.

4.   Take a Walk in Another Person's Shoes

Talk with other people about what it's like to be them; if it's alright with them, ask them about their issues and insecurities. Ask them about their perceptions and opinions about the experiences that you shared.

5.   Check on Your Biases

Everyone has their own personal biases, some people keep it to themselves, while others let them all hang out. Unfortunately, your biases prevent you from effectively listen and empathize with the other person. Biases are often centered around age, gender, and race. Don't think that you don't have any biases whatsoever, everyone has them, you probably are not fully aware of yours yet. Observe what you think about when you first meet someone – what assumptions do you automatically make, what conclusions do you immediately come to?

6.   Cultivate a Health Sense of Curiosity

What could you learn from the new guy at the office, the one you believe is "inexperienced"? What can you learn from the cashier at your local convenience store? When you ask questions, you also develop a much stronger understanding of the people around you.

7.   Ask Better Questions

In connection to the first point, it is not enough that you are just curious, you also need to learn how to ask the right kinds of questions. At every conversation that you have, always prepare at least three insightful, maybe even provocative, questions for your colleagues or your clients.

When you have more empathy towards others, you can actually feel what they are feeling. In fact, when you have attained attunement after your Reiki training, you might even be able to feel the emotions that other people are feeling.

Chapter 11. All You Need To Know About Reiki Energetic System

The Reiki energetic system works from **three places in the body**. Working with these, starting with these whenever you face an issue, can help balance yourself to face anything.

These are:

Earth Energy (*Hara* – below the navel about 3 inches (8 cm), the core of everything according to Usui.)

When the term hara is mentioned, it references the "lower" hara. The symbolic energetic center for *Earth Ki* (life force or energy that flows through everything). Within that center, original energy is stored. This energy is the essence of your life, energy you were born with, and provides your life's purpose. This original energy is a direct connection between you and the universal life force, and it is not just the energy you received from your parents at your conception.

Heavenly Energy

This is a symbolic energetic center holding *Heaven Ki*. This energy is directly connected to your spirit. If you are connected to this center, you might see colors or experience psychic ability. It is important to stay centered and not become unbalanced. Using this energy in a balanced way will allow you to see beyond the immediate.

Heart Energy

This is a symbolic energetic center holding *Heart Ki*. Energy from this center is connected to emotions. This is 'human' energy that is connected to human experience. You can understand your life's process through this center – from childhood to adulthood and back to childhood. As a child, you lack experience, but as you grow, you turn into a child with experience.

All of these energies are important, particularly when it comes to Reiki. Being in tune with them can help you to use them to your advantage.

Five Elements

Five element Reiki focuses on the **five main elements**: Wood, Fire, Earth, Metal, and Water. This is not to be taken literally, but is more about the qualities that these elements embody. Each element works in its own way, but they all need each other and to work in harmony to be effective.

5 Element Reiki has a good explanation of this:

"Water creates Wood by nourishing it. Wood feeds Fire by being fuel, Fire produces Earth as ash through combustion, Earth produces Metal as minerals, and Metal feeds Water by becoming condensed essential fluid (Earth's core is molten iron, mercury is liquid at lower temperatures, for example). Then, the process repeats with a new set of conditions."

By applying these elements to the body, they relate to Reiki very well:

Wood

Wood represents the eyes. Any issues with eyes can be linked to an imbalance in the liver or gallbladder, headaches, and aggression. Vision issues can lead to poor decision-making, which is why we need to keep it balanced.

Fire

Fire represents the ears, heart, and small intestine. The heart protector is associated with hearing, and the small intestine is associated with sound, so this is all linked. A fire imbalance makes it difficult to listen to others.

The tongue is also represented by fire, so any speech impediment is linked.

Keeping a balance with fire and water is incredibly important.

Earth

This element is represented by the flesh. Connective tissues and fat tissue. A wasting disease is down to an imbalance in the earth element. The mouth, stomach, and spleen are also linked.

Ideas are associated with the earth, so if someone is having trouble creating ideas, then this imbalance may be why.

Metal

The nose is linked to metal, and because of this, so are the lungs, the large intestine, and mucus. Any breathing issues or funny smells is a metal imbalance. The skin is also linked.

The best time of day to help conquer a metal imbalance is between 3:00 and 7:00 a.m.

Water

Water is represented by our kidneys. But it's also linked to our willpower, survival instinct, and sex drive. Issues with it can be seen in kidney stones, kidney and urinary tract infections, bone diseases, loss of hair, some types of watery diarrhea, menstrual disorders, insomnia, and constantly cold hands and feet.

The best time of day to deal with these issues is between 3:00 and 7:00 p.m.

To live our best life, all of these elements need to be working at their best, and working in harmony as well. Seeing the signs for an imbalance in any elemental area gives a practitioner a clear idea of what work needs to be done.

Seven Chakras

The word 'chakra' might seem like a newer concept, but it actually dates back to 600-2000 BC (source). It's also associated with Yoga as well as Reiki. Chakras are concentrated centers of energy in the body that are designed to keep us functioning at optimum levels.

The seven chakras are associated with positive well-being and correspond to the nerve ganglia directly, which are attached to the spinal column. The chakra positions relate to the endocrine glands, which secrete directly into your bloodstream, and are associated with an organ or bodily function.

They are centers of energy inside the human body that link to emotions, behaviors, and feelings. So, when these are blocked, there are issues that follow.

The **seven chakras are located**:

Base of your spine

Lower back and abdomen

Between navel and sternum (solar plexus)

Heart

Throat

Between eyebrows

Crown of your head

These are often associated with colors as well, as shown in the diagram above. The chakras in the lower part of our body link to basic instincts, and the higher ones govern our thoughts, behaviors, and characteristics.

So, now that you know where the chakras are, we're going to look at **how to feel them**. It may not happen right away, but if this is important to you, then you should keep trying until you do:

Start with finding a quiet peaceful place to sit with your eyes closed. Take a few deep breaths and let any stress fall away.

Focus on your body; start at the base of your spine and imagine a spinning red light there. Sit with that feeling for a while.

Move your attention up a little closer to your belly button and feel the warm orange light there. Feel it move with your breath.

Now focus on the area just above your belly button and sense the intense yellow light.

When you reach your heart, the light becomes green. You can place your hand on your heart to really connect.

Move to the dip in your throat. It's bright blue. If you need to

swallow, then do so.

Head to your eyebrows and your third eye. As the indigo light flashes there, you become wiser.

At the top of your head, the spinning light is violet. This light connects you to the universe.

For further reading on this subject, check out the <u>Mind Valley Blog.</u>

Keeping your chakras balanced and making sure everything remains harmonious inside the body can be done in a number of ways, including:

Reiki

Massage

Yoga

Meditation

Exercises

Holistic Medicine.

A lot of these suggestions are things that you can do alone to balance your chakras. It isn't something that you need to visit someone else for, which is great news, because a blockage can be very problematic for you.

Conscious Lifestyle Mag has an in-depth guide to balancing your own chakras, but here is **an exercise you can practice** to get you started:

Put yourself in the mind-set, or energy state, of the

emotion you desire. Start by letting go of expectations of, especially those, or attachments to, the outcome of this exercise.

Bring your knees up, putting your feet flat on the surface beneath you, while you lie on your back. Inhale through your nose, then breathe out through your mouth. Be sure to relax your jaw.

Think of your breath expanding your belly just like a balloon. When you exhale, squeeze your Kegel muscles and flatten your lower back against the surface beneath you. There will be a gentle rocking of your pelvis as you breathe.

Imagine pulling energy from your root chakra – the base of your spine – as you breathe in. The energy will follow your thoughts; you won't have to push or pull.

Inhale, moving your energy from the root chakra to the sacral chakra. As you exhale, the energy circulates back to the root chakra. Keep moving this energy between the chakras by inhaling and feeling it rise to the sacral, then exhaling and letting it drop to the root. Repeat, and you will notice the energy moves easily – nearly on its own.

You can enlarge the circle you've established by breathing healing energy up to your solar plexus chakra. Squeeze your Kegels as you exhale. Repeat this, as well. When you feel this is complete, shrink the circle to send the energy between your solar plexus and sacral chakra.

Keep breathing and squeezing your Kegels as you enlarge this circle of energy to move from your sacral chakra to your heart. When you feel this is complete, shrink the circle to send the energy between your heart chakra and solar plexus. This is moving the energy from sacral to heart, then solar plexus to heart.

Now make two circles of energy; one, between the solar plexus and throat, and two, a small circle between throat and heart. Vocalize when you reach the throat if you aren't already doing so, for example, sighs or moans, even "oohs." This helps to create a deeper chakra healing and move energy. As the momentum builds, energy circles may start moving through the chakras on their own.

Inhale to move energy up from the heart chakra to your third eye, and exhale to move energy down to the heart chakra. Repeat this, followed by creating a small circle between the third eye and throat chakras. Roll your eyes up as you send energy into your third eye, but keep them closed – imagine you can see out of the top of your head. This helps your energy rise and your chakras to heal and achieve balance.

Your next energy circle moves from the throat to the crown chakra, which is followed by a small circle formed between your third eye and crown chakras.

Continue breathing and rocking your hips to move the energy in circles, giving your body the space to go through the full process of chakra healing and energy body rejuvenation.

Healing and keeping these balanced is a great way to overcome the demands of everyday life. Stress is unavoidable, and it puts a strain on our energies that leaves us blocked and risks illness, whether that be mental or physical.

Insider Tips

Here are some **tips to help you determine if your**

chakras are blocked:

Root (Red, the base of your spine, Earth) You feel sluggish.

Stress is unrelenting because of a reliance on external circumstances.

Your career and finances are less than ideal. You have abandonment issues.

You have a strong self-hate.

You need to work on getting this open to have better communication and a deeper openness with the people in your life.

Sacral (Orange, below your belly button, Water) You struggle with sexual intimacy.

You feel abused, and that sex will be painful.

You move from one relationship to another, searching for love.

Healthy sexual experiences are important to life, and a block in this chakra cuts off a very powerful energy inside of you.

Solar Plexus (Yellow, above your belly button, Fire) You feel powerless and like a victim.

You give power away to try and maintain relationships. You struggle to achieve your goals.

You suffer from anxiety and stomach pains.

You need to unblock this chakra to regain your power so you can live a more successful, fulfilling life.

Heart (Green, center of your chest, Air) Fear of commitment.

You have high walls so you don't get hurt by love *again*. You struggle with love and compassion.

You hold grudges.

Your weak heart chakra can lead to heart disease, asthma, and allergies.

Finding comfort in relationships and giving love means you will receive it much more easily. Your life will feel much lighter with this chakra unblocked.

Throat (Blue, bottom of the neck, Sound)

Fear of speaking up and expressing how you feel.

You go along with others, even if it makes you uncomfortable, which leaves you frustrated.

You often have a sore or blocked throat.

Speaking your truth is freeing, and having it heard is even better. Reiki can be wonderful for helping with this chakra.

Third Eye (Indigo, between your eyebrows, Light)

You feel disconnected from life and struggle to find any meaning.

You have trouble with decision-making, particularly when it comes to your spiritual path.

You feel frustrated and get a lot of tension headaches.

You need confidence in your life's path to get any kind of satisfaction from your existence. Clearing this blockage will benefit you greatly.

Crown (Violet, top of the head, Thought) You feel lonely, insignificant, meaningless.

You disconnect from your spiritual self and connect to material possessions instead.

You suffer from migraines and tension headaches.

Unblock this to gain an immense gratitude towards yourself and your life. This will also reconnect you to spirituality.

PROVEN TIPS TO Transform Negative Energy

To purify the negative energy in your life and to transform it into something more positive, here are some suggestions that work not just on you, but on the life that surrounds you:

Declutter – the mess in your house can accumulate stagnant energy and block the flow. It's amazing how getting rid of clutter can help clear out the mind.

Smudge – burn sage, lavender, or cedar as you walk through the house to clear out the negative energy.

Reiki – the symbols can also help clear out any negative energy.

Crystals – clear quartz, black tourmaline, and amber are great for purifying bad energy.

Salt – salt baths or a salt lump can transform negative energy.

Reiki can remove blockages that have been hindering

you, which makes it particularly helpful in transforming negative energy and keeping energy flowing smoothly. Positive intention alongside the healing energy in the Master's hands can remove negative energy, even negative emotions and thoughts, to leave you feeling lighter.

Chapter 12. The Importance Of Reiki To Daily Living

Though no official documentation had yet been published to support the alleged benefits and cures of Reiki, many had already posted through the internet their experiences with Reiki. To sum them up, here are some important facets of Reiki which are applicable to contemporary lifestyle.

Hand art

Reiki is founded on energy movement. It is administered by placing of the hands. The healing virtuosity has been practiced safely for so many years. Also, as Reiki is directed by Divine Awareness, it cannot do any damage.

Thus, it can fine tune accordingly to every individual's requirements to create a result that is appropriate. The goal of Reiki treatment is to cure emotional, transcendental, and physical hurt through the diffusion of "Universal Life Energy."

Healing from afar

What distinguishes Reiki from the many natural curing therapies is its ability to convey healing from afar. What is interesting is that the uses of Reiki are not limited to people in direct physical contact with the therapist. It can also be projected to give healing to those in far remote places. Hence, Reiki creates a bridge between the dispatcher and the recipient. The receiver may also be an individual, an animal, a plant, an object, a place, an event or a happening.

Plant therapy

You can direct Reiki healing by putting your hands on the exterior sides of the vessel where the plant grows. This will enable you to treat the roots and the whole body of the plant. Another option is for you to project Reiki to vegetation from a distance.

Reiki fusion

Reiki supplements and fuses well with all other therapeutic modalities and has received recognition in medicinal settings. According to Time, the National Health Services sanctions Reiki and has designated a Reiki therapist in the Middlesex Hospital, London, to cure young leukemia patients living through the painful side effects of chemotherapy.

Reiki is currently also being utilized as a complementary remedy for the treatment of usual, acute and lingering ailments, in some hospices in the United States of America, and many other countries as well. It is not surprising that physicians and nurses are nowadays getting educated in Reiki.

Versatility, minimalism, effectiveness and easiness of use

Reiki can be convenient in various walks of life. It is capable of tackling a host of circumstances involving living and inanimate substances having blockages arising from imbalances of energy. As you concentrate and direct Reiki to a substance, place, occasion, situation, or occurrence, you will be able to get rid of blockages by harmonizing the flow of life force.

Beginners may try executing Reiki for training and building confidence in the following circumstances:

Advanced predetermining through remote Reiki for triumph during presentations or presentations

Augmenting the efficacy of medicine taken, may it be in capsule, tablets or liquid form

Cleaning and charging quarters in your house or work area by utilizing Reiki symbols in the corners of the said location

Cleansing water or liquids

Closing the house from bad energies, such as burglary, fire and force entry

Encouraging your inherent creative capabilities

Enriching meals

Reconciling with your past

Refining relationships with the spouse, work superior or colleagues

Starting your computer, car or any gadget

Self-protection from harmful energies in populated locations, such as train compartments, schools and cinema halls

Quit addictive habits, such as over-eating, cigarette smoking or drinking liquor

Veterinary cures

Animals, especially birds, horses, cats and dogs seem to build an affinity with Reiki. They also permit people to dispense Reiki to them with no problem at all.

Reiki can be a huge benefit to various conditions by helping you manage the pain, let go of emotions related to the symptom and aid in healing of the ailment. A few of these conditions that Reiki can cure are:

Anxiety

Arthritis

Asthma

Back pain

Colds

Depression

Lack of self confidence
Low self esteem

Migraines

Flu

Skin conditions

Ulcers

As we close, here is a list of when a Reiki treatment is beneficial to a person:

You are not sick but want a soothing treatment;

 You just want to heighten your energy levels;

You are on medical treatment;

You have cancer and/or going through chemotherapy;

You broke a bone and sporting a plaster cast;

You are an in-patient at a hospital;

You are on the family way; or,

You need a complimentary therapy.

"Healing may not be so much about getting better, as about letting go of everything that is not you - all of the expectations, all of the beliefs - and becoming who you are."
- Rachel Naomi Remen

Conclusion

We're finally at the end of the book. From the meaning to the techniques, you have learned what Reiki is and how it can be beneficial for you. It may have a bit of a tricky history and a mixed reception worldwide, especially with the many naysayers out there, but as you have learned, a lot of people think that it has allowed them to feel better and refreshed. Others can even say that the pain they once felt is gone because of it. They even get better sleep, too. And many have also integrated Reiki so well into their lives that they have ascended through the levels, got their attunements, and become practitioners themselves. Thus, they can share what they have learned with others.

Reiki has also been a great healing method. Even when the techniques are a bit challenging to do, they have turned into natural skills as time has passed by and revealed that energy can be cultivated with patience and perseverance. Even the simple act of meditation has become a growing trend in the world of Reiki.

Furthermore, Reiki healing is not just about the techniques themselves. It is also about fulfilling principles, being open to everyone, knowing that within ourselves is the energy we've all had right from the start, integrating the essence of the symbols that represent Reiki, and sharing what we have learned to everyone else who needs it.

After all, who would have thought that a rich doctor who went on a 21-day fast would envision the symbols that would build up the foundation for Reiki? With what Dr. Mikao Usui taught his students, his legacy for cultivating energy has lived on. Since then, it has touched many lives, built different types, branched out to everyone from all religions, and provided a new kind of light to millions of people.

Still, do not think that ascending to the highest Reiki level entails that your journey is over. No, it has only just begun. You will find the path towards learning more about Reiki and how it will benefit and bring you wonders that you have never thought possible in your life. It is also a way to see that Reiki has evolved.

Eventually, you may realize that Reiki is not just a

healing method that you can learn and master: It can also be a lifestyle that will help you cultivate the energy you have waited for so long to have. It will be a way for you to carve a new path with opportunities and show you that you can control your fate.

You may not be able to control everything in life, but if you can channel the energy on the things you can, it will fill you up with the kind of light that you will never forget. Reiki can show you that deep within your heart is a light that you can use to heal yourself and others.

So, what are you waiting for? Go for it, practice Reiki techniques, and feel the energy flow from within!

Book 3 Buddhism For Beginners:

Eliminate Anxiety and Stress through Mindful Guided Meditation. Discover Happiness & Inner Peace as a Zen Mind thanks to Clear & Simple Transcendental Mindfulness Techniques.

Introduction

What Is Buddhism?

So, what exactly is Buddhism? There are different definitions, as there are different perspectives on what Buddhism is. There are even different branches of Buddhism based on regions, schools of thought, movements etc. For the purpose of this book, Buddhism will be defined as a lifestyle rather than a religion or a philosophy. This lifestyle will teach you how to conduct yourself in order to make the best of your environment; the ultimate goal of this lifestyle is to maintain peace and happiness. As I mentioned in the introduction, I had suffered as a prisoner of my own anger for years. By adopting this lifestyle, I now know how to control my emotions and have been able to find happiness and peace of mind. By continuously practicing the teachings which I will bestow upon you, I am able to maintain this newfound serenity.

As this book is a practical guide, I will not delve too deeply into the history of Buddhism. However, it is necessary to have a basic understanding of some key data so that we can see how it was implemented to solve problems, and how centuries later it still holds practical value.

Siddhartha

Siddhartha Gautama was a prince who, being from a regal background, was raised surrounded by opulence. All that he desired he could have. As an adult, he got married and carried out the duties of a prince. He lived a life that others could only dream of and that any common person, whether in the past or present (and I expect in the future), would envy. Siddhartha was happy with his life; he had not a complaint in the world.

His life was sheltered until he ventured out one day to see what the outside world was like. During this trip, he came across an elderly man, an ill person, and finally a corpse. The sight of these three had an effect on Siddhartha. As someone who had lived within the boundaries of affluence, Siddhartha had never been exposed to the frailty of old age; nor was he acquainted with illness or death. He realized that the wealth he was born in could not afford everything. He too was not immune to old age, illness, and eventually death. In this instant, the luxuries which surrounded him ceased to bring him any pleasure. He felt a great unease when he reflected upon the reality of the world. These realities began to take its toll on Siddhartha's well-being and his state of mind. He eventually realized he would have to find a way to deal with these realities. Little did he know, that his journey and the lessons he learned would eventually become teachings, now grouped together as Buddhism.

After seven days of meditating and contemplating, Siddhartha realized that to achieve a peaceful state one had to train one's mind. He would share his learnings with others and would eventually become known as "Buddha" which is the Sanskrit word for "awakened."

I want you to pause and reflect for a moment. Do you see any parallels between you and Siddhartha? Forget about his being called Buddha, which deifies him and can make one feel that they can worship him, but not relate to him. Have you ever struggled with your own peace of mind due to the harsh realities that life brings us? What steps have you taken to cope with the prospect of becoming ill, the stresses of your career, the worry that comes with having a love for your family and friends? Have you done anything at all? I imagine that you, just as I used to, struggle with coping with these realities. While you might not be a prince or princess living a life of affluence, you can relate to Siddhartha and the emotions he felt when he witnessed the horrors he had been sheltered from.

You must understand that we cannot control or predict what the world has in store for us. Instead, we must learn how to train our minds to react to these situations without letting them weigh us down. Like Siddhartha, we must awaken.

Though he was born in opulence, in his adult life Siddhartha displayed immense compassion for others who were not of his social status. As you reflect upon the world you inhabit, you may feel there is a great lack of compassion. This could be that the rich do not show compassion for the poor (the opposite of Siddhartha); it could be that we are apathetic to the suffering of others; it could also be that we always think the worst of others. Have you ever gone to a shop, paid for a product, and then waited impatiently as the shop attendant tried to calculate how much change they owe you? You may think that the shop attendant is a fool and cannot understand simple mathematics. But did you think that perhaps they have had a long and stressful day? Perhaps they have had to deal with disgruntled and aggressive customers since the early morning and are overwhelmed with stress that even something as simple as giving the proper change seems like a challenge to them.

The Teachings

Think about the following for a moment. You may even want to write down your answers to keep track of your current state of mind:

1. How often do you lose your temper?

2. How often do you lose your temper or become anxious about the most trivial matters?

3. How often do you give someone the benefit of the doubt?

I am sure you can guess what my own answers to the above three questions were before I found Buddhism. I would frequently become angry, and more often than not, it was over trivial matters. I never gave others the benefit of the doubt and always thought the worst of them. This is what caused my relationships to break apart; if your answers are similar to mine, the same may happen to you and this is what I hope you can avoid.

Of course, this is easier said than done. But it is attainable and I will ask you to be patient. Incorporating the teachings of Buddhism will not happen overnight, but I want you to commit to adopting these teachings no matter how difficult they may seem. Let us look back to those three questions. To resolve them, I will actually address them in a different order.

How often do you give someone the benefit of the doubt?

Our lives are rushed and hectic. Often, the days seem like a series of inconveniences. We regularly feel sorry for ourselves and want others to feel sorry for us. But do we ever feel sorry for others? Do others feel sorry for us? You might be well- acquainted with your daily troubles, but others are not. Think back to the example of the shop attendant I gave. Have you ever had to deal with someone's temper and thought, if only they knew what I was going through? If you expressed the troubles you were facing directly, perhaps people would control their temper toward you.

And what about considering other people's troubles? Do you ever think about what others are going through? We are so caught up in our own problems that we seem to think that the stresses of life are exclusive to us. But any rational mind knows that this is simply not true. If you see someone swerve slightly on the road, do you think they are drunk, irresponsible at driving, or texting on their phone? The Buddhist mindset would either not speculate or presume it was something out of the person's control that caused them to swerve; maybe this person has an illness and experienced sudden pain. Surely they could not control the swerve if that was the case. Regardless of why they actually swerved, the Buddhist trains his or her mind to believe that the person is innocent. It does not presume the worst about people. If you give someone the benefit of the doubt, you automatically are more compassionate toward them. The focus is not on the inconvenience of the situation, rather, you develop an understanding for the other person and you subliminally wish them well.

The Buddhist mindset means not getting frustrated with the shop attendant who took the time to give you the proper change. The Buddhist mindset would silently wish the shop attendant well. The Buddhist mindset would understand the hardships of the shop attendant and presume the shop attendant has had to deal with stressful situations throughout the day. It is, of course, possible that the shop attendant has not actually experienced any such situations. It is possible that the shop attendant is lazy and doesn't care about providing good customer service. But giving the shop attendant the benefit of the doubt is not something I recommend for the shop attendant's sake; it is recommended for your sake. You will not be overwhelmed or enraged by the situation because you will believe the best of someone else. You may know people who try to see the best in everyone, and while you may consider this naive at times, this attitude does help one cope. Buddhists cannot change others, but they can change their reaction to others.

How often do you lose your temper or become anxious about the most trivial matters?

I am embarrassed to confess that I have been guilty of this. Even if anger is a natural emotion, is it really natural to become furious about matters which do not have dire consequences? Much of this is due to our innate, presupposed need to react to everything and anything. As news stories are available and produced constantly, we are always expected to think and form opinions about those stories. Think of how much outrage you see on a daily basis on your social media accounts. Much of what you see is unnecessary. There is no need to react to everything. While the teachings are not asking you to rid yourself of emotions or opinions, you must know where to direct your energy. Directing it toward trivial matters is a waste of energy.

I was once standing in a long line in the post office during the December holidays. On this particular day, the post office was understaffed. Needless to say, the line was moving slowly and impatience increased rapidly. A customer in front of me kept complaining loudly. He was upset that the post office was understaffed; he spoke about the customers currently being attended to and complained that their packages were large and therefore caused the attendants to spend more time with their transactions. He loudly offered suggestions to improve the situation. He then looked at the gentlemen behind him and managed to get him to join him in the complaining. During this time, I was deep into my study of Buddhism. Had I not been, I too would have joined in the complaining; knowing myself, I could have given these two gentlemen a run for their money with my anger problems. However, I was not upset or annoyed by the slowness in the post office. I knew that waiting in a line, while tedious, did not have dire consequences. The fact that I had to wait a little and spend more time than desired was a trivial matter. There was no need to react. I could not control or alter the situation in any way. The first gentleman who complained could not offer any solutions either. Could he ensure that more attendants would be in the post office to speed things up? Was he going to start working on the spot to help the rest of us who were also stuck in this never-ending line?

Think back once again to what the essence of the Buddhist mindset is: you cannot control a situation but you can control your reaction to as well as your perception of it. I was stuck in a long line same as the men who were complaining. In fact, it was worse for me as I was not at the front of the line as he was! But I knew I could not control the situation. Instead of being angry at the lack of attendants, I was grateful for the two attendants who were there. I was sympathetic to the stress that they had to face in having to deal with a throng of customers. I had no ill feelings toward the customers who may have held up the line because of their complicated transactions. I gave them the benefit of the doubt, and, as a result, I did not get angry over a trivial matter.

How often do you lose your temper?

Ah! Now we reach the big one. Controlling your temper will not be easy. And anger is especially difficult to control as I know from my own experience. The root of much of our anger is disdain and contempt. This actually comes back to the benefit of the doubt. The reason we carry so much disdain is because of our perception. I was once working in a shop and tending to a customer. After a long interaction, the customer asked for some information regarding the product. I excused myself and told the customer I would consult my colleague and return. Upon returning to my customer, I saw that another colleague was talking to them and asking them how everything was going. I was furious! I thought that my colleague was trying to take this customer from me and therefore steal a potential sale (and thus commission) from me! I told her that I was helping this customer, to which she gently responded, "I know, I just wanted to say 'hi' to my neighbor."

As it happened, said customer was, in fact, the next door neighbor of my colleague who was simply making small talk, not trying to steal my potential commission. Now, let us imagine what would have happened if my colleague had walked away before I could approach her and the customer. I would have assumed that she was trying to steal my sale and I would have felt disdain for her; I would probably have been suspicious of her for the remainder of my time at that job. Thankfully, this was not the case. But as I reflect upon this situation now, I know that as someone who had difficulty controlling my anger, I would have been furious if she had not clarified her actions.

In the above situation, I could have unnecessarily held a grudge towards my colleague. But what about a situation in which my disdain would have been justified? What if my colleague had seen an opportunity to steal my sale and did so? Surely, I would be justified in having disdain toward this act. Surely, it would not be irrational for me to be suspicious of her henceforth. Buddhist teachings do not tell us not to be angry. Nor do the teachings tell us that disdain or contempt is wrong. It does not weigh the good and bad of anger and disdain. But it does warn us of the dangers of holding on to these emotions. My incorporation of Buddhism has not rid me of any feeling of anger

- but it has helped me control it. My anger does not consume me and fewer things make me angry. This is because I have actively worked to disallow anger to consume me.

You may be familiar with the concept of 'sin' in many religions. In Buddhist philosophy, there is a belief that we all have a kindness and a good nature which we must bring out. When I was an angrier man, I was not an evil man. However, as my anger had gotten the better of me, my compassion and my gentle side had been suppressed.

If you hear a news story, how quick are you to form an opinion? How likely is this opinion going to enrage you? Maybe if you paused and reflected before forming an opinion, your feelings about it would be different. One constant that you can take from these three points is perspective. Change your perspective to rid yourself of unwanted anger. This is what Buddhist teachings have to offer and you can already see that if one implements these teachings, it can positively affect one's life. How may I have treated the shop attendant if I had not given him the benefit of the doubt? How may I have reacted to the post office scenario if I did not have compassion for the staff? How may I have behaved around my colleague if I did not know that she had no ill intentions?

Take a moment to reflect on situations which you could have handled better. As you progress through this book, I will provide you with practical exercises to ensure that next time, you do handle these situations better.

Chapter 1. The Basic Concept

Paying on this book the whole Buddhist teaching would be impossible. However, it is doable to get familiar inside the basic concept that you'll be able to apply in your health. Knowing these basics will help you review the way you live up to now and find out how you can increase your lifestyle just how that could satisfy you most inside sense of your enlightened state.

Then again, this is not an unexpected transformation. You might even get contrasting some of these concepts, mainly if are derived from a belief that disagrees with all the claims with the Buddhist practice.

A.   Life and also the Material World

The notion of Buddhism in life and the material world revolves around the belief in reincarnation. Here, the repetitive cycle of birth, death after which rebirth is named the Samsara. This cycle often happens inside the six plains of existence. Renewal on a certain plain is usually derived from the Karma, or the deeds sowed as seeds by a person within a lifetime. These seeds may do tremendous or bad. Consequences of these seeds could happen within precisely the same life if the seed is sown or upon the following cycle of rebirth. Karma is influenced only through the individual who planted his or her seed. This idea of Karma often results in ignorance from what could be the true enlightenment if anyone is not able to continue with the path to nirvana.

Rebirth then becomes the entire process of successive lifetimes. These lifetimes all start in the moment of conception towards the moment of death. A sentient being can be reborn in any of the six plains (or five plains depending in the branch being followed). These plains are the Naraka, Preta, Animal Plain, Human Plain, Asura, and Deva. Each succession is relying on cause and effect regarding the sowing of the seeds of Karma.

Naraka is the realm comparable to what other beliefs define as hell. It has to be understood though that there can be various forms of Naraka depending on the being that's reborn in this plain. Naraka technically takes shape from how a being viewed hell from your previous lifetime causing this to be realm particular on the sown Karma of the last lifetime.

Preta, on the other hand, maybe the ghost realm. It sometimes shares its existence with the human field thus making the beings within these realms capable of interacting collectively in certain circumstances.

The animal realm shares the same reality in the human field. Still, the beings within these realms are viewed different life forms. This concept could technically be the way to obtain the idea of most Buddhist vegetarians not to eat meat.

The human realm is technically the realm where you are reading this article book as in the moment. Alternatively, in a very sensitive, it could be the realm the location where the author wrote the written text you are reading basing on Buddhist beliefs.

The Asura realm could be the plain for lesser deities for the people beings in a position to reach a specific a higher level of enlightenment. Still, this plain could be home to demons also which may technically be argued capably to reach an enlightened state in their own right.

The Deva realm could be the plain committed to the deities, angels, and spirits who can attain the highest type of enlightenment.

B.   The Suffering (Causes and Solutions)

It is time and energy to see the causes with the suffering inside the human realm basing on Buddhist beliefs. To indeed see why part, you need to learn two central teachings.

First, you must learn about The Four Noble Truths. According to Buddhism, suffering (Dukkha) might be explained through its causes and also the ways that it can be eased and then improved. The first truth then focuses on the reality that suffering exists. A person must realize that there is undoubtedly suffering in your life as a way to truly understand it.

The second truth is the undeniable fact that suffering has their origins. Once pain is accepted, it's time for it to seek out its source. Once the background is available, it will be clearer why it causes the sufferings of life.

The third truth deals while using the proven fact that each supply of suffering carries a solution. You must accept first that any problems can be ended and therefore it is just not eternal. In a feeling, it works with keeping hope being a fact and necessity in your life.

The last truth reveals the route to locating the solution for that suffering. This truth is only able to be attained if the sentient being is capable of accepting the previous three without hesitation fully.

The second Buddhist with instructions on a need to learn will be the Noble Eight Fold Path. This teaching can help you accept The Four Noble Truths of life. The eightfold is divided into three divisions, each having specific folds under his or her instructions.

The first division relates to wisdom. The first fold under this division could be the Right View. It means you need to view reality as it can be and never the way appears to get based on how you want to notice. The next fold will be the Right Intention it indicates you need to know what you need with regards to rejecting and thus freedom from a preference of reality.

The next division concentrates on ethical conduct. The first fold here could be the Right Speech. This fold indicates that everything has to be spoken should be true yet mustn't hurt, euphemisms should come in handy. The next fold is the Right Action which states that you must act in the best way you cannot hurt anyone. The last fold in this division will be the Right Livelihood. It should speak for itself but to clarify it is finding your ends meet in techniques cannot hurt or compromise other beings or Lives.

The last division may be the concentration. The leading fold with this division is the Right Effort, meaning you must have the will to improve yourself further and not dwell about the level in which you are not going to continue. Next fold is the Right Mindfulness. This fold of Right Mindfulness states a person with the current scenario in your life without trying to hide from yourself any information on whether it can be good or bad. The last fold could be the Right Concentration that states that you should hold power to concentrate your efforts by combining the applications of all the folds into one existence in your health. Right meditation may be a way of amplifying it further.

C.   Reasons and nature of Existence

This goal is also the fact drives everyone to get with an answer to the question of what makes someone happy. In reality though, if your answer is using the Buddhist tradition, happiness can only be defined through the individual that asked the question.

One the definition becomes concrete then a road to contentment is see-through. The nature of existing then can be determined now since anyone who asked already knows what he wants to do in life.

The next step for you then is usually to become see your face who will likely be thinking.

D.   Liberation

Now that you be aware of question you'll want to think about it is possible to start to try to liberate yourself through the bonds which are hindering you. You are given a blueprint to begin things out.

Chapter 2. Who Was Buddha?

Buddha was the name given to a former prince named Siddhartha Gautama who became a messenger of peace, and taught others to stop inflicting pain and suffering upon others. He originally was the son of a king, which allowed him to live a very lavish lifestyle full of wealth and luxury. The time period of his existence was about 500 B.C. or roughly 2500 years ago. He was born in a place called Lumbini and raised in Kapilavastu for the first 29 years of his life which is now in Nepal. Nobody knows the exact date, but it was around this era. We do know that he brought his teachings to the eastern region of India, which is why Buddhism is popular in that country and its surrounding countries.

Siddhartha Gautama

Back in the days of Buddha, there were very few wealthy people. Siddhartha felt lucky that he didn't have any worries and could be a totally free thinker. As he dwelled in his thoughts, he realized that bad things could still happen to him even though he was rich. What if he fell down a hill or got a deadly disease? Money wasn't going to save his life. After Siddhartha came to this realization, he made a decision to walk away from his life of luxury at his royal palace to see new realizations on life. Siddhartha went on a journey to meet four specific kinds of people; an old man, a sick man, a monk and a dead man. Siddhartha believed that each of these men could teach him different things about life and death. For example, a dead man will teach him that he cannot escape death, an old man will teach him he cannot escape getting old and a sick man will teach him he cannot escape getting sick.

After meeting with those three men, the monk would be the final person Siddhartha would meet. The monk represented all that was holy and would encourage Siddhartha to become a holy person himself. The only condition was that Siddhartha could never go back to his life as a wealthy prince ever again. Siddhartha agreed to these terms and spent the rest of his life trying to be a holy person seeking answers to important life questions. The questions are "Why do people have to suffer?" and "What is the cause of suffering?" Siddhartha believed if he could answer these questions then he could find a solution to fix these problems and stop people from having to suffer anymore. It was through mediation and prayer that Siddhartha found the reasons for suffering. He took his newfound knowledge and began sharing it with other people. As time went on, Siddhartha became known as the "enlightened one" to those around him. The Indian word for this name is called Buddha, which is what people referred to him as ever since. Those who believed in his teachings and followed his advice became part of the Buddhist religion, or religion of Buddhism, based on his name.

Buddha continued to teach his truths throughout eastern India for the remainder of his life. He never wrote any kind of holy book, or bible, like you would find in other religions. However, a collection of his teachings and spoken words were collected over the years and eventually compiled into a book known as the "Tipitaka." It was originally written in the Pali language, which was an ancient Indian language that is no longer used. After Buddha's death, his teachings had become so wide spread that others followed in his footsteps. That is why the Tipitaka was written. Buddha had remained the primary figure and symbol of the Buddhist religion. In the Indian city of Sarnath, there is a stupa (a Buddhist relic) called the "Dhamek Stupa" that marks the very spot where he delivered his first sermon to his first disciples after getting enlightenment. The place has become a popular attraction for both Buddhists and tourists interested in Buddhist history.

Buddha's life

Buddha began his life as the son of a king. His parents were King Suddhodana and Queen Maya. Buddha's real name was Prince Siddhartha Gautama and he was born around 500 B.C., although the exact year is unknown. Siddhartha grew up in a beautiful palace in Kapilavastu, which was the capital city of the Shakya kingdom of Nepal. Siddhartha was troubled as a child because of his confusion about life and death, especially after his grandfather died. He did not understand why his grandfather had come down with a terrible illness and just died from it. This was after he had wished for his grandfather to stay alive. These thoughts would plague him until adulthood.

Buddha left his life of comfort to find the truth

Siddhartha always wondered what life outside the palace was like. He never had any reason to leave because the king spoiled him with material things and everything else he could want. Siddhartha even married a beautiful woman by the name of Yasodhara on his 16th birthday and stayed with her in the palace for the next 13 years. It was when he was 29-years-old that he finally wanted to see what life was like in the outside world. When he journeyed away from the palace, he ended up meeting four men on his journey. He met an old man, a sick man, and a dead man. It was at this point that he realized there was a lot of suffering out in the world and that other people's lives were not as lavish and luxurious as the one he had been living. This made him feel bad, so he then went on wondering what he could do to help fix this problem. One day he found his answer when he met a monk who happened to be wandering by. The monk told Siddhartha that he gave up all his possessions in order to go on a journey to end the suffering in the world. This intrigued him, and so he decided to follow this very same path in his own life.

Siddhartha made a decision to permanently leave his palace and throne in order to become a wandering monk just like the one he had met. He even cut off all his hair because he felt the hair was a reminder of the worldly lifestyle he left behind. Then he dressed himself in raggedy robes and just wandered away to new locations while trying to figure out how to stop suffering.

With each new place Siddhartha arrived, he studied with the wisest teachers in hopes to learn about how to end suffering. Unfortunately, he did not learn much from any of these teachers and he was still without answers. For the next six years, he purposely put himself through hardships in order to have the experience of being poor. He thought this would lead him to the answers he was seeking, but they did not. After these six years, Siddhartha realized that depriving himself of food and luxury would not bring him any of the freedom and answers he was looking for. So he began to eat healthy again and regained his strength. It was at this point that he decided to use meditation as a final alternative. Siddhartha sat underneath a fig tree in Bodh Gaya (in the state of Bihar, India) and vowed never to leave that spot until the answers came to him. His deep meditation led him to the conclusion that we are the cause of our own suffering. Everyone endures suffering in this world because each of us tries to get ahead in this world and gather possessions, while neglecting people in the process. If we care more about people and less about possession or material things then suffering would decrease.

Siddhartha (now Buddha or the "awakened one") traveled to Sarnath in India and met up with five holy men which whom he shared his newfound knowledge with. These men understood Buddha completely and later became his disciples. For the next

45 years of Buddha's life, he traveled with his disciples

throughout India to teach others about how to end suffering. He had all sorts of people listening to him, beggars, slave girls and even kings. Buddha was a kind person and was loved by everyone he met in his travels in India. He was never angry, rude, or violent; not even to the people who disagreed with his teachings. After his death at the age of 80, future disciples would carry on his teachings. Today, there are over 480 million Buddhists in the world, with the majority of them in countries around India.

Basics of Buddhism

Buddhism is a very popular religion around the world. It originated in eastern India about 2500 years ago by a man named Siddhartha Gautama, who later became known as Buddha. There are currently over 400 million Buddhists in the world, which is about 7% of the global population.

Basically, the goal of Buddhism is to reduce the suffering we put on others and ourselves. This suffering originates from being materialistic, violent, superficial, liars and cheaters. Buddhists are taught to not be any of these things, but rather kind and loving to all people. Not only will this reduce suffering, but it will help Buddhists get into a better life during their rebirth phase.

Statue of Buddha at the Tokyo National Museum

Buddhism was founded by a man named Siddhartha

Gautama, who lived 2500 years ago around 450 B.C. He was the son of a king, which means he was a prince. Gautama got to live a lavish lifestyle, but soon later realized that most people don't live like he does. Once he experienced the pain and suffering of the outside world, he realized that he needed to find the causes of suffering and ways to stop it from happening. This eventually led him towards a new lifestyle where he abandoned his throne and became a wandering monk in search for answers. Eventually, he found the answers and made it his life's duty to teach others what he had discovered through deep meditation and prayer. People started referring to Gautama as Buddha, which means the enlightened one.

Buddha's teachings were comprised of four noble truths that taught people the reasons behind suffering and the ways of overcoming it. Buddha taught that all suffering has a cause, but it also has an end. The only things in life that are definite are sickness, aging and death. Suffering is not definite, but highly likely because people constantly cause it to happen. The Four Noble Truths offer solutions to reduce the causes, which in turn reduces the suffering. The first truth simply identifies the existence of suffering. The second truth determines the reason for suffering. The third truth is about how to end suffering, which teaches that you have to achieve Nirvana. This is where you are finally free of all pain and suffering, which means you don't have to go through a rebirth period again. All Buddhists want to achieve this period, but they need to have all their karmic debts cleared. In other words, they have to be as good as they can be during their life and follow all of the teachings of Buddha. The best candidates for Nirvana are the Buddhist monks. They actually live a solitary life inside a gated community, where all of the monks can practice the teachings of Buddha without any outside interference. If a Buddhist doesn't achieve Nirvana, then the fourth noble truth teaches that they go on to the wheel of samsara. This wheel sends them down either a good or bad path, which determines their fate for the rebirth.

Karma is a big part of the Buddhist religion. Despite what many westerners think, karma does not mean the result of doing something. Buddhists think of karma as a willful action, and that your actions determine your outcome. Those who get stuck in a repetitive course of action will likely endure the same fate upon themselves. For example, if you were a violent person in your life, then that violence will cause you pain and suffering at the end of your current life, and possibly in your next life as well. That is why Buddhists try to be as good as possible in order to keep their karma positive.

Chapter 3. Where Do I Start?

Indeed, you are welcome to the world of Buddhism. The practice of Buddhism is such that it transcends all bounds of religions. Yes, there are those who choose to take Buddhism as religion. You don't need to take it as such, for it only becomes your religion when you make it to be. Buddhism is about ending suffering through enlightenment and eventually attaining Nirvana – that state of no bad perceptions, of eternal bliss, joy, peace, and harmony, where serenity reigns in abundance.

Where should you start? Well, first of all you must know that life is whole, and as such, it cannot be compartmentalized into material life, religious life, spiritual life, and the rest. By gaining this knowledge, so would you awaken to the universal truths about suffering that are not held hostage to false beliefs, practices, and traditions. To gain greater insight, take the initial step to walk the path to ending suffering. And as you walk, you will grow the urge to learn more and finally flourish as a person. Buddhism is about whole life without compartmentalization. Remember: there is no distinction between spiritual life and daily life, no distinction between body and soul, and thus, just as they both come, so do they both leave.

Thich Nhat Hanh once said "It is not important whether you walk on water, or in space, the true miracle is to walk on earth." This gives a reflection as to how ordinary Buddhism is. It is about you in your own ordinary ways. To Buddhism, loving-kindness and compassion are the greatest miracle a human being can perform.

"If we could see the miracle of a single flower clearly our whole life would change." – Gautama Buddha

Do Awake

To awaken is to become aware, which is the sole purpose of truth. The greatest truth is that spiritual life and daily life are one and the same. Thus, practicing kindness and compassion in your daily life is indeed leading a daily spiritual life.

To awaken is to become aware of what is happening within and around you. Always ask yourself "why I am doing/saying that I'm doing/saying right now?" and "how am I doing that? I'm here and present? Am I one hundred percent committed to what I'm doing? If not, why is that? What's the reason my thoughts are somewhere else?" Ask yourself where you are going in your life. Where have your past decisions taken you?

Another important question that you should be aware of is connected to the people around you. Always take a moment to think about what your words or actions will do to these people and how will they react. Mind you that what you do and say also affects your own emotions through other people's reactions, so that your unwholesome words or actions can create a vicious circle for your entire environment.

You should also apply this practice of presence to even the most trivial things, like brushing your teeth, eating breakfast, or taking a walk. You should always be focused on what you're doing right now. You may find yourself surprised how much there is to discover about yourself and about your life, even in these little things. That's the only way to become present. If you're not present, you're simply wasting your life, because your life is here, it's now, it's in this very moment. There's no past, there's no future, yet –

no one ever experienced "past" and no one ever experiences "future", because that's impossible (something you should really think about) - and the only moment for taking action to make your future happy and bright is now anyways.

I can't even count how many times I hit myself in the head or fell over on the icy road because I was everywhere in my thoughts but not there, living my real life. These trivial "countless mindless self-injuries" led me to see a bigger picture of my life. When I couldn't be mindful while cutting bread or washing my hands, how on earth could I be focused and concentrated on important aspects of my life? Obviously I couldn't. I was distracted from A to Z. Then I realized how faraway I used to be when meeting my friends and spending time with my family. I would think about my job or business or other future plans, but then, back home, I would think about my friends instead of doing my job. That was nonsense and a big waste. And so then I started from focusing on the smallest everyday tasks and things. I started asking myself these simple but important questions. Everything's changed now.

You must not only observe but also engage in truthful inquiry of everything around you. More so, you must question your very own beliefs, your very own traditions, words of others, words of 'supernatural beings', authority of ancient scriptures, elders, priests, teachers, etc. That's the only way to find YOUR, not someone else's, truth. Buddhism teaches us that the world is not dualistic. It's not black and white. There is universal truth in Nirvana, in the enlightenment, in "suchness", but you can't be given the truth directly, you can't just obtain it without experiencing it. The Buddha shows you the way, but you have to walk it on your own.

My personal philosophy is to always abandon all the beliefs I can't defend from my own and others' attacks. I often watch movies or read books that are totally against my perceptions and beliefs, and can even be offensive to me at some levels. So often I feel that curious kind of "pain" inside me, whenever I read that something I believed in was not true, didn't work, and made no sense. That always leads me into further inquiries.

If I can't defend a particular belief under a crossfire of difficult questions and problems, if there's a crack on the glass that is going further and I can't do anything about it, if I can't explain to myself why I believe so, if I don't see how that's going to serve me and the people I love – I just quit the philosophy or a certain belief. At the times when I was particularly in love with backpacking, I really enjoyed engaging in discussions (often in peoples' cars when I was hitchhiking, or in planes) about how I was irresponsible, how the traveling was going to make me catch a tropical disease and eventually make me broke and unhappy...how I should've never quit my job and how a university education was the most important thing in the world.

That way, and only that way, I could feel that everything I was doing made just perfect sense to me. I could strengthen my beliefs and be sure that the path I chose was perfect for me. It allowed me to stand firm on my own ground without any distracting doubts. I could never understand why so many Muslims and Christians (say, my parents) didn't want to read atheistic books such as "The God Delusion", why marijuana smokers didn't want to watch any serious academic medical testimonies and reports other than "how tetrahydrocannabinol is a panacea medicine for every kind of sickness" (not that I have anything against it), or how Buddhists didn't want to read books stating that Buddhism is just a hippie, outdated kind of pointless

B.S and how it's totally useless in serious people's everyday lives.

If you can't defend your own beliefs, WHY on earth would you

stick to them? It's like being in a relationship with a person you don't like that doesn't like you either, who is rude and unattractive to you... or building a high ladder out of rotten sticks. The rungs have to be solid!

You are going to step up on them!

Thus, you must empty your mind of any held beliefs, attitudes, and prejudices that you cannot support. Yet, you must do this in the most sober, respectful, tolerant and non-violent way. Only by discovering that a given belief is an affirmation of your very own experience and discovery should you give it a chance - not to get fixed onto it, but as the knowledge that you must keep on interrogating.

Do walk the path to ending suffering

The path to ending suffering is to experience the Four Noble Truths. This path encompasses a four-step process:

1.   Diagnose your suffering: Pain is a reminder of

your very own suffering. It may be spiritual, psychological, mental, emotional, social, or physical. Each of these pains is an alarm that alerts you of the need to do something - yes, diagnose your suffering.

2. Determine the cause of your suffering: The cause of your suffering rests in deep in your mind. Yes, the external circumstances may arouse your stimuli, but how you choose to experience it makes the difference between you suffering or not.

Thus, the cause of your suffering is the intent or Karma that

you've embraced in your mind.

3. Discover the path to recovery: The path to your recovery is that which leads to a complete end of all your sufferings - your ultimate attainment of enlightenment.

4. Carry out your treatment: The only lasting cure to your suffering is enlightenment. Like any cure, it is administered in a gradual dosage. The dosage for ending suffering comprises of the milestones you undertake on the Noble Eightfold Path.

Let me show you a practical example of a process which can be used in this context. If you're unhappy, you should inquire into the one who is unhappy. What do I mean by that?

Let's say that your unhappiness is caused by a particular relationship. Your action should not necessarily be to change the relationship itself (although you might really want to do it as well if it's really not going anywhere), but to turn towards yourself, the "I" who is unhappy. So you ask yourself: "What is this 'I'?" Because the unhappiness that "I" feels is not necessary being caused by just this relationship - "I" has also felt exactly the same unhappiness at other times in your life for completely different reasons.

It was the same feeling, but had numerous different causes. If

it's caused by lots of different things, no single thing can be a cause of this happiness. So that maybe you should question the "I" who is so often unhappy, because that's exactly the one constant that is always the same in all of these experiences? The causes may change, but the "I" is always the same "I".

You use the word "I" many times during the day, so think

of it now - what are you exactly referring to? You are probably referring to the person you used to call "I", that is your body, the collection of your memories, feelings, thoughts and perceptions, right?

So then you notice: "My thoughts are always coming and going... but I'm not always coming and going. I'm just aware of my thoughts. I thought I was my thoughts, but actually that's not the case." Then just observe the thoughts – feel as they come and go. You will see that you are just observer of your thoughts. So often you don't even have to continue them at all if you don't want to. They are constantly changing. You are not them.

Then proceed to your emotions - of being lonely guilty, sad, etc. You will also notice that your feelings appear and disappear, but you - your awareness – is still there. Let's say that you were upset in the morning, but you're just OK in the afternoon – so that emotion went away – do you feel that part of yourself vanished, too? No. You're still there. So you can't really identify yourself with your emotions.

Then you do the same with your sensations – you can pinch yourself or brush your hair and then stop – they also come and go.

Your images, the sights and the sounds you hear – all these

appear and disappear, but you don't.

So then you come to interesting realization. You thought that you were a "package" of your thoughts, feeling, emotions and sensations – but then you notice that they are constantly changing, coming and going, and you're something separate from them.

You are aware of them.

The only thing that has always been there in your life is this "observer" who has always been aware of all these emotions, sensations, thoughts, feelings and the whole world around. A witness.

So then you start redefining of what you used to call "I". Then you can ask yourself again: "what is this sensation of unhappiness"?

That's not "I" who is unhappy. The "I" is just a perfectly peaceful, unlimited space of awareness, through which all these emotions and feelings constituting "unhappiness" go.

So then you may become intrigued and ask yourself, "What is that present awareness that is always there, that knows my experiences but is not made of these experiences, that is not made of thoughts, feelings, perceptions, and sensations?" That may result in changing your focus from all these passing sensations, the "package", and paying more attention to the present and aware "I", the background, the unrestricted space, the essence of your being. Who is aware of that? Well, it is aware of itself. It is aware of your experience. It is this "I" that is aware of itself. Then, you should start looking on yourself instead of your thoughts and feelings.

And then, finally, you may turn back to your feelings again, and notice that they're long gone and your unhappiness is nowhere to be found.

The cause of unhappiness and suffering is mistaking yourself

- the "I" - with the train of emotions and feelings – and as long as you do that, you will have a bad relationship with yourself, so to speak – suffering is misunderstanding your true essence and the nature of things.

Take the ultimate responsibility of ending suffering upon you;

1   Take steps to understand the three universal truths

2   Take steps to understand the four noble truths

3   Take steps to understand and practice the eight-fold paths

4   Keep the five commandments wholly

"Peace comes from within. Do not seek it without." - Gautama Buddha

Take steps to understand the three universal truths

The following are three important universal truths that you must embrace in your practice of Buddhism.

1.   Nothing is lost in the universe – This is a reminder that you should not grieve overly due to your loss of whatever you may have attached yourself to. Everything that does exist including you, your loved ones, and all your belongings are part and parcel of this one indivisible universe. Therefore, the universe as a whole loses nothing. Not even your death is a loss to the universe, for upon your death, your body returns to the various elements of the universe from which it originated from. Christians express this as "from dust to dust and from ash to ash." Thus, from where you came from so shall you go back to – the universe. Yet, you won't go anywhere since you came from nowhere, for you are not somewhere, except you being the whole universe. So, of course you will be sad when you lose something or someone – that's perfectly normal and sane for us in this earthly life when forms change their appearance - and the point's not in becoming an emotionless robot (rather on the contrary!). But don't torture yourself over that. Everything's going to be just alright as there's no real distinction between all human beings, we really are all just one big whole.

2.   Everything changes – Nothing in this universe is static. Even the earth that seems static is on the move, hills and valleys come and go, oceans form and disappear, rivers

flow and dry, stars appear and implode, beings gain life and then die, etc. Thus, you must embrace change as inevitable. You must be open to change in your life.

3.   Every cause has an effect – this teaches you that nothing happens without a cause. Yet every cause that results into your suffering is an effect of your intent, or Karma. The best way to understand the cause of your suffering is to understand the Four Noble Truths.

Take steps to understand the four noble truths

The Four Noble Truths are truths about our suffering;

1.   There is suffering and suffering is common to all – Suffering is not what happens to us but what we intend, say, and do about what happens to us. Thus, your intent, words, and actions are not confined to you, but they flow like ripples from the vibration of your thoughts, words, or deeds in a restful ocean, causing disturbance across the ocean.

2.   We are the cause of our own suffering – We cause our own suffering by the bad karma that we cultivate within

our minds.

3.   We can end suffering by doing away with that which causes suffering. We can end suffering by cultivating good intents. Good intents, or rather good karma, will enable us to seek enlightenment about our suffering and thus be able to end it.

4.   The path to end suffering is enlightenment and everyone can be enlightened. The path to ending suffering is that which brings you to the realization of the existence of the Eightfold Paths.

Chapter 4. Examples Of Closeness Between The Two Cultures

Are Western and Zen culture really that far? The word creates the world, and throughout the book I will give you examples that can show you that many of the things we do, or that are part of our Western culture, already have something of Zen in them and could make our journey easier. But we lack the awareness of it, and someone to help us do it. Only then can we say: "I am doing something applying the principles of Zen".

There is a writer who can represent a trait-d-union between the West and Japan, and she is the Belgian Amelie Nothomb. The daughter of a diplomat, she was born and raised in Japan, even though she left her native country when she was a child and followed her father in China and other Far Eastern countries. The latter makes some mention in a book called "Biography of Hunger" and elsewhere, but Japan, one of its rockstar literary production (really prolific) and Nothomb makes us know many aspects, even grotesque and paradoxical. In fact, I discovered aspects of Japan that I didn't really know by reading Nothomb's books. I would like to focus on one step.

In "Metaphysics of the tubes", she, an unmanageable child, is calmed by a piece of Belgian white chocolate.

Have you seen Kill Bill, Quentin Tarantino's eastern western? Do you remember the scene in which the Bride (Uma Thurman, for instance), wakes up after a very long coma? What moves first thing? The feet. This has a very Zen meaning, and we must not exclude that the reference is wanted, given the director's interest in that culture.

Drieu La Rochelle he was a French writer who went down in history because he was a Nazi, a Stalinist, a collaborator and a suicide seeker. He wanted to annihilate his own self to merge with the universal whole. Although not very edifying, it is another example of closeness between the West and the East. Isn't one of the principles of Buddhism Nirvana, that is, the place where all subjectivity is lost?

Anyone who has studied a bit of philosophy knows that much importance is given to the senses as data collectors that the mind then reworks, and also knows that our mind shapes the shape of the world. Man is the measure of all things, is a principle of Renaissance philosophy, and finds its analogue in one of Zen.

He also knows in the early days that he sought the first principle, the element of which all beings are constituted. Thales hypothesized that it was water.

Excluding for reasons diametrically opposed Thales and the Nothomb, we do not know if the cases we have seen above derive from a knowledge of oriental culture, or anyway of an influence, or if they are simply the result of a coincidence (another principle dear to Zen) and, ultimately, we don't even care. What interested us was the fact that we are not so far away, and we will return in the course of the book. We understand that some things we do are already zen, only that we need to work on it.

Zen, Network and the world

We mentioned before the vegan cook imitated by Maurizio Crozza. Now let's talk about another character from the Genoese comedian, Napalm 51. Who is Napalm 51? Napalm 51 represents the haters. The haters, the word itself says it, but surely you will already know it, they are people who vent their anger on the Internet, especially on social networks. We leave out the question of fake news because it goes beyond this context, even if the two concepts are often linked, and let's focus on anger. If Napalm 51 began to listen to their own feelings, even the negative ones, they would be able to understand and accept them, finding a more peaceful way of expressing and controlling them. Because we all have moments of anger, and anger must not be repressed, but we must only not let it turn into rage.

The main point is that for Zen every man is enlightened, only that all those obstacles that prevent the light from radiating must be eliminated. Zen and practices help us do it. In this way, the hater character created by Crozza would stop insulting, and even click and share compulsively. The abuse of the Internet that many do is a form of greed 2.0. Also for this reason the Zen advises to switch off the mobile devices from time to time, at least during meals. It absolutely does not ask to live without, because it has fallen into the world and is indeed a way to live better within it. Why, let it be known, "The Buddha, the Divine, dwells in the circuit of a computer or in the gears of the change of a motorcycle with the same ease as atop a mountain or in the petals of a flower".

Zen does not even want us to renounce pleasure and gratification, or that we punish ourselves in penance. It simply tells us that we must seek the source of happiness within us, so that it is more stable and more lasting. Events outside of us can change, indeed they will almost certainly change and some will be painful. If we entrust our happiness exclusively to the outside world, when things go wrong, how will we do it? On the contrary, the happiness that comes from within will not be subject to so many changes. Let's take it as a useful tip. But do you advise us to be insensitive to the pain of others or not to feel them? Absolutely not. Pain exists, it must be accepted and Zen helps us do it.

Of course, superficial things can give us pleasure, and pleasure should not be rejected, but we will find true happiness by coming into harmony with our deepest part.

Jung spoke of me and The Self, and for him dreams are the bridge between the two components of our personality, while for Zen it is meditation.

Someone will dispute: but if we already have these habits, why bring up Zen? I refer above all to that of counting up to ten. Because there is a difference, which is that we understand that Zen has negative feelings, and we accept them. We say that it is as if there were a sort of splitting thanks to which we perceive our negative part (or obscure, as some claim). We are aware of this. In general, some uses that we have in the West or that we are adopting in the West are bricks that help us build our Zen home, but we must also put other types of bricks and, what matters most, the house will be special. In short, it is not enough to put chopsticks to be a Japanese restaurant. We must also pay attention to the elements that we have and which they lack, and also to understand that in some cases it is a structural non-presence. I refer to the almost total absence of speculation, as we have already seen. A bit like a fat-free kitchen. Amelie Nohthomb said that Japanese monuments are built and designed to be admired in the dark. One more case in which the absence of something, in this case the light of the sun, becomes structural.

The second objection is that there are ways to channel anger, such as sport and artistic sublimation. Well, those who already succeed in these ways, probably don't need Zen. The point is that Zen is not only useful for managing anger and aggression.

Chapter 5. The Buddhism Philosophy

Every human being is the author of his own health or disease.

☐ Buddha

Noble Truths

Through Shakyamuni Buddha's enlightenment, we find the core of Buddhism. In Buddha's first teaching of Dharma, we learn of the four noble truths: the suffering, the cause, the end, and the pathway to the end. Each truth provides a foundation for a greater understanding of life.

Generally speaking, we all crave happiness. One may argue that happiness or unhappiness comes as a result of cause and effect. It is through the Buddha's teaching that we can find a greater understanding of this basic cause and effect. The awakening of Buddha took shape through his life experiences. In these experiences, he found a common point of reference in all people. As the Buddha looked into the world, he found what is now known as the first noble truth, suffering or Dukkha. That suffering is not as simple as pain, or even death. That there are lessons within suffering to understand: physical suffering, mental suffering, and even suffering in life.

1.   The First Noble Truth Life has inevitable suffering
☐Buddha

These lessons provide a guide to enhanced understanding of this first noble truth. Physical suffering appears in many ways. Take for example an elderly person experiencing joint pain. She may find it difficult to move without worry or fear of breaking a bone. As the body grows older parts that once worked well begin to deteriorate. The eyes cannot see as clearly or the hearing becoming muffled. Yet, the old or aging are not the only to experience physical suffering. The young, even the middle-aged realize suffering in the form of disease or the pain that is brought on by loss or death. The first lesson of this noble truth is that suffering is unavoidable. Regardless of the outside appearance understand that we all suffer. That living what seems to be a carefree, or happy life will too experience suffering in some way. What is evident is suffering is an experience different to us all. The pain you bear the only you truly understand how it feels. An example of this may be a husband caring for his sick wife. Her body riddled with an incurable disease, regardless of how much he cares for her he cannot trade places with her. He cannot remove the illness and put it into his body, nor can he take away her pain. She is the only one who can endure her experience.

Through the Buddha's teaching, we recognize suffering as an unavoidable part of life.

2.   The Second Noble Truth There is a cause to our suffering

☐   Buddha

This brings us to the next lesson of suffering within the mind. Just as physical suffering takes on many forms, so does mental suffering. Feelings of depression, sorrow, or anxiety are just a few forms of mental suffering takes. People suffer in grief over the loss of a friend or loved one. Young people experience frustration when parents enforce rules or do not allow them to have things they desire. Adults experience dissatisfaction that no matter how many hours they work they still struggle to pay the bills. All of these examples are experiences of mental suffering, the feelings of pain that arise from being separated from our desires. With this metal suffering, we recognize that suffering is certain.

Understanding that both mental and physical suffering is necessary for life; Buddha speaks about how happiness is real but not lasting. Take for example a person being given a pastry. They feel happy that they were giving this pastry, as it temporarily relieves the hunger within their body. Yet once the body uses that fuel there is suffering again, as the body feels the need to refuel. This person is experiencing the sensation of suffering; because the attachment to happiness was not lasting. Many feels that the distraction of temporary pleasures allows them to escape the feeling of suffrage. Buddha teaches not to take solitude in these momentary pleasures, yet to look at the bigger experience to find a more substantial end to suffering.

Through acceptance that suffering is part of life Buddha came to the realization; that to find the end you must understand the cause. The second noble truth is the cause of suffering. In Buddha's observance, people gave evidence that the individual's desire causes suffering. These desires are more deeply understood through the three roots of evil: greed, ignorance, and hatred. The first evil is that of greed. This can be seen in the desire that something will improve life. In Buddhism greed is represented by the rooster often referred to as Lobha. An example of greed would be the desire to elevate popularity, such as being driven to wear a designer brand, with the goal to gain popularity. As well greed can take the form of selfishness, holding onto things that we no longer need just for the sake of having them. When in reality there are others suffering that would benefit from the kindness. Greed can also arise in ignorance or Moha represented by the pig. It is important to understand that ignorance is not just the uneducated. It finds more fundamental standing in the inability to see the truth in a situation. In ignorance, the mind can become so fixed on an outcome that it cannot see any other solution. Often this ignorance will bread in the final root of evil hate, Dvesha represented by the snake. Hate arise as a response to the judgment of others, or the desire to have what someone else possesses. Through Buddha's teachings, he expresses how these causes provide a guide to the end of suffering.

3.   The Third Nobel Truth There is an end to suffering Buddha

The discovery of the pathway to happiness is found in the third noble truth: the end to suffering. The Buddha taught that it is possible for one can achieve supreme happiness, that the path is guided though ending of suffering. It is not uncommon for a Buddhist to spend a lifetime seeking out happiness. Understand that there are different levels of happiness, freedom from craving, freedom from ignorance. The journey to happiness can start small with a simple commitment to the improvement of spiritual activities or finding greater joy in simplicity. Begin with the understanding that the Buddhist realizes happiness can flourish when greed is extinguished. No matter the surroundings the Buddhist can live with the ability to overcome desires. As the Buddhist accepts there is no need for judgment or animosity, he can comfortably co-exist with others who harbor ignorance or hate. The Buddhist free from desire, ignorance, and hate can experience greater happiness bringing him closer to his goal allowing his journey to arrive at the ultimate destination, enlightenment.

Which is the end of suffering? Imagine enlightenment as pure liberation, a total freedom from suffering. Enlightenment requires many qualities two of which being perfect wisdom and great compassion. With this perfect wisdom, the Buddha is able to understand the nature of all experiences, and situations. As well as with great compassion, the Buddha can help others conquer their suffering. Nirvana is a blessing that comes along with enlightenment. It is the extinguishing of the fires of greed, delusion, and hatred within. As an individual achieves nirvana they are not transformed into a heavenly realm, nor do they disappear. Nirvana happens within the mind where the spirit reaches supreme happiness, a spiritual joy, free of emotions and fear. The Buddha believed that nirvana is obtainable in our lives, he believed that living in bliss was the answer to end suffering.

4.   The Fourth Nobel Truth

The end to suffering is contained in the Eight-Fold Path.

☐   Buddha

Ending suffering requires an understanding of the fourth noble truth: the path leading to the end of suffering. The Buddha was not always an enlightened being. He began his life as a prince living a life of privilege in his father's palace. After renouncing his position, he became a wandering monk. In this experience, he found himself at the extreme opposite of his once known lavish life. He spent years with no comforts, tortured in his thoughts before he came to the realization that neither the life of poverty nor wealth lead to happiness. That the only way to obtain pure joy was to find the middle path. The middle path provides the guidelines for the treatment of suffering. Through Buddha's studies, he found that using the Noble Eightfold Path as a formula, it provides a guide to the ending of suffering. This guide helps to develop personality, and character encouraging a virtuous life. With each of these noble truths, the Buddhist grows in understanding of finding a way to peace and happiness.

In the end, these things matter most: How well did you love?

How fully did you live? How deeply did you let go?

☐ Buddha

Chapter 6. The Different School Of Buddhism

Buddhism is almost three thousand years old, so it is no longer surprising that it is divided into several schools or doctrinal institutions. These schools fall under two main foundational groups, namely the Theravada and the Mahayana.

Theravada Buddhism literally translates to "The Ancient

Teaching," while Mahayana Buddhism literally means "The Great Vehicle." Mahayana Buddhism has two sub-sects, namely the Traditional Mahayana and the Vajrayana, or the "Diamond Vehicle."

Theravada Buddhism

Theravada is the most widespread branch of Buddhism in South Asia and Southeast Asia, especially in Cambodia, Sri Lanka, Myanmar, Thailand and Laos. The Theravadins refers to the teachings of the Buddha based on the Pali Canon, which is the earliest collection of Pali scriptures of the teachings of the Buddha.

Ananda, the personal attendant and cousin of the Buddha, was the one who meditated intensively on the sermons of the Buddha to commit them to memory. Thus, after the Buddha's death, he taught the senior monks to recite and memorize all of the Buddha's forty-five years' worth of sermons.

In 29 BC, the Fourth Buddhist Council in Sri Lanka wrote down all the oral teachings and categorized them into three divisions - the "Basket of Discipline" or the Vinaya

Pitaka, which were teachings regarding the traditions of the Sangha, or the monastics; the "Basket of Discourses" or the Sutta Pitaka, which were the sermons of the Buddha and his closest disciples; and the "Basket of Higher Doctrine," which provided the philosophies of the Dharma in detail. Together, these books are called the Tipitaka, or more commonly known in the West as The Pali Canon.

Some say that the Pali Canon is like the Bible of the Buddhists. However, practicing Buddhists themselves do not regard it as gospel and do not treat it as divine truth. Rather, they encourage aspirants to study the teachings, assess for themselves the meanings, and more importantly, apply the teachings in their lives to determine whether they hold the universal truth or not.

Theravada Buddhism teaches the concept of vibhajjavada, or the "teaching of analysis." According to this doctrine, insight should be derived from the experience, practice of knowledge and critical reasoning. Theravadins also place emphasis on the need to listen to the advice of the elders and regard this as of equal importance as one's experience and practice of Buddhism.

Theravada is highly conservative when it comes to

practicing Buddhist teachings, particularly among its monastics. Theravada is clearly distinct from other schools in that they believe the arhat, or those who have attained nirvana, are incorruptible. The Mahayanists, on the other hand, believe they can still regress. Another distinction between Theravada and the other schools is that the Theravadins believe that insight comes suddenly, not gradually.

One important doctrine of Theravada is the Seven Stages of Purification, which they prescribe as the path to follow towards enlightenment. It is believed that every sentient being is fully responsible for his or her enlightenment, actions and karma. They highlight the importance of gaining knowledge through practice and personal realization over belief and faith on what is written in the Pali Canon.

The Seven Stages of Purification, or the Visuddhimagga, is divided into three parts:

The first part consists of the first stage of purification, which is the Purification of Conduct or the sila visuddhi. It describes the rules of discipline, the steps to take on how to find the right temple to practice Buddhism, and how to find the right teacher.

The second part consists of the second stage, Purification of the Mind or the citta visuddhi. It explains the various stages of concentration, particularly the practice of the "Calming of the Mind and Its Formations" or the Samatha.

The third part is made up of stages three through seven, namely the Purification of Overcoming Doubt (or kankha vitarana visuddhi), the Purification of Knowledge and Vision of What is Path and Not Path (or maggamagga nanadassana visuddhi), the Purification of Knowledge and Vision of the Course of Practice (or patipada nanadassana visuddhi), and the Purification by Knowledge and Vision (or nanadassana visuddhi). These describe the Four Noble Truths, the practice of vipassana meditation, and the other concepts of Buddhism, such as the five khandhas and ayatanas. It highlights the various types of knowledge gained once an aspirant practices the teachings.

According to Theravadins, meditation is the most important practice to attain enlightenment. There are two types of Theravada meditations, namely Samatha and Vipassana.

Samatha is literally translated as "to make skillful". It refers to meditation, which enhances one's ability to concentrate, visualize, achieve and calm the mind.

In this type of meditation, the person should meditate on a particular object. In Theravada, there are forty traditional objects, called the kammatthana, where the person should meditate on.

The first ten are the objects that one can directly sense. These are air, water, earth, fire, wind, blue, green, yellow, red, white, enclosed space, and bright light.

The second ten are the objects of repulsion. These include a swollen corpse, discolored, bluish corpse, fissured corpse, rotten or festering corpse, dismembered corpse, gnawed corpse, worm- eaten corpse, bleeding corpse, mangled corpse and a skeleton.

The third ten are the objects of recollections. The first three are the Three Jewels: the Buddha, the Dharma and the Sangha. The second three are the recollections of the virtues, namely: liberality, morality, and the wholesome attributes of Devas. The final four recollections are of the body, peace, breath and death.

Four of the objects are the stations of Brahma, namely unconditional kindness and goodwill, sympathetic joy over another being's success, compassion and equanimity or even- mindedness.

The next four objects are the formless states that are infinite space, infinite nothingness, infinite consciousness, and neither perception nor non-perception.

The next object is the aharepatikulasanna, or the perception of disgust to foods. The last object to meditate on is the group of four elements – the fire, earth, air and water.

By meditating on the kammatthana through Samatha meditation, a person can then enhance his jnana, or skill of the mind. As soon as that happens, he can move on to practicing Vipassana.

Vipassana means "abstract understanding" or "insight". It is the second type of Theravada meditation, which focuses on gaining insight into the real nature of truth or reality. Per Theravadins, nirvana can only be reached if one practices in life the Noble Eightfold Path, including mindfulness meditation.

In modern Burmese Vipassana, the meditation consists of four stages. In the first stage, the person concentrates on discovering the connection that the body and mind are as one. It is also to see phenomena as impermanent, or appearing and ceasing. In the second stage, the practice of meditation no longer becomes an effort, but one that is purely enjoyed. In the third stage, the feeling of joy in practicing meditation disappears and what remains is happiness.

In the final stage, the person attains pure mindfulness, which will then lead to direct knowledge. It is also in this stage when the person gains insight on the true nature of reality, and it is that all phenomena are impermanent. After gaining this knowledge, the person reaches nirvana, which is the highest goal of all Theravadins.

Mahayana Buddhism

Mahayana, or the "Great Vehicle" was traditionally called the Bodhisattva Yana or the "Bodhisattva Vehicle". It is regarded as the "vehicle" that will bring the Bodhisattva (those seeking to become Buddhas) to nirvana for the benefit of all sentient beings. The foundational teachings of Mahayana are all based on the belief that all sentient beings have the chance at attaining universal liberation.

Many Mahayanists believe in the existence of supernatural bodhisattvas, who are utterly devoted to the perfections, to liberation of all sentient beings, and to the ultimate knowledge.

Unlike Theravadins, the Mahayanists believe that attaining nirvana is not the ultimate goal in Buddhism. Rather, they believe that one should resolve to free all sentient beings and not just the self from samsara. Those who wish to follow this aspiration are the Bodhisattva.

The Bodhisattva intend to achieve this aspiration as quickly as they can so they can benefit an infinite number of sentient beings. High level Bodhisattva who achieved the

Six Perfections are described as immensely compassionate beings who possess transcendent wisdom.

An interesting thing to note about Mahayana Buddhism is their cosmology, which consists of different words and Buddha- realms in which the different Buddhas and Bodhisattvas reside. They also teach Buddha Nature, which focuses on describing the sacred nature of the Buddha so that sentient beings may emulate him and become Buddhas themselves.

Historians find it difficult to trace the roots of Mayana, yet it is more widely practiced than Theravada. Mahayana began in India as well, but later it spread across Asia, particularly Bangladesh, Bhutan, China, Indonesia, Japan, Korea, Malaysia, Mongolia, Nepal, Singapore, Taiwan, and Vietnam.

As mentioned, Mahayana has two sub-sects, Traditional Mahayana and Vajrayana. Buddhism teachings practiced under Traditional Mahayana today are the Japanese Zen, Korean Seon, Chan, Pure Land, and Nichiren. The teachings practiced under Vajrayana are the Tibetan, Tiantai, Tendai, and Shingon Buddhism. You can further explore all these on your own, but for now, let us discuss

Japanese Zen Buddhism in particular, for it is one of the reasons why many are drawn to Buddhism in the first place.

Traditional Mahayana: Japanese Zen Buddhism

Japanese Zen Buddhism originally came from Chan Buddhism, which was developed during the Tang Dynasty in China. Those who practice Zen focus on developing self-control, the practice of meditation, insight into Buddha Nature, and the practice of this insight in one's life not just to benefit the self but also others. Zen relies more on practice and being taught by a teacher over knowledge of the Buddhist doctrine and sutras.

The practice of meditation is the core of Zen Buddhism. One can do it through meditation of the breath, of the mind, through Koan, and through chanting. Zen meditation or zazen is often done in the lotus sitting position. During meditation of the breath, the person is focuses entirely on the movement of his breath or on the energy found below the navel.

In meditation of the mind, the person needs to acknowledge his stream of thoughts but should not become involved with them. He should simply let these thoughts arise then fade away.

The Zen meditation of Koan is when the Zen practitioner uses a paradoxical riddle called a Koan to provoke enlightenment and test his progress. The Zen teacher will quietly assess the student as he presents understanding of a given koan.

Now that you have some ideas about the two main schools of Buddhism and the Japanese Zen Buddhism, you may be curious to know which one you should follow. However, what makes Buddhism unique compared to the other religions of the world is that it does not tell you to follow doctrine based on faith. Rather, the Buddha emphasizes on practicing the Noble Eightfold Path then realizing the true nature of reality for himself.

By following the path, you will know for yourself whether you wish to achieve enlightenment as is aspired by the Theravadins, or go beyond that and teach the path to other sentient beings as well, as defined by the Mahayanists.

Chapter 7. Philosophy And Practice Of Zen Buddhism

Zen is a branch of the Mahayana Buddhist tradition and is fundamentally based on the teachings of Siddhartha Gautama, the historical Buddha and founder of Buddhism. However, through its history, Zen also received influences from the diverse cultures of the countries it has passed through.

Its formative period in China, in particular, determined much of its identity. Taoist teachings and practices exerted considerable influence on Chinese Chan. Concepts such as wuwei, the fluid nature of reality, and the " non-carved stone" can still be identified in Japanese Zen and related schools." Even the Zen tradition of "mad masters" is a continuation of the tradition of Taoist masters. Another influence though minor came from Confucianism.

Such peculiarities have already led some scholars to argue that Zen as an "independent" school outside the Mahayana tradition or even outside of Buddhism. These positions, however, are a minority, the vast majority of scholars regard Zen as a Buddhist school within the Mahayana tradition.

All Zen schools are well-versed in Buddhist philosophy and doctrine, including the Four Noble Truths, the Noble Eightfold Path, and the parasites. However, Zen's emphasis on experiencing reality directly, in addition to ideas and words, always keeps it within the limits of tradition.

This openness enabled (and allowed) non-Buddhists to practice Zen, such as the Jesuit priest Hugo Enomiya-Lassalle, to also receive the Dharma transmission and a lot of other non- Buddhists.

Zen Practices and Teachings

In general, the teachings of Zen criticize the study of texts and the desire for worldly achievements and focus on a dedication to meditation (zazen) as a way of experiencing the mind and reality directly. However, Zen does not become a quietist doctrine - the Chinese Chan Baizhang (in Japanese, Hyakujo, 720-814), for example, devoted himself to manual work in his monastery and had as his motto a saying that remained famous among Zen practitioners: "A day without work is a day without food."

Zen has a long tradition of meditative work, from manual to refined activities such as calligraphy, ikebana, and the famous tea ceremony - in addition to martial arts, with which Zen has always been connected to.

Zen is not a style of intellectual or solitary practice. Temples and centers of practice always assemble a group of practitioners (a sangha) and conduct daily activities and monthly retreats (sessions). Also, Zen is seen as a way of life, not just as a set of practices or a state of consciousness.

Zazen

For Zen, experiencing reality is experiencing nirvana. To experience reality directly, one must detach oneself from words, concepts, and discourses. And to separate yourself from this, one must meditate. Therefore, zazen ("sitting meditation") is the fundamental application of Zen.

When meditating, the practitioner sits over a small round cushion (the zafu) and assumes the lotus posture, the posture half lotus, the burmanesa position, or posture seiza. Joining his hands, a little below the navel (doing the cosmic mudra), he half- sits his eyelids, resting his eyes about a meter in front of him. At the Rinzai School, practitioners sit facing the center of the room. At the Soto school, they sit facing the wall.

Then the practitioner "follows his breath," counting each cycle of inspiration and expiration, until it reaches ten. Then the cycle begins again. In the meantime, your only task is to maintain a relaxed, open mind, concentrated but without tension, and be present in the "now" of the moment, without being led by thoughts or ruminations. When this happens, he returns to focus on counting. The more experienced practitioners, whose power of concentration (samadhi) is greater, can refrain from counting or following their breath. By doing so, they will be practicing the type of zazen called shikantaza, "just sit down."

The duration of a meditation period varies according to the school. Although the traditional period of meditation is the time that an incense stick takes to burn (from 35 to 40 minutes), schools like the SanboKyodan advise their students not to meditate for more than 25 minutes at a time, as meditation can result in inertia. In most schools, however, monks routinely meditate between four to six periods at 30-40 minutes each every day. As for nonspecialists, Master Dogen said that five minutes a day were already beneficial - what matters is consistency.

During monthly retreats (sessions), however, activities are intensified. With a duration of one, three, five, or seven days, the retreat routine provides nine to 12 periods of 30-40 minutes a day, or even longer. Between each zazen period, practitioners "rest" doing kinhin (walking meditation).

The Teacher

As Zen gives relatively little importance to the written word, the role of the teacher is crucial for the practitioner's training. Generally, a Zen teacher is an ordained person in any school who has been permitted to teach the Dharma to others.

A central part of the whole Zen tradition is the notion of the transmission of Dharma, that is, the idea that there is an unbroken lineage of teachers who, from the Buddha, transmitted and received the teachings and attained at least some degree of attainment. This notion originated from Bodhidharma's famous description of Zen:

"A special broadcast, out of the scriptures; Without depending on words or letters; Pointing directly to the human mind;

Contemplating their nature and attaining Buddhahood."

When a teacher is officially recognized as having reached a certain degree of attainment and is admitted to the lineage of masters, he is believed to have "received the transmission of the Dharma." Since at least in the Middle Ages, this "mind-to-mind" transmission from master to disciple has played a vital role in all Zen schools. During the transmission ceremony, the new teacher is presented with a letter genealogical mapping of the entire lineage, from Buddha to himself.

Honorary titles attached to teachers who received the transmission of the Dharma include: in China, Fashi and Chanshi ; in Korea, Sunim and Seon Sa; in Vietnam, Thay; and in Japan, Osho ("priest"), Sensei ("teacher") and Roshi ("elder teacher"). In general, one speaks of a "Zen master" only about renowned teachers, especially the medieval or the ancient.

The Illumination

In Zen, enlightenment is generally called satori or kensho. The kensho is the initial glimpse, so to speak, of the true nature of reality and of itself. It's a shallow form of enlightenment. Satori, on the other hand, is a more profound and more lasting experience in which the practitioner has an intense experience of Buddha's Nature, and sees his "original face."

But it is not a visionary experience. Although some people suppose that the experience of enlightenment should lead those who experience it to universes of intense light or something that is worth it, the testimony of Zen masters contradicts this hypothesis. When asked about how his life was before and how he stayed after satori, a modern Zen master replied, "Now my garden looks more colorful."

In enlightenment, the practitioner is not distracted.

Another common assumption is that when being enlightened, the flow of thoughts stop, and the practitioner stands as a polished mirror, reflecting the actual reality without ideas that will hinder it. On the contrary, dreams do not stay - what happens is that the practitioner gives them up, lets them go, forgets them, and forgets himself. When the Fifth Patriarch, Hongren (in Japanese, Daiman Konin, 601-647), decided to choose who would succeed him, he proposed to his disciples that they try to capture the essence of Zen in a poem; the author of the best poem would be his successor. When they received the news, the monks knew who the winner was: Shenxiu, Hongren's oldest student. No one bothered to compete with him. They just waited, and Shexiu wrote his poem and hung it on the wall:

"This body is the Bodhi tree. The soul is like a bright mirror. Take care that is always clean,

leaving no dust accumulates on it."

All the monks liked it. Surely Hongren would enjoy it too. However, the next day there was another poem hanging by the side, which someone had preached during the night:

"Bodhi is not like a tree.

The bright mirror shines nowhere:

If there is nothing from the beginning, Where does dust accumulate?"

The monks were amazed. Who would have written that? After a while, they discovered: the author of the poem was Huineng, the cook of the monastery. And realizing his achievement, it was to him that Hongren extended his cloak and his bowl, making Huineng the Sixth Patriarch.

Radical Teachings

Some of the traditional stories of Zen describe masters using strange methods of education, and many practitioners today tend to interpret these stories overly literally.

For example, many are outraged when they hear stories like that of Master Linji, the founder of the Rinzai school, who said, "If you find the Buddha, kill the Buddha. If you find a Patriarch, kill the Patriarch." A contemporary master, Seung Sahn, also teaches his students that we all need to kill three things: kill our parents, kill the Buddha, and kill our teacher (in this case, Seung Shan himself). However, it is clear that neither Linji nor Seung Sahn was speaking literally. What they wanted to say was that we need to "kill" our attachment to outside teachers and things.

When visiting temples or Zen practice centers, beginners who have read many of these stories and expect to find iconoclastic teachers are often surprised by the conservative and formal nature of practices.

Zen and Other Religions

Since the mid-twentieth century, Zen has been open to interreligious dialogue, having appeared in countless meetings and conferences around the world. Perhaps the most representative figure of Zen in this dialogue is the Vietnamese monk Thich Nhat Hanh, shortlisted for the 1967 Nobel Peace Prize, who has been engaged in interreligious dialogue for decades and keeps images of both Buddha and Jesus on his altar.

In Zen temples and centers of practice around the world, it is common for many non-Buddhists to attend activities and practice zazen. This practice is generally well accepted by teachers, since Buddhism is a religion of tolerance that sees other religions as valid spiritual paths, and is open to anyone who only wants to meditate without any religious affiliation.

In some schools, one of which is Sanbo Kyodan, the acceptance of practitioners of other religions is so high that without needing to leave their religion, a practitioner can receive the Dharma transmission and become a teacher.

Statements like that of the former Pope, who called the Dalai Lama "godless," naturally had a considerable and (of course) adverse effect on the masses of the population.

Therefore, most people are unaware that the Buddha did not regard himself as either God or a messenger of God. He merely explains that the teachings Dhamma (Pali) or Dharma (Sanskrit) can be experienced through his meditative vision (of contemplation). Furthermore, Buddha refers to the self-reliance of the individual himself in learning this technique and urges against a dogmatic adherence to his teaching. Self-responsibility is the highest here.

Zen and Meditation

Likewise, Zen is the school of Buddhism that takes reflection as a direct way to reach awakening. All schools of Buddhism also take meditation as a practice and try, through it, to achieve full awareness, however, it is Zen among all the different traditional schools that take meditation as the primary tool to reach this achievement.

The word Zen is of Japanese origin and is derived from the Chinese word Chan, which is what was called Mahayana Buddhism practiced in China from which Zen arose. In turn, the word Chan is a transliteration of the Sanskrit word Dhyana. The term Dhyana describes the experience of meditative absorption that occurs after an effective concentration. In the ancient discourses of the Buddha, up to eight different levels of this absorption are detailed.

Observing our nature and awakening to Buddhahood. Buddahood happens when you reach your ultimate enlightenment. Zen considers that any person has, not only the potential for Enlightenment but also Buddhahood itself in his experience, this is a very particular feature of Zen Buddhism. When practitioners become involved with any aspect of their practice, be it conscious attention, compassion-or whatever-they assume that that quality is already inherent in their experience. Consequently, the method consists of opening up and discovering what already exists in its condition, this makes Zen practice very positive, affirmative, and allows its practitioners to progress naturally and directly. In essence, Zen affirms that we are all Buddhas and training helps to discover this fact more deeply.

A peculiarity of Buddhist ethics can be found in Zen Buddhism. Here, the prohibition of intoxicating means is emphasized, this is related to the fact that in Zen Buddhism, the right mindfulness has a significant role. Moreover, intoxicants prevent a clear and always alert mind. Another peculiarity that only occurs in Zen Buddhism is the great importance of goodness and compassion. In Zen Buddhism, the idea of universal love is emphasized as much as the concept of charity in Christianity. That is why nonviolence, peacefulness, and love of one's enemies are sought.

Chapter 8. American Buddhism

Much talk is currently going on in Buddhist circles about how Buddhism will create in America, so here is my input.

Generally, Buddhism has taken on the way of life to which it has moved, and I accept that American Buddhism will be no particular case. I further believe that American values will reflect profoundly in the Buddhisms that, in the long run, become "American Buddhisms."

Be that as it may, what are available American values?

Is it accurate to say they are Mom, God, and Apple Pie? Or then again, is America going another way, a weird way that comes consistently nearer to verifiable Buddhist values?

The family in America is being broken with almost a half separation rate. Numerous people are not wedding and permanently living respectively with single momism drifting toward right around a standard. This is lamentably the present reality paying little heed to what we might want that reality to be.

Mother (family), regardless, has lost a portion of its conventional values.

What about God? In Germany, just 15% state that God is significant in their lives. Is this the pattern in America too? As per Pew Reports, it is.

What's more, Apple pie? When's the last time you prepared one?

Are Americans usually enriched with affection, sympathy, and a positive attitude? Not really. If we are sensible and found some hidden meaning of all the news stories and governmental issues, the dominating American attribute is wild autonomy. They don't call the Fourth of July Independence Day to no end.

The fascinating thing is, the Buddha felt a similar way. He left the shows of his time, which for his situation was the well-off lifestyle of a ruler and lived as a bum in the woodland for a long time, practically starving to death attempting to discover genuine responses for himself about how he could get away from the desolates of maturity, ailment, and passing.

Supposedly, when the Buddha was conceived, a sage anticipated that he would either turn into an incredible world ruler or become a sacred man that would spare the world. (The birth accounts of the Buddha and Christ are uncannily comparable).

Since the Buddha's dad, a lord in his own right, needed nothing to do with heavenly men, he protected the fellow from any possibility of his seeing the dark side of life that may raise spiritual inclinations. So he orchestrated three manors for the ruler who stayed under 'house capture' carrying on with a debauched lifestyle. No delight was obscure to the sovereign.

At some point, he convinced his charioteer to escape the stronghold to glance around. At the point when the Buddha saw an older adult, he didn't realize what it was! His charioteer guaranteed the Buddha that even he, the extraordinary ruler, couldn't get away from this destiny.

At that point, he saw a wiped-out man and, after that, a carcass. His charioteer again guaranteed him this is the thing that the Buddha himself was bound for. Presently, the

Buddha left his young spouse and day-old child and entered the woodland alone either to discover the response to death.

Americans are do-it-yourselfers. We don't need anybody instructing us on how to do it. We loathe similarity. Latently tracking like sheep is repulsive to the majority of us.

The Buddha was similar; he walked out on his Hindu religion, which didn't offer him the responses he looked for, and instead scanned for truth inside himself. He discovered it, and later educated for one reason and one reason only, as he said - to free people. He turned out to be free himself when he was 35 years of age and instructed for a long time from that point.

Americans have traveled along these lines also, right? Toward freedom? Support in general church administrations where we are determined what to accept and the proper behavior is declining, isn't it? Truly?

Americans increasingly need a "hands-on" way to deal with their spiritual life, not spoon-encouraged pablum. Isn't this valid?

We inalienably are starting to comprehend that freedom must be found inside and are beginning to scrutinize the old fantasies that "companions, family, church, profession, and riches" satisfy us. Right?

In actuality, encounters, getting these things and clutching them can ordinarily create severe pressure, isn't this valid? Where does your pressure originate from? Something contrary to what we're attempting to achieve, which is total freedom, is supplanted by complete anxiety.

The constant battle to develop, and after that keep - spouses, wives, companions, family, church, profession and riches - is distressing, and trusting that these will bring about total freedom is a conspicuous paradox paying little mind to what we are persuaded. Is this false?

These things, things that are outside of us, cause pressure when we attempt to collect and then clutch them. They are very guiltless in themselves, yet it's the craving to amass and afterward guarantee these people and things as our very own that high feelings of anxiety bound with envy, uncertainty, and dread. In any case, we don't see this, isn't that right? Since we have gotten tied up with these things as being ethical.

How about we be genuine? Buddhism, in its most perfect structure, is counter-social. It runs contrary to the natural order of things, of conventional wisdom, or the possibility that we should be profitable and commit ourselves to the material improvement of society.

What a stunner! Correct? One will contend that, if we, as a whole, lounged around pondering our navels, society would fizzle. I will react that Steve Jobs pondered his maritime!

A few Americans are starting to scrutinize the present model of society that is increasingly getting to be no-nonsense. Is it true that it isn't valid? The disparity of salary, vagrancy, whatnot. This scrutinizing is being reflected in changes of frames of mind toward religion, governmental issues, fund, and even family values - the first turn focuses where societies are produced.

Americans, being free and not sharp about being determined what to do or what to believe, are increasingly scrutinizing the conventional wisdom that forfeits one's internal development for the benefit of a materialistic society. It boils down to 'make easy money' or who gets injured, refrains from getting well-off deep down. One strategy reinforces its enemy, and the other obliterates its foe. Exacting primary concern, free enterprise with no respect to social values slaughters the pursuit of internal ethicalness, while the pursuit of inward prudence fortifies society all of society.

Buddhist Monks, who in some American eyes simply lounge around and ruminate and are a delayed society, are alternately adored by Asians who comprehend that the more profound excellencies are to be developed and respected because these are what guarantee a fair and placated society. Asians put resources into their priests just as their 401ks.

Globalization financially manages that social orders increasingly should give a ton of consideration to profiting. In short, vitality or intrigue is left for spiritual pursuits. In a zombie- like trance, we go to class, find a new line of work, profit, bring up children, grow old and die - if we are fortunate. In the game that we are unfortunate, we get left behind and die as poor people

- no cash, no spiritual arousing.

We may go to church and accept what they let us know, yet only sometimes do we search inside for our truth; we take someone's story and accept it as our own. We accept wholeheartedly that we will go to paradise or any place our specific religion reveals to us that we are going. We never question that. In any event, we never did.

A mix of expanded insight, expanded access to data, and expanded mindfulness that real joy - the power of societal achievement - leaves us ailing in apparent freedom, has all consolidated to scrutinize what, at one time, was viewed as blessed truth - that achievement implies a big bank account.

Perhaps because a big bank account is increasingly getting to be distant for the regular specialist, or possibly because our profound values are changing, something is causing the old solid beliefs to disintegrate.

As I would see it, American Buddhism won't create along the lines that conventional Buddhism has created in other nations or along paths that customary Christianity has created here. This will be unique; it will be radical and an impression of a development of the spiritual life.

A blast of enthusiasm for yoga and contemplation once chuckled at by everything except hardcore hippies during the 60s is a sign where Buddhism is going. These are close to home pursuits not associated with any gathering and, in spite of most Eastern religions, where the societal spotlight is carrying on with an upstanding life and liberally providing for the religious association. Americans instead go for the throat of individual, religious and spiritual experience.

We are not especially keen on being upstanding or high or buckling down in society and after that offering cash to an association; we are progressively keen on creating ourselves inside until we change from pressure balls to placated and confident people. Strikingly enough, the Buddha valued these sorts of apparently narcissistic people over ones who pondered others before they considered themselves.

The Buddha realized that, until an individual turned out to be free themselves, they couldn't generally help other people become free.

(We're talking edification here).

He said there are four sorts of people: Those who don't help themselves or help other people. The individuals who help other people yet not themselves. The individuals who help themselves, however, not others. Furthermore, the individuals who help themselves and others.

The fourth classification is simply the most elevated - the individuals who help themselves and others. The following most astounding is the individuals who help themselves, however, not others. Notice this is higher than the individuals who help other people and not themselves. What's more, the least individual is one who helps neither him nor herself nor others. Americans fall in the third class - until further notice, helping themselves and not helping other people. Anyway, this third classification transforms typically into the fourth as the individual turns out to be spiritually best in class.

So, as it were, the Buddha was counter-societal, recommending that we remove time from our material pursuits to examine ourselves internally.

Is Buddhism Real for Americans?

Like Christianity, Buddhism has numerous branches. The original regulation that the Buddha taught his monks is known as the Theravada or the Teaching of the Elders, yet this profound teaching might be excessively unusual and terrifying for regular Americans.

This disagreeability isn't unordinary when we think about the more profound teachings of numerous religions, for example, Kabbalah in Judaism and Orison in Christianity. Individuals, for the most part, talk a decent tale about God, however, would prefer not to go there truly, selecting instead for natural wonders, for example, sex, cash, power, security, and excitement. Recognizable things.

For precisely these reasons, some Buddhist branches, for instance, Zen, Tibetan, and numerous different divisions of Buddhism, have divided from the original, severe Theravada, making their specific image of Buddhism easier to understand, and have consequently appreciated incredible accomplishment in pulling in supporters, while the Theravada remains, to some degree, dark in the more significant part of the world.

Theravada is called (Hinayana) the "little vehicle" since it advanced originally to a predetermined number of individuals who were intense in their practice, i.e., the Buddha's Sangha of monks or pupils, who had just one desire at the top of the priority list: Enlightenment.

In present-day times, Theravada has developed into, for the most part, a ` social religion where service and practices of liberality, innocuousness, and adoring generosity have supplanted the shady traditions of the Buddha and his pupils. In any case, these grim teachings are as yet practiced by devoted Buddhist monks in the remote woods of Sri Lanka, Thailand, and other Southeastern Asian nations, a practice moderately unaltered from the Buddha's occasions, teachings that I was lucky enough to take an interest in while living in backwoods of Northeast Thailand.

Zen, Tibetan, and different branches are called Mahayana, the "enormous vehicle," which is progressively friendly and where hoards can, without much of a stretch, fit into the boat. Mahayana changes the original teachings with the goal that they are palatable for the more extensive crowd. A mix of Buddhism, German Romanticism, new age, and light and love appears to function admirably in the U.S.

Hinayana, or the original Buddhism, never adjusted the Buddha's original teachings to pull in more devotees, since this technique has demonstrated, more than 2600 years, to be the quick and sure street to edification. Being completely discerning that this adherence to the exacting tenet constrained its prominence, Hinayana never adjusted its course and has subsequently made do for a long time, generally under the radar, since it is the spot one goes to get the original, significant Buddhist teachings that work.

Despite the fact that a bunch of individuals ever get a craving to go this far, enough from the beginning of time have perceived the Theravada as the genuine article. The numbers, even today that have turned out to be illuminated by rehearsing as the Buddha initially taught, is a demonstration of its viability. Thailand stays relentless at about 93% Theravada Buddhist, and Sri Lanka about 70%, with huge Theravada populaces in Cambodia, Viet Nam, and Laos. There are around 100 million Theravada Buddhists worldwide and approximately 2 billion Mahayana Buddhists internationally checking China.

Buddhism is moderately new to America, coming here just around fifty years back through scholarly channels and Asian migration. Likewise, Buddhist writings have only been somewhat, as of late, converted into English since the mid- 1900s, so Buddhism is in its earliest stages in America. Zen Buddhism landed here for the most part during the 50s, Tibetan Buddhism during the 60s, and Theravada Buddhism during the 70s.

After Buddhism arrived, it engaged westerners, given its coherent methodology - for what reason would it be a good idea for you to accept what another person discloses to you except if you can demonstrate it valid for yourself? (Which is really what the Buddha said). What's more, the demonstrated strategies for Buddhist practice spoke to westerners, practices intended to free one mentally so one can carry on with a tranquil, mollified life, instead of being a "work in advancement" where there is only, from time to time, any work... or on the other hand, advancement!

What the Buddha taught, when connected, prompts individual flexibility from stress and significant comprehension of life, restricted to recycled understanding that isn't the aftereffect of individual knowledge, yet the consequence of what another person or some data let you know.

This logical methodology of testing and then encountering knowledge for yourself, including illumination, quickly spoke to America's optimal of independence and the intrinsic propensity to be wary about what others state (show me rather), which may be a reaction of media publicizing and a developing contempt of sorted out, definitive religions.

Strangely enough, the practice of contemplation, when practiced effectively, brings about improved knowledge mirroring a consciousness of numerous great qualities, some of which are simply going to the bleeding edge on school grounds, for example, dealing with our earth, (not contaminating and deforesting just to profit), thinking about every single living being, trustworthiness, and harmony.

Be that as it may, regardless of anything else, when the most profound parts of Theravada are investigated, and it comes down to the truth of issues, numerous westerners flee and look for a haven in the natural environment. You could state that Asians are somewhat harder in such a manner.

The Theravada Buddhist teachings negate the world - against the world in a manner of speaking, against the flood of regular cognizance. Along these lines, Theravada will never be well- known in the world, as the world exists.

The Buddha said the world's way is the method for desire, of needing and thirst, and all things considered essential burden us with negative drives, for example, childishness, daze aspiration, scorn, mercilessness, and unpleasantness, and in the long run brutality and wars. He said that the worldly pursue their thirsts, feeling that the objects of their desires, when gotten, will fulfill them. In any case, rather than joy, this longing for wishes and the subsequent sticking to them after they are accomplished become the prime reasons for our pressure. He takes care of business down to the bare essential of human experience, which runs contrary to the natural order of things in our psyches that genuinely accept that we can be upbeat by craving and getting things. It conflicts with all present rationale and what we allow to be valid.

He announced that, when we stop this hankering and sticking to our objects of desire, at precisely that point, the can brain become glad and free. In any case, who might accept that?

He doesn't get into God or paradise since he recommended that those things are only contemplations and minds, the very deeds that shield us from seeing with intuitive knowledge and won't help haul out the bolt of discontent. Also, imaginings and contemplations cover our actual envy by a mental transference of obligation. Just by unraveling discontentment in advance in the domain of reality can the mind, at that point, advance into super-mundane states. Something else, super-mundane states are just envisioned and not so much experienced or accomplished. It is these supermundane states that make Buddhism a religion as opposed to just a way of thinking.

For instance, the Buddha recommended investigating this body of ours, investigating the truth of it that we escape, rather than looking outside to gods or the sky. He said this is the main spot that the truth can discharge us. I accept this is reliable counsel, supposing that we can't confront the truth of our own body, which is directly here before us to see, by what means can we ever plan to uncover the truth of different things progressively convoluted and far off?

Also, when we know the truth of this body and brain of ours, the reality of everything outside turns out to be mystically clear too.

Chapter 9. The Three Principle Practices Of The Buddhist Path

The path of enlightenment has a few principles that are the foundation of Buddha's teachings. These principles are divided into three categories, which are prajna, sila, and samadhi.

Prajna

One of the first principles of the Buddhist path is prajna, also known as wisdom. Prajna is regarded as enlightenment, which is the main focus of Buddhism. When it comes to prajna, wisdom is a lot different than knowledge. Knowledge is what you know, a collection of facts. Wisdom comes out when you are most calm and pure. It's obtained through meditation and cultivation and comes at the end of your path.

Sila

The word sila translates to moral values and is important in the path's progress as it's the foundation of qualities. There are two principles that sila is based on, and these are the principles of reciprocity and equality. When the Buddhists speak of the principle of reciprocity, they are speaking about the golden rule: "Do unto others as you would have done to you." When Buddhists talk about the principle of equality, they are speaking about the equality of all living things, including the equality of security and happiness.

Samadhi

Samadhi translates to mediation. As a Buddhist, you want to obtain pure freedom, which you can do through mental development. You need to purify the mind, and the only way to do this is through meditation, or samadhi.

All three of these practices work together in order to purify the mind so that you can obtain complete freedom. You can't have one without the other.

Chapter 10. The Four Noble Truths

When Buddha started teaching about his enlightenment, he started with the Four Noble Truths. In these truths, Buddha is teaching about suffering, its cause, how there is an end to suffering, and what to do so you can end suffering.

Dukkha

Dukkha is the truth that states that suffering exists. Dukkha is real and universal, and there are several causes of suffering. Some of these causes are sickness, the impermanence of pleasure, and pain. Dukkha states that our suffering often starts because we have a desire that we can't fulfill.

No matter what we want, we continue to suffer because when we reach one goal, we want more. This is human nature, and Buddhists feel that in order to fully reach the path of enlightenment, we need to understand dukkha and take control of it so that we can control our suffering and take the next step toward entering the pure state of mind. An example of this is money. How often do we state that if we just had more money we could buy a nicer car or a bigger house? However, once we attain this level of wealth, we still want more money because we want more things.

Samudaya

Samudaya states that there is a cause for suffering, which is the desire to control things. Some people refer to this as the cravings or thirst for things that we can't have at the moment. There can be many forms of samudaya, such as the desire for fame, craving of sexual pleasures, and the desire to avoid unpleasant sensations, such as anger, jealousy, and fear. Buddhists also state that this craving creates karma, which is what makes you want more. When we suffer, we are ignoring karma because we are too worried about our own selfish desires and wishes.

When we let suffering take over, it's because we've let go of what really matters and started to focus on our wants. For instance, we start looking toward our neighbors to see what they have in life, and we begin to want that. We want the bigger car, the bigger house, and nicer clothes. We work on trying to impress others instead of focusing on compassion, understanding, keeping our minds clear, and karma. We also start blaming others for our own problems instead of looking inside ourselves to see if we can find an answer and cure for our problems.

In the eyes of Buddha, anything that made you unhappy or took away your peace was a cause of suffering. When the word suffering came to Buddha, it didn't just have to do with seeing people become sick, die, or get physically hurt. It also had to do with allowing ourselves to become unhappy, clouding our minds with unwelcome thoughts, such as "I have this, but it's not good enough, so now I want this."

Nirodha

Nirodha gives us the realization that there is an end to suffering, and this comes when we finally reach the liberation of nirvana. In Buddhism, the only true way to end suffering is to end your wants and wishes and your selfish desires. You need to become free of those thoughts. In order to do this, you need to understand the right view from the Eightfold Path. Only then will you be able to realize that suffering can end if we let go of what we want and find happiness within ourselves. Once this is attained, we let go of all the cravings we have and are truly free of our suffering.

Megga

Megga is the fourth Noble Truth, which states that the only way we can work toward ending our suffering is by following the Eightfold Path, or the Middle Path. To end suffering, you need to follow a path. One of the best ways to understand this path of ending suffering, along with the Four Noble Truths, is to look at this as if you had an illness. For example, dukka is the diagnosis. This is the part where the doctor tells you what illness you have, and you come to realize that you have this illness. The next step of the process is finding the cause. What caused this illness? In other words, what caused this suffering that you've realized is inside of you? The third step, which is nirodha, is the treatment phase of the process. Now that you have observed you're suffering and you've found the cause, you can come up with a plan to help treat the suffering. The final phase, which is megga, is the recovery phase. This is the part where you've been able to get through the suffering and you're liberated.

Of course, it's important to realize and remember that no matter how hard we try, we can't get rid of suffering in the world. It's just part of life, and we need to learn to deal with it and, at times, overcome it. We suffer when we are born; we just have no remembrance of it. We also suffer when we are growing up and growing old. We also suffer because of death and other situations that happen in our lives, such as heartaches. Buddhism isn't about getting rid of suffering or finding ways so you don't have to feel like you are suffering; it's more about working to ease the suffering. Buddhism can work to try to give you an understanding of your suffering and why suffering exists in this world.

Chapter 11. What Is Karma?

Here are some questions that Buddha remained silent on. There were known as undeclared questions. They are as follows:

Questions on the existence of time in the world:

1.   Is the world not everlasting?

2.   Is it?

3.   Or both?

4.   Or neither?

Questions on the existence of the world in space:

1.   Is the world bounded in space?

2.   Is it not bounded in space?

3.   Or neither?

Questions about personal identity:

1. Is it self-indistinguishable from the body?

2. ... or is it dissimilar to the body?

Questions about life after death:

1. Does the Buddha exist after death?

A monk named monk Malunkyaputta asked Buddha these questions expecting him to answer them. The monk cannot accept Buddha's silence on these questions, so he ventures forth to search for the Buddha himself in an attempt to answer these questions. But he got nothing and was left to explore Buddhism more to find the answers himself.

Strictly speaking, the meaning of karma refers to any action, intent, and deed by a being. It summarizes the spiritual way of cause and effect, meaning the actions and intentions of a being help shape what the future for that being will look like.

In a general sense, having good intentions and doing good things strengthens your good karma and promotes the possibility of you having happiness in the future. On the other hand, having bad intentions and doing bad things can lead to bad karma, which makes experiencing pain and suffering a big possibility.

In traditional Buddhism, karma specifically refers to one's actions being based on having good intentions. Such intentions would then determine the being's cycle of rebirth and reincarnation. The word used to describe the "effect" of karma is karmaphala. You can think of karma as the seed and karmaphalas as the fruit of that seed.

When you practice Buddhism, you believe that your karma is what keeps you chained in rebirth in the afterworld. The concept of rebirth is also called reincarnation. It is described as the cycle of life and death within the realms of the afterworld, driven by desire, hatred, and ignorance. The only way out of this cycle is by following the teachings of the Buddha.

Karma is a process and according to the Buddha, karma is not the only thing that determines how your life will go, but rather that is is apart of the factors that affect your future, with other factors being in relation to the nature of being and circumstantial. It moves in a fluid and dynamic, rather than in a mechanical, linear manner. In fact, not all factors in the present can be attributed to karma.

Be careful not to define karma as "fate." Karma is not some form of godly judgment imposed on a being that did good or bad things. Rather, it can be defined as it's the natural result of the process.

In other words, doing a good thing would not automatically entail you to a big future full of happiness, and vice versa. After all, while certain experiences in your life are a result of your actions in the past, how you respond to those is not yet determined. Of course, such responses to circumstances would then lead to their own consequences in the future.

Every single human being is constantly changed due to karma. For every thought, action, and word being said, a certain kind of energy is released in different directions of the universe. These energies have the power to change and influence all other human beings, including the being that put the energy out there.

As you learn to discipline the mind, you also learn to control the karma that will happen in your everyday life and that is a big thing. This means that you limit your suffering and are able to live with that high energy in a positive way and positively influence the people that are around you. Your inner voice of calm is the voice that is able to control the voice of criticism and anger and it is the one that helps you to become the type of human being that is able to work with the limits of karma and keep everything in a positive manner. This is important, butyou do need to pay attention to your solutions and make sure that they are not close-minded and that they bring upon you the good and bad thoughts and energies of others.

Chapter 12. The Teachings Of Buddhism

The Way of Investigation

The very first teaching of Buddha is to investigate everything and not accept anything that is based on blind faith. He advised people to discover the truth of everything and anything that they encounter. He pointed out that most of the problems were induced by believing in things that are not based on tradition. The right way to accept things is to have an open mind and dig a little deeper into the development, origin, and characteristics of things, just so that you know the whole truth about everything. Similarly, he said that people should only explore Buddhism after investigating meditation and thinking about Buddhism while using meditation.

Four Noble Truths

During the course of Buddha's life, especially while

working towards reaching enlightenment, Buddha discovered the four noble truths. These are the truths you need to accept and understand if you want to reach complete happiness and peace in your life.

The first truth of Buddhism is the 'Truth of Dukkha', which states that each of us is affected by some sort of suffering in this world. There are two types of suffering: physical and mental. Mental problems are the emotional disturbances we experience after going through a traumatic experience or difficult time in life and physical suffering refers to the physical harm, pain, and injury we experience.

The second truth in Buddhism is 'the truth regarding the creation of dukkha'. This truth explains that the main cause of suffering is your ignorance and desires. Ignorance is not being conscious of the reality of things and just completely living a life of delusion. Desires refer to all of your wants that make you indulge in practices that bring different kinds of harm and pain to your life.

The third truth in Buddhism is 'the truth pertinent to the ending of all suffering'. This truth states that by working on eliminating all of the things in your life that are negative or bring negativity from your mind and life, you can rid your life of all sufferings and reach the state of complete peace, serenity, and happiness.

The fourth truth to Buddhism is 'the truth of following the middle way that ends all dukkha'. This truth is said to contain complete peace and happiness. You need to follow the middle way, also known as the eightfold noble path. By following this path, you can live a more balanced life, which is neither careless nor too difficult. It is just perfect and helps you live a perfectly happy and beautiful life.

Eightfold path

The eightfold noble path is known as the middle way that sets out the guidelines you need to follow to deal with every type of hardships and sufferings. This way of life compromised of eight rules that you follow when you are following Buddhism.

Samma ditthi or right view/understanding: You need to reevaluate your understanding of things and view things the right way so that you can gain complete insight into them. This means correcting your view of this life and not getting attracted to the worldly pleasures and desires because when this happens, you become very involved in this world and strive just to obtain those pleasures that will eventually result in suffering. Try to mentally understand what you really desire in your life that will ultimately bring you the absolute happiness in your life and not just temporary happiness that is brought to you by the worldly possessions and desires. Secondly, you need to understand that you inflict suffering on yourself with or without knowing it, so end it and correct your vision of things.

Samma Sankappa or Right Thought: Next, you need to focus on correcting your thought process, which can be accomplished if you correct your intention. For that, you need to reject the pleasures the world tries to dangle in front of you and instead bring love, kindness, and compassion for others in your thoughts.

Samma Vacca or Right Speech: You need to work on correcting your speech and the way you speak to people, which can be done if you practice abstinence from bad grammar, gossip, cruel speech, arguing, and idle chitchatting.

Samma Kammanta or Right Action: You must improve your actions and correct them by giving yourself a cleansing and ridding yourself of all sorts of sexual misconducts, destructive, and illegal actions.

Samma Ajiva or Right Livelihood: You need to work on the way that you make a living and must not do anything that will harm any other living being. Buddha instructed that you absolutely cannot practice these five professions: dealing in ammunition and arms, dealing in the flesh (butcher), dealing in sex and human trafficking, dealing in any sort of drugs, and dealing in any poisonous substances.

Samma Vayama or Right Effort: You need to correct your efforts. For that, you need to think in the right direction which may be a different direction. The sixth, seventh, and eighth factors are interlinked and closely related.

Samma Satti or Right Mindfulness: You need to work on reaching the state of mindfulness, which means you need to be aware of everything that is happening inside you and around you. This can be reached by practicing the eighth factor.

Samma Samadhi or Right Concentration: Lastly, you need to work on your concentration and focus. You must be fully concentrated on a subject to be aware of it and to understand it better. Right effort, concentration, and mindfulness can only be reached with meditation; hence, meditation is a very important tool of Buddhism.

By following these eight factors, you can live a more balanced, smooth, and composed life that is free of all sufferings.

Karma

Karma refers to actions that humans make and the law of action. It states that every single action has a reaction. If you do bad things, bad things consume your speech, body, and mind and harm you, then you will get painful results that you may not like. If you are living a life full of hardships, then it is a reflection of the bad things you chose to do.

Rebirth

Buddha believed in rebirth. He states that the reason why some people are born rich or poor is because of the good or bad things they did in their previous lives. According to Buddha, a person is born many times and rebirth goes far beyond the human realm and into the spiritual realm. He believed that people could be born as an animal, a bird, or even a spirit. The different realms that exist within are the human realm, grim and lower realms, ghost realm, animal and bird realm, and heavenly realm. Human beings can come or go into any of those realms if they desire.

The Six Lower Realms of Desire

Most sentient beings are trapped within these six lower realms. They do not get to move from one realm to another in a linear fashion, however, but in a more dynamic way of depending on their karma and the other factors that come into play. Here are the six lower realms:

1.   Hell

In Buddhism, this realm is called the Naraka. In it, you experience a complete state of pure hostility. You feel as if you do not have any free will to choose how you want to act, in the sense that you seem stuck in circumstances that are far beyond your control.

Those who are trapped in this realm are the ones who find it extremely difficult to hold back their hatred, anger, and frustrations. These beings have the constant urge to destroy everything around them including themselves. They see everything as hostile and threatening, so they will always feel claustrophobic towards their surroundings. Be warned that it is very difficult to escape from this realm.

2. Hunger

Traditional Buddhists call this realm the Pretas or the world of the hungry ghosts. Those who are in this realm are the beings that have never-ending appetites that come with extreme amounts of obsessiveness. Such qualities affect the thought of these beings and their actions that pertain to their wants and desires, whether they be wealth, power, fame, and pleasures of the flesh. This addiction is never satisfied and it only heightens as it is fed.

Beings who are in this realm find it almost impossible to have any self-discipline. Their search for pleasure affects them to the point where they begin to not care for the wellness of the people around them. This is a state of mind that is very easily interpreted by people today and is something that everyone can work on to try to correct their sense of need that resides within themselves. Many people learn from their own experiences as they go on in living their lives. It is just a matter of applying or not what they learned in order to stay away from the being obsessive or from the mistakes that they have once made.

3.   Brutality

This realm falls under the Buddhist world of the animals. These beings are trapped in thoughts and actions that are done on pure instinct, with absolutely no sense of morality. This means that their judgment has no reasoning to it whatsoever.

Being in this realm means that you only live in the present moment and not in the way that Buddha teaches mindfulness, rather in the way that they take advantage of others for selfish reasons that only help them. Not unlike how predators kill and stalk their prey when they are hunting in the wilderness. They also can't help but manipulate people in their favor and for personal gain.

Again, this is something that can be worked through

simply by being able to understand your own weaknesses and then learning how to overcome them in a healthy way. Changes in the life of someone may signal a change of direction and this is needed to rise from this state, where morality is the main problem you have to worry about.

4.   Arrogance

In traditional Buddhism, this realm is described as the world of the asuras and the demigods. Beings trapped here are those that are completely engrossed in jealousy, selfishness, and the obsession to win. Another distinctive quality of these beings is their constant desire to be on top in all aspects of life that they consider relevant and important to them. Although having these traits in the modern world may be considered beneficial, in the long term, it will destroy the being. This is because they end up valuing their own beliefs and egotistical ways more than the wellness of the people they care about around them. Being too competitive will also hold you back from being compassionate towards others because they are considered other beings.

5.   Passionate Idealism

In traditional Buddhist teachings, this realm falls into the world of human beings. It is the one where the beings have developed very advanced thinking skills and awareness that is discriminating. The most common trait in this realm is to be too ambitious with one's ideals.

While this realm presents some benefits, especially as it can help to motivate you into reaching enlightenment, it can also lead to suffering due to the desire of reaching perfection. In the same way, we criticize people who try to be perfectionists themselves, because their self-criticism holds them back from every reaching true enlightenment. This sense that everything needs to be perfect can stunt your spiritual growth immensely, which is hard for perfectionists to understand. For example, when learning how to meditate, a perfectionist may try too hard and achieve very little because of that. They need to let go of their need to be perfect in a world that is constantly changing and accept the changes that will happen, making them flexible towards that sort of thing. They must also try to really understand and remember that there is no perfect individual in this world.

6.   Rapture

Traditional Buddhists associate themselves with this realm. It is known as the world of gods and/or Devas. In this realm, this is most often referred to as the heavenly realm, the beings live very short lives, but with strong feelings of pure happiness and pleasure.

It cannot be changed that the beings in this realm only get to stay for a short amount of time. This is because the feeling of the rapture is momentary, and eventually, the being would then go back down to a lower realm.

The Four Higher Realms of Nobility

The four higher realms of nobility represent the ways of a traditional Buddhist in the way that they must exert all motivation and willpower to be able to let go of their desires in the mundane world. This is in order to understand our connection with nature and become our true selves.

The seventh and eighth realms are learning and absorption. They are referred to as the two vehicles in Mahayanist Buddhism. This means that when they find themselves in those realms, they are on the way to reaching the most important realms.

However, because of the presence of desires and the focus on oneself, specifically, to increase wisdom and gain insight, this is called being still within the samsara.

7. Learning

In Buddhism, this realm is represented by the Sravabuddha world which is essentially the realm of the enlightened disciples of Buddha.

In this realm, beings are in a state where they are seeking knowledge of the truths and self-improvement to become spiritual leaders and teachers. Specifically, they will try to seek guidance from some kind of mentor or guru. Such form of guidance, if not coming from a guru or mentor guru, can be obtained from texts and other pre-recorded information.

To come out of the lower realms and into this one, your inspiration should be built on motivation to learn and have an open mind towards the true nature of the world. This is a positive realm to be in because you are receptive to lessons and you are constantly being taught. You will also question things and find that gurus will give you examples so that you can understand more in your life. This is a time when you may be reading a lot or only going to classes just to widen your knowledge and understanding of Buddhism and how it works.

8.   Absorption

This particular realm is the world of pretyekabuddha, or "a Buddha on their own."

Beings who have reached this realm are those that seek the truth only based on their own observations and efforts. Typically, those who are in this realm have discovered that while external sources are useful, one's true learning experience come from the truly superior. Therefore, beings that are in this realm have chosen to seek truth and wisdom through internal discernment.

This will also apply to the people that have learned to meditate and have the self-discipline to take learning matters just one step further. Once you do begin to learn and understand, this state is one where you may want to improve the way you meditate to such an extent that you have a bigger understanding than you did before from it. You will be able to concentrate sufficiently and gain much from everything you are learning and have been taught.

Chapter 13. Becoming A Buddhist

If you are still here, it might be because this book has sparked a deeper interest in you and you would like to know how to get started. All the before mentioned theory may seem complicated and you might be asking yourself: "ok, but where do I begin?".

Over the past few years more and more people have approached the philosophy of life dictated by Buddhism, one of the oldest religions spread in the world, founded on the Four noble truths. The term Buddhism indicates in the strict sense a set of traditions, practices and spiritual techniques, currents of thought deriving from the different interpretations of doctrine, evolved over time. But which is the most suitable path to follow to embrace the Buddhist lifestyle and religion?

As you already know, Buddhism is based on a set of rules defined as the "Four noble truths", originating from the Indian itinerant ascetic Siddhārtha Gautama between the 6th and 5th centuries B.C. Originally based on spiritual discipline, Buddhism has taken on philosophical importance over the centuries, denying the existence of the gods.

From India, Buddhism subsequently spread to Southeast Asia and the Far East, from the 19th century to the West, involving a growing number of people. Approaching Buddhism means proving oneself able to go through different passages eliminating haste, requiring a deepening of the long-term sacred readings.

The first step to be taken to approach Buddhism, in order to be able to understand the fundamental concepts of this religion and philosophy of life, consists in the deepening of sacred readings and literary volumes for beginners currently available on the market. Subsequently it will be possible to address specific Buddhist associations located within your territory, starting a progressive approach to the meetings, letting any doubt or perplexity emerge during the confrontation.

To become a Buddhist you will have to change your lifestyle through gradual daily steps, changing your habits in a completely positive way, starting with the practice of beneficial actions and attitudes towards others. Buddhism is also based on the importance of meditation. Learning the art of meditation requires a great deal of experience and practice, making use of the directives made available by the various associations and of a profound contact with one's inner self, under the observance of the fundamental principles of everyday Buddhism and consistency over time. Within this path, we must arrive at a stabilization of inner happiness, making choices that can improve the quality of one's life and others'.

So, let's end this book with a list of simple steps that you can start implementing today to begin your journey towards Buddhism.

- Read the book "Siddharta", as it is one of the most

important books that talks about Buddhism in a profound yet beginner friendly way. It is a must, so get a copy as soon as you can;

- Experiment with vegetarianism and a healthier diet. It may seem a secondary step, but by changing up your nutrition you will soon experience benefits in every area of your life. It is a great way to get your feet wet, so do not overlook it;

- Start meditating. Do not worry if at the beginning you are not very good at it. In this first phase, it is important to establish new behaviors, that will ultimately help you become more and more connected to Buddhism. We have a lot of books that go into the depth of meditation, so feel free to check them out on Amazon and Audible.

•   Find other Buddhists and hang out with them. As simple as it may sound, spending time with people that are practicing Buddhism on a daily basis will help you grow faster and avoid the most common mistakes.

Just by following these easy steps, you will be on your way to deepen your knowledge on this fascinating philosophy.

Chapter 14. 55+ Mindfulness Tips For Beginner's

55+ Mindfulness Tips for Beginner's

I have this list in a file on my computer that I can reference whenever I feel the need to refocus. I hope these tips have the same positive impact on your life that they did in mine.

1.   Whenever you need to relax, simply concentrate only on your breathing and allow your subconscious to take over.

2.   When driving, turn off all music or talk radio, experiencing the sound of silence. It takes a bit to get used to. You'll feel like something may be missing. However, after time you'll see that with silence you're able to otherwise fill your mind with different perceptions, many of which are very rewarding. Practicing this can leave your mind calmer, quieter and much more focused overall.

3.   Eat slower than normal. Try eating a meal in silence each week as an experiment. This will help you experience the eating more fully. You may also want to cut out reading, listening to music, or watching TV while you're eating. Eliminating these things will allow you to become more attuned with how you eat and will give you more awareness when you're eating among other people.

4.   When you're working, use your breaks to really relax instead of just pausing on what you're doing. For example, instead of having a drink and talking with your fellow workers, take a short walk and meditate.

5.   Be aware of how often you're letting your mind dwell on past memories or future possibilities. Is this something that is necessary? Are these memories affecting you negatively? The future and the past are places we visit for planning and learning. However, many of us end up living in the past or future, instead of focusing on the here and now. Don't let yourself fall into that trap.

6.   Use your environmental cues as a reminder to continually center yourself. Allow the cues around you to help signal to yourself that it's time you take a minute to pause, take a deep breath, and become more aware of your bodily sensation. When you do this it allows your mind to

settle down and regroup.

7.   When going to work and stopped at a light, take a moment to pay close attention to what's around you, where your mind is at, and your breathing.

8.   When your done with your work day and you're walking to your vehicle, focus on your breathing and the air around you. Listen to any sounds you hear. Your goal is to be able to walk without the feeling of being rushed. You shouldn't feel anxious to get home.

9.   When you get home after work, be sure to say hello to everyone in your home. Look into each of their eyes when doing this. Afterward, take about 5-15 minutes to stay quiet and still. If you happen to live by yourself, enter your home and embrace the quietness of your environment and the feeling of that silence.

10.   Spend some more time in nature. I take long walks and hikes whenever possible.

11.   Notice how your mind is constantly judging things. Don't take these judgments too seriously. These thoughts aren't who you are.

12.   Practice listening without judging. It's harder to do than it sounds.

13.   Don't feel forced to always be doing something. If you have some free time take that time to simply be.

14.   When walking, be aware of how your weight is shifting, the sensations you feel in your feet. Focus more on yourself and less on where you're headed.

15.   Take some time to focus only on your breathing. Feel the flow of your breath and how your chest rises and falls.

16.   Take notice of what you're doing while you're doing it. Try and be in tune with all your senses.

17.   When you're eating, notice the texture and colors of your food as well as how it tastes.

18.   If your mind begins to wander to negative thinking, bring it back gently to your breath.

19.   Remember your thoughts are only thoughts, You aren't obligated to react to them or even believe them.

20.   Think of all the activities you do that you tend to zone out in. Some examples are texting, doing chores, web surfing, & driving. Take some time and practice being more aware when participating in these activities.

21.   Practice short bursts of mindfulness. Our brains react better to shorter sessions of mindfulness many times throughout the day, rather than a few long sessions of being mindful.

22.   Pick out a prompt to help you remember to be mindful. It could be getting a cup of coffee triggers you to take some time to be mindful, or hanging your coat up when you get home from work. Whatever triggers help you remember to practice mindfulness on daily basis will work just fine.

23.   Learn to properly meditate. Mindfulness is a skill we need to learn and sharpen over time. Being able to meditate properly will allow you to accomplish this.

24.   Practice being mindful while you're waiting.

Whether it's in line or at a doctor's appointment, these moments are great opportunities to practice being more mindful.

25. Practice first thing when you wake up in the morning. I find this helps me set the tone for the rest of my day and gets my body more in tune with my surroundings. Take a few minutes before you start reading your paper, watching TV, or getting ready for whatever tasks you have on hand that day.

26. Right after waking up, before getting out of your bed, focus on your breathing. Observe at least 5 mindful breaths.

27. Be aware of changes in posture. You need to stay aware of how your mind and body feel when you're going from lying down, up to sitting, up to standing, up to walking. Notice your posture from one transition to the next.

28. Use any sound you hear as a bell for mindfulness. Really use that opportunity to listen and be present.

29. During the course of your day, take a moment from time to time to focus on your breathing. Observe 5 mindful breaths.

30. Pay attention when you're eating. Consciously consume your food, bringing awareness to tasting, chewing, and swallowing. Realize that your food was connected to something that helped nourish its growth.

31. Bring awareness to talking and listening. Can you listen to someone without either agreeing or disagreeing, disliking or liking, or planning what things you'll say when it's your turn to talk? While talking, can you simply state what you need to say without understating or overstating? Are you able to notice how both your body and mind feel? The more you practice being aware and present the easier it'll get over time.

32. Focus some more attention on your normal everyday activities. These include washing, brushing your teeth, and getting dressed. Try and practice bringing mindfulness to each of these activities.

33. Notice any points on your body where you're feeling tight. Try and breathe into them, while exhaling let go of any excess tension you feel. Do you have tension

stored in any part of your body. For example, your shoulders, neck, jaw, stomach or back? If so, try stretching and practicing yoga at least once each day.

34. Before bed, take a moment to bring some attention to your breathing. The same as you did when you wake up in the morning. Observe 5 mindful breaths.

35. Create a 15 minute invite on your calendar regarding mindfulness for each day and be sure to commit to always spending that time with yourself.

36. Take breaks from your job to help gain perspective on what you're doing.

37. Find some other people at your job who are interested in becoming more mindful and practice your mindfulness together.

38. Find a mindfulness mentor. This can be anyone practicing that you can get advice from and can talk about your practicing with.

39. Focus on individual tasks instead of trying to multitask.

40.   Try and take a walk outside every day leaving your phone behind or turned off.

41.   Try riding a bike to work. You'll need to be mindful if you're biking through some traffic.

42.   Pause and center yourself for about 30 seconds at your job before diving into the work you have to accomplish.

43.   Turn a unused closet or room into a meditation space.

44.   Implement boundaries to help let your mind shut off. For instance turn off your phone after 9 pm or don't bring it in your bedroom before going to sleep.

45.   Don't beat yourself up if you get distracted. There will be days that are far more hectic than others.

46.   They call it "practice" for a good reason – It takes a lot of repetition to properly develop your mindfulness muscle.

47.   Not everyone will develop there mindfulness habits at the same pace. For some it may take as little as 8 weeks. For others it will take longer. Just keep going and you'll get there eventually.

48.   Don't get dragged down by your problems. Problems can be an opportunity to grow. Learn to recognize problems and solve them.

49.   Don't wallow in your past. Live each day without regret. The more you look to the past the harder it will be to enjoy your time in the present.

50.   Always create new goals for yourself. Give yourself something to look forward to each day.

51.   Take time to appreciate yourself. If you can't learn to find value in yourself you'll have a hard time finding it in others.

52.   Learn something new everyday. Even if it's something small. Continued growth and knowledge will only benefit you in the long run. Making mistakes is par for the course. It's only that we learn from our mistakes that matters.

53.   Appreciate the small things your friends and family do for you. Do small things for the people in your life to show how much you care.

54.   Mindfulness is not something to do a few minutes a day. Over time it should become a part of your life. The goal is to bring more awareness and compassion to every situation you find yourself in. Learning how to be more mindful in all situations will only benefit you long term.

55.   Try out aromatherapy to increase your focus. I've found that smell helps me focus more than chants or mantras. Most people don't think to try aromatherapy. I know I didn't at first.

56.   Have an open and clean space to meditate in. You want as little distraction surrounding you as possible when meditating. This especially rings true when you're first starting out. Try to find an area that is free of clutter and

distraction when meditating at home.

57.   Let in some air and natural light to your meditation area. Many people, myself included, are able to focus much better when breathing in fresh air and surrounded by sunlight.

58.   Choose the kind of meditation that resonates with you. Don't practice a form of meditation just because it's what someone said you should do. Learn the different methods, and decide for yourself. The more comfortable you are, the better chance you'll have at sticking with it. While I enjoy mindfulness meditation and walking meditations, my partner prefers yoga and guided sitting meditations.

Chapter 15. Important Festivals In Buddhism

Much like any other religion, Buddhism is not meant to be practiced in solitude. It is for this very purpose that the Buddha asked lay Buddhists and monks to take refuge in the Three Jewels.

When there's a community to fall back on, one feels stronger in their practice of Buddhism. But this community (sangha) does not assemble just to reflect on their lives but also to celebrate certain practices faith. But that's not all: they also get together to celebrate certain moments in the Buddha's life so many years ago when he gained enlightenment.

Buddha Statue

That said, one must remember that Buddhism has spread throughout Asia and these communities found in a number of countries celebrate certain days based on the schools of Buddhism that they have adopted.

To document each and every one of these festivals would be an arduous task. So, with that said, let's look at the ten most important festivals followed by those who are practitioners of Theravada, Mahayana, Vajrayana and Zen Buddhism. So, even if Buddhism has a rich 2500-year history to draw from, all Buddhists share one thing in common: they clearly acknowledge the life of the Buddha and give precedence to his teachings.

Vesak

This is the most important festival day in Buddhism since it celebrates the birth, enlightenment and death of the Buddha. Since the first full moon day in May occurs on different dates each year, there is no fixed date.

The name "Vesak" is derived from the Indian name for that particular month of the year. On this day, Buddhists are reminded to attempt leading noble lives, practice the quality of loving-kindness and foster peace among all humans.

Not only do Buddhists visit their temples but they celebrate this day with a lot of happiness where they offer their priests vegetarian food, candles and flowers. An important ceremony called the "Bathing the Buddha" ceremony is also conducted along with much chanting and praying. This ceremony reminds Buddhist practitioners of the need to purify one's mind from hatred, avarice and ignorance.

Vesak Day celebrated in Indonesia

In addition, gifts are also placed at the Buddha statues located in temples and which shows the respect and appreciation that Buddhists have for the Buddha. That said, each country that celebrates this day incorporates aspects of their culture when they celebrate this important Buddhist festival.

Sangha Day

The Buddha was said to visit the Veluvana Vihara in Rajagaha and this day remembers that very visit. It was on this day that 1250 'arhats' returned to the same monastery to pay their respects to the Buddha while also listening to him give his very first sermon of the Patimokkha. What is amazing about their return is that the Buddha had not summoned them for the sermon.

Buddha giving the Patimokkha sermon

Also known as the Magha Puja Day, this festival honors the 'sangha' without which the austere practices as considered necessary in Buddhism would be difficult to follow through one's own.

On this day, people exchange gifts while also committing themselves again to the practices and traditions left behind by the Buddha. Not only do they clean their homes but they also study the Pattimokkha and attend a procession with candles on this day. Sangha Day is generally celebrated on the full moon day in March.

Nirvana Day

This festival celebrates the day when the Buddha passed away. The Buddhists believe that in his passing, he found freedom from suffering and the struggles that come with physical existence. Even if the Buddha died at the age of 80, he spent most of his life teaching his followers the importance of attaining Nirvana. The reason for this is because whoever did achieve such a state would find themselves released from samsara or this never-ending cycle of births and deaths.

Parinirvana Day

On this day, Buddhists not only read the Parinirvana Sutta which documented his last days among the living but they also go to their respective temples as well. Meditation is also a common activity by Buddhist practitioners on this day. Presents and foods are also offered when visiting the temples.

Even if the subject of death can be depressing to dwell on, the Buddhists view it as important to being able to appreciate the lives that they lead. The impermanence of life and one's own attitude to death is often examined on this day too.

Kathina

This festival that focuses on alms-giving takes place in October or November each year. A large amount of money is given for the upliftment of the poor and the needy. Commonly remembered as the rainy season during Buddha's time, monks have been known to stay in a single place for three months or so. This period of seclusion, prior to the Kathina festival, is called 'vassa'. This festival marks the end of that time and when monks have to go out to spread the Buddha's teachings for the rest of the year.

Nun with robes on Kathina Day

In particular, lay Buddhists give cloth to the monks that they can use to make a new set of robes before they begin their journey. This includes other necessities that might make the monk's journeys comfortable. Having said that, this period of offerings lasts for almost a month. Interestingly, no monk is permitted to organize such a festival as it really depends on the generosity of the lay Buddhists.

Dharma Day

It was at the Deer Park in Sarnath that the Buddha first informed the ascetics that he was responsible for the turning of the wheel of 'dharma'. Celebrated on the first full moon day of July, this day, it is one where Buddhists remember the very first few moments of Buddhism as we know it.

Dharma Day Celebrates the Beginning of Buddhism

In addition, they also reflect on what their lives would be

without this wisdom that the Buddha offered his first disciples. People also contemplate on the first time they came across the Dharma and how it has impacted their lives. Even if this is a crucial moment for Buddhism, people rejoice in having come across the Buddha's teachings along with their friends and

family.

New Year Day

The Buddhist New Year Day is celebrated at different times in different countries. While the Tibetan Buddhist usually celebrate this day on a full moon in March, countries that practice Theravada Buddhism celebrate three days from the first full moon in April. Countries that practice Mahayana Buddhism generally celebrate the New Year on the first full moon day in January.

The Losar Festival

In Tibet, this is a very important holiday as it is celebrated for three days in a row. Known as Losar, Tibetans visit their monasteries and make offerings. The monks themselves spend this time cleaning up the monasteries. These activities are only symbolic of what "Losar" stands for in Tibet. A time for

purification so as to welcome in the new.

Observance Day

Also known as Uposatha, this is not a particular day that has special meaning in Buddhism. How this observance day consists of four holy days of each month that include the new moon, full moon and the quarter moon days. Observed only by Theravada Buddhists, there is a renewed focus on Dharma by Buddhist monks on these days. They solemnly commit themselves to follow the Dharma in observing the eight precepts as taught by the Buddha.

Food Offerings on Ancestor's Day

Ancestor Day

Primarily observed by Buddhists of the Mahayana sect, the reason why this day is observed is the belief that the gates of hell are opened on the fifteenth day of August. It's a time when deceased ancestors come back to visit the living.

During this period, food offerings are made so as to provide comfort to the ghosts that emerge through these gates. Also, people visit cemeteries to remember and make offerings to their ancestors.

This day, which is also called 'Ullambana', is based on the story of Maudgalyayana who rescued his mother from hell. Buddhists are reminded of the importance of filial piety through this story and which has culminated in the observance of Ancestor Day. It must be said that Buddhists living in Cambodia, Laos and Thailand observe this day as well.

Final Thoughts

If one must use a metaphor to describe Buddhism, it has to be that of the proverbial iceberg. We see very little of the iceberg at the surface until we delve a little deeper. Even if Siddhartha or even a modern-day Buddhist teacher such as Thich Nhat Hanh might not seem so educated, one thing is certain after you read their thoughts. They know and practice the development of wisdom as opposed to merely accumulating practical knowledge.

It's the very reason why people still use Buddhism as a model to run their lives even if attaining 'nirvana' seems a daunting task. Probably this is because the Buddha preached a universal message: one of suffering and how each and every one of us could transform that suffering.

When one looks at the Four Noble Truths and the Eightfold Path, we see an intelligent framework set in place for Buddhist practitioners to apply to daily living. Unlike a number of rules that are found in other religions, it's clear that the Buddha understood the imprecise nature of his philosophical teachings nature of Buddha much like philosophers such as Aristotle and Plato. Still, even if the terms we have looked at seem rather archaic, the depth and interconnection of these teachings become more and more apparent with each passing day. After all, human experience has hardly changed over centuries. We still have the same sorrows, joys, challenges and struggles as our ancestors had. So, it's really up to us to use the principles of Buddhism in a way that suits us individually.

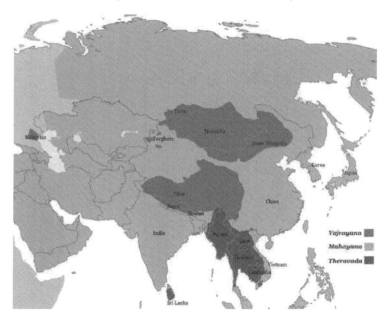

Map of the main modern sects of Buddhism

Up until now, we have tried to stick to Theravada Buddhism which stays close to the teachings of the Buddha. This was the scope of the book as it was for beginners. However, if reading this book has inspired you to learn more about this way of life, then it would be wise to continue with reading the various pitakas that are the mainstay of the three main schools of Buddhism – Theravada, Mahayana and Vajrayana Buddhism.

It would also be wonderful if you could deepen your knowledge by following up on the works of popular Buddhist teachers in today's world given how difficult it might be to understand languages like Pali, Sanskrit, Chinese and Tibetan. Or even joining a community of Buddhist if you so desire.

Thich Nhat Hanh in Paris

In closing, here's a stanza from a poem written by Thich Nhat Hanh that elegantly captures the heart of a real Buddhist practitioner:

Since I learned how to love you,

the door of my soul has been left wide open to the winds of the four directions. Reality calls for change.

The fruit of awareness is already ripe And the door can never be closed again.

Let us remember these words always as we move forward on this path to peace and liberation!

Chapter 16. Bringing Buddhism into Your Everyday Life

As you have journeyed through this book, you have consumed a lot of information pertaining to Buddhism. You are likely a bit overwhelmed right now – there really is a lot to take in. In fact, this book only barely touches the top of all of the teachings of the Buddha. However, you are likely to have a general understanding of some of the most important aspects of Buddhism by now. The next question is to determine if you want to bring Buddhism into your life. If you want to learn more about Buddhism, there is plenty of information and resources available to teach you. If you have read this book and decided that you would like to give Buddhism a try, you must still continue learning. This book is merely a guide for a beginner. In no way does this book encompass all that is Buddhism.

With that said, as you start your journey down the path to enlightenment, you may wonder how you actually get started on bringing Buddhism into your daily life. No, you do not have to start wearing robes, and no, you do not have to join a monastery. There are no secret clubs to join, no Buddhist secrets to keep. The journey to enlightenment is just that – a journey. It has to start somewhere, so why not start with the first step? Here, in this final chapter, you will discover some easy ways that you can start to incorporate Buddhism into your everyday life.

Practicing Buddhism

The best way to start practicing Buddhism is to find a Buddhist center. Here, you will be given much more in-depth information about the teachings of the Buddha. These centers are made for beginners and established Buddhists. The atmosphere is going to be welcoming because, well, that is the way of the Buddhist – love, kindness, and compassion. There will be plenty of written information you can take home with you to study on your own. There will also be Buddhist teachers who will assist you in understanding all of the teachings. You will learn how to meditate, an essential aspect of Buddhism. The reason that it is always best to seek out a practiced Buddhist for teachings is because there is only so much information and understanding you can take from books and articles. Having a teacher to discuss your studies can be a great tool for traveling down your path to enlightenment with more ease.

As you begin your path to enlightenment, you need to learn all that you can about Buddhism. There are different paths to enlightenment, so you must study each one to find the path that fits your life the best. The different paths of Buddhism usually have the same basic ideas, but incorporate their own understandings of the Buddha's teachings into the path. So, you will find variances between the paths. There are thousands of books available to teach you about Buddhism. It is important to focus on one aspect at a time. If you try to cram in all of the Buddha's teachings as fast as you can, you are never going to understand what you are learning. You will also likely just get overwhelmed and fed up, leading you to give up on Buddhism.

A Buddhist teacher can help you with so many questions and aspects of Buddhism, so that you make the best choice for you. A teacher can also monitor your readings and studying, so that you stay focused without getting overwhelmed. However, not everyone has immediate access to a Buddhist center, so you may need to make the first steps on your own. Choose a specific aspect of Buddhism to study and learn. You want to absorb absolutely all of the knowledge of the aspect until you have a complete understanding. Only then should you move on to another aspect. Take your time with your studies. Utilize the internet to find other Buddhists online who will answer your questions and help guide you on your path.

You can start off slow, just simply learning some basic Buddhist terminology. You can start at the beginning, and delve deep into the story of the Buddha and the origins of Buddhism. The goal is to choose a place to start, stick with it until you really understand it, and then move on to another area of study. You can study as much or as little as you feel comfortable doing. Some people want to immerse themselves in Buddhism from the beginning – they are just that excited to go down the path of enlightenment. However, others choose to take a more cautious journey, taking their time with the teachings, asking all of the hard questions, and gaining as much insight as possible before taking even one more step. You decide how you want to learn about Buddhism – you are the only one who knows what is best for you.

Community is a crucial part of Buddhism. Buddhists need each other to learn from and to help guide. You need a strong, smart support system during your path to Nirvana. You cannot learn all that you need to learn alone.

If there is not a Buddhist center near your location, then take to the internet. There are plenty of Buddhist forums, groups, websites, etc. that are full of practicing Buddhists who will provide you with the encouraging support system you need. They will also give you a place to take your questions, your anxieties, your concerns, and learn how to release all of them. Online groups can even help you with meditation.

One way you can bring Buddhism into your everyday life is to just take the time to sit every day. Sitting in peace and quiet is your first step towards mindful meditation. If you cannot sit still for a few minutes each day, completely still, then you have to keep practicing. Meditation requires a stillness of the body and the mind. So, start off with just sitting quietly. You do not necessarily have to worry about clearing your mind yet. You just want to ensure you can sit still for a bit of time. Start with five minutes each day. As you become more comfortable with just sitting in peace, add more time to each session. Eventually, you can start to bring meditation into the session.

Since Buddhism is a way of living your life, you have to be prepared to make many changes, especially in your awareness and understanding of the world around you and of your own mind. Awareness is a key point of Buddhism, so learning a proper meditation method is ideal. You must be able to clear your mind, to attain a level of purity in your mind that will lead you to enlightenment. You can practice meditation at home, on your own, with information you learn about meditation. You can practice meditation in a group setting with other blossoming Buddhists. You will likely find online groups where you can meditate "virtually" with a group. As long as you learn how to meditate, and you go further and further with each session into reaching that supreme level of a pure mind, then you are on the right track to enlightenment.

To bring Buddhism into your everyday life other than studying and meditation, just start living a kind and compassionate life. You want to put forth positive, happy energy in everything you do because, as you know, karma is watching. So, live your life knowing that karma will always find you. You are going to struggle during your Buddhism journey. There are going to be negative times as you learn more and more about the true nature of reality. You will likely have to face some hard truths about yourself and the way that you live or feel. Just keep going forward. You are not going to become a full-fledged, enlightened Buddhist in just a few weeks or months. You are looking at years of studying and practicing and changing and living your newlife before you reach Nirvana.

While this probably sounds overwhelming, it will be worth the effort and the wait. Once you reach the level of enlightenment, you will no longer struggle with letting go of clinging, with accepting that all things change, with living a simple life, and with total awareness. You will be awakened – you will be like the Buddha. You will have a full understanding of your mind, your life, and your actions, as well as your feelings and thoughts. You will be a Buddhist, and your future will be very bright.

Conclusion

What exactly is Buddhism? A religion? A philosophy? Buddhism is a religion, but it is not! Is Buddhism a philosophy? Yes and no!

Philosophically, the Buddha explained what we faced with as human beings - we suffer (eventually, we become old, become ill, and die in addition to all the other ailments of life). He further explains there is an apparent reason for this suffering - that we can end the pain - and how we can complete the pain. The Buddha logically pointed to the workings of the Universe as cause and effect, and how Karma fits into the entire picture.

Unlike most philosophies based on the power of reason and theory, Buddhists use direct experiences instead. Real understanding and insight result from perfecting specific abilities such as meditation, mindfulness, and body and mind investigation with little speculation. It's just about direct experience.

Since there is something that cannot be explained in

Buddhism (the Buddha called it Nibbana), Buddhism narrowly defined as a religion. This excellent quality of Nibbana characterizes Buddhism as a religion.

However, unlike other prevalent religions, Buddhism does not believe in a creator God. Nor does Buddhism believe in a soul or anything that accumulates good or evil on its journey through time. Therefore, Buddhism is not religious in a broader sense. A Buddhist counts only on his efforts for his salvation; there are no saviors to save them. These encourage Buddhists to be very responsible for their actions and will generally pay close attention to how their actions influence others, hopefully positively.

Buddhists believe in rebirth, which differs from reincarnation. So what is reborn in Buddhism? Only the karma or actions of the last body. Actions (Karma) are impersonal, and this tendency of old activities is what the new body assumes. If the elderly person were angry, even the new "person" would probably have mad tendencies. But the new person will not be reincarnated, "Bob."

Where do the extras come from?" In Buddhism, there are many planes of existence, thirty-one, to be exact.

The exciting thing about the Brahma gods, according to Buddhism, is that they are still so deluded as to believe they created the universe! The increase of the world population results from all these other kingdoms that deposit their occupants on the earth or other planets. It's a vast universe!

Another good question is: "If there is no personality reborn, who is it that lights up and reaches Nibbana?" We can hypothesize that the "self" or personality we think is real, is only a fabrication of thought (this can confirm by meditation), and when Nibbana is reached, what never existed in the first place no longer exists now.

The difference is that we know it now. Who knows? Only the mind and the mind are simply the present emanations of that transcendent reality to which Buddhism refers, called Nibbana: the immortal, the shapeless, the unborn, the immutable. This is the reality we cannot know directly; the pure awareness called by things like; emptiness, emptiness, sunyata. This pure awareness creates awareness through our mind and our sense organs so we can exist, but this awareness is not part of existence itself; it is a reality. Therefore, we cannot know him directly because we caught in presence, and therefore we are not real. And truth, on the contrary, does not exist.

Finally, people are increasingly asking what they need to do to become Buddhists. It's easy: no baptism, no grades, nothing like that, just a commitment to finding the truth within you. It is among you, and you. You are your teacher. Buddhist precepts are useful, Buddhist teachings are helpful, Buddhist groups and monasteries are helpful, but they are only suggestions for working with yourself. You have to do it; nobody will do it for you. There are no sins or damnations in Buddhism, only karma, which is a universal truth and not just a Buddhist truth. You will be responsible for your actions.

Book 4 Third Eye Awakening:

Increases Mind Power, Clarity, Concentration, Psychic Awareness through Meditation. Align Your Chakras and Activate the Kundalini Energy and Decalcify the Pineal Gland.

Introduction

The third eye opens the door to higher consciousness. It enables you to look beyond the realms of the known. Since time immemorial, it has been referred to as the all-seeing eye. Even when scientific knowledge of the humankind was limited, it was hooked to the idea of the third eye that could enable humans to look beyond the point of the known.

The third eye has always been seen as a mystical vision

source. It enables you to see things in far greater detail. It enhances your experience of the world. If your third eye is active and functioning well, you will have the ability to see clearly, and your sense of perception will be sharper. You may be able to feel things that no other normal person feels.

We all have this ability, but it often isn't fully developed. We call it the sixth sense or a gut feeling. It indicates that things are not the way you are looking at them. You do not have a scientific reason to believe the way you are feeling, but somewhere deep down inside you know that you are right. This unexplainable knowledge is known as the third eye.

The third eye is often referred to as the inner eye or the all-seeing eye. It makes you clairvoyant and enhances your precognition abilities. Our ancestors have always believed that an active third eye can lead to out of body experiences and visions.

The ability to possess psychic abilities and greater powers has always been the quest of humankind. We have always wanted to know more than we already know. There have always been limitations to the things we can know. The third eye defeats all such known boundaries, and that's why it is revered so greatly.

Our ancestors were hooked to this idea and believed that there was some greater power within ourselves that could allow us to know more than we knew. Across all the ancient cultures of the world, you will find the mention of the third eye in some form. Western and Eastern cultures alike have believed in the idea of the third eye.

The pineal gland in your brain is considered to be the link to the third eye. People have believed it to be the physical location of the third eye. Science kept on considering it a vestigial gland for a long time. However, modern research has demonstrated that it isn't a vestigial gland after all. It performs several crucial functions like the stimulation of several important hormones. It also regulates your circadian rhythms. Some researchers also believe that the pineal gland releases several hormones that can induce different states of consciousness.

Understanding the concept of the third eye and activating it can help in gaining higher consciousness. It can help you in gaining clarity of thought and vision. Working of the third eye can enhance your cognitive abilities and make your instincts sharper. It will also demonstrate the ways through which you can enhance your abilities to see things clearly.

Chapter 1 What is the Third Eye?

The third eye is a term reserved for a physical and spiritual part of the body. The pineal gland, in its physical form, is a gland located at the top of the spine that connects with the brain. Physiologically speaking, this endocrine gland has many functional purposes within the body. It is often referred to as the third eye outside of scientific circles. If you were to look someone squarely in the face, the pineal gland would sit just above both eyes, right in the center, like another eye, hence its name.

The pineal gland produces hormones like melatonin and serotonin, which play a big role in regulating sleep patterns and contribute to the overall mood. Without this gland, the body would not recognize normal fluctuations in light, making it difficult to fall and stay asleep in a normal pattern. In the bigger picture, the body would not be able to recognize summer from winter, aside from the change in temperature. The pineal gland exists in most vertebrate animals, and therefore, keep the entire ecosystem running on the same clock, based on sunlight.

While the functional purposes of the pineal gland are generally known, there has always been a bit of mystery surrounding the small gland. Early scientists assumed that this gland was highly important because of its location within the brain. The tiny gland sits dead center between the right and left hemisphere of the brain, and deep under its tissues, almost like the function of the rest of the brain is to protect this small piece. Think of the meat of a walnut encapsulated tightly in its outer shell.

The idea of the pineal gland being a third eye in the spiritual sense is much more powerful than the pineal gland's physical properties. It has long been believed by many cultures that this third eye holds the key to life, and that is no small task. The power of the third eye goes above and beyond recognizing light patterns, and is for channeling energy and light, which is what drives the body.

The power of clairvoyance, seeing the future, is also associated with a strong pineal gland. The idea is that a clairvoyant person has a very strong connection with the universe. This knowledge transcends time and allows you to sense things that will happen in the future. It is not necessarily as depicted on television. A clairvoyant does not necessarily see things happening in the physical sense but through energy.

Many people also see energy in a physical sense. There are auras of energy that surround each and every living thing. The energy emitted takes many different shapes and colors, depending on positive and negative energy. The third eye communicates with the energies of the universe in this way, and learning to recognize these energies is important for ultimate guidance. Many say that negative energy is depicted as red, while positive energies are much lighter, white or shades of green. You would not willingly walk into a room full of people with red auras if you could see them, would you? Likely not, but the average person only sees the room full of people, and enters anyway.

Opening the spiritual eye means seeing the world in a new light, recognizing the connections between your inner energy and that of the universe, and sensing or seeing the energy all around us. Throughout history, the third eye has been celebrated as the utmost in knowledge, education and higher being. Having a well-functioning third eye means having a connection with the higher energy, a God, Gods or any combination thereof depending on classic culture.

We can see the impact of the third eye throughout

history in art. Early on, the pinecone became synonymous with the pineal gland. In fact, the name pineal comes from 'pine.' The pinecone had graced this planet with its existence long before any other plant species on earth. It is ancient in nature, and its perfectly aligned spiral structure represents energy and perfection in the deepest senses. Looking through art works throughout the centuries, even dating back to the ancient Egyptians, we see pinecones. It is meant to symbolize divine wisdom and our spiritual soul.

Hindu and Indian cultures also use the pinecone to depict the highest enlightenment and wisdom of their gods. In Hindu culture, all of the gods are depicted in art and lore with pinecones, with Shiva being the most prominent. Indian culture depicts the god Kundalini, with an awakened third eye, bringing wisdom, love, and joy.

The third eye isn't restricted to Eastern cultures, it also spans from Mexico and the Central American region, and even with the Native Americans indigenous to North America. While the traditions and rituals to harness the power of this third eye vary, the outcome is the same. People throughout history have recognized the third eye as the window to their soul, and the connection to their universe.

With all of this discussion of the history of the third eye, it is important to remember that modern man also possesses the pineal gland, the third eye, and a spiritual connection. As time wears on, it seems that humans have become much less connected with their spiritual selves, and the power of the third eye is waning. The importance of spiritual connection often falls by way of modern medicine and factual evidence for what ails us.

What we need to remember is that the spirit is wholly in charge of our physical being and that the energy of the universe is boundless and never-ceasing. We cannot be happy and healthy with a spirit that is unwell. Therefore, it is vital to nurture our third eye and our spiritual connection just as we would treat our bodies well. We need to embrace our spiritual culture and reconnect to be whole, and functional, and human.

If you are looking for science, there is that too. It has been found that the calcification of the pineal gland can be the cause of many physical and mental ailments. This calcification happens when minerals and other elements build up around the gland, causing a decrease in function. Calcification presumes that calcium is the major problem, but other elements, like fluoride and chlorine, also increase the calcification process.

As we age, calcification increases, disrupting sleep patterns and creating overall stress within the body. This stress can manifest itself in a number of ways, including weight gain, chronic disease, and a dysfunctional immune system. Studies have also linked calcification to Alzheimer's disease and memory loss in general.

This gland also produces DMT, a chemical that has been associated with so-called hallucination, and loss of consciousness. This chemical allows us to dream, to enter another world. The idea of this being a hallucination is a fallacy created by man to explain the phenomenon. Those guided by their spirit can recognize that the loss of worldly consciousness and entrance into a higher plane is their soul transcending the body and time as we know it.

Many people have vivid, very real dreams, while others don't. It is believed that the lack of DMT creates a dreamless sleep, and the soul remains stuck within the confines of the body. It is unable to escape and collect wisdom from the universe. Many say they can also find this transcendence through the practice of meditation, a very advanced skill.

These changes in function and behavior can be directly related to a decrease in melatonin DMT and serotonin, but have also long been described in a spiritual sense as losing one's connection with the spiritual universe.

The energy of the universe is all-knowing and helps guide our lives. Being connected helps ensure a steady path in all aspects of life, as the universe gives you the insight and wisdom you need via energy patterns. For example, when you are in a good place, you are surrounded by positive energy, which your body is attracted to. Your third eye has a keen sense of encroaching negative energy, and if you are truly guided by it, can be avoided.

Do you feel connected to the universe? Do you have a keen sense of your surroundings? Do you feel you make good decisions? It is hard to know if the path that you are on is the right one, but there are usually clues. If you feel as if you have no destined path in life, or that you keep making choices that lead you to negativity, you are likely not in touch with your third eye.

This can be a helpless feeling. Imagine that you have cast offshore in a boat with no oars and no sails. The boat aimlessly floats, with no way of steering through deep swells and rogue waves. If this sounds like your life, it is time to reacquaint yourself with your spiritual being. All of the positive energy and wisdom you need lies dormant within you. It is only a matter of harnessing that power to make positive changes in your life.

Learn to decalcify your pineal gland, reconnect with your true self, and with the endless energy of the universe. Your life is special, and you are meant to live a meaningful and productive life. Now is the time to do it.

Chapter 2 Process of Unlocking the Third Eye

Electro-magnetic field pollution can be among the most influential Pollution and can be emitted by cell phones, Wi-Fi, microwaves, transmission masts, power grids etc. and they interfere with our regular connection to nature's frequencies keeping us in an artificial Electro Magnetic field frequency.

The most effective brain wave that is transmitted emulates natural frequencies of the earth and interchangeably too without the pollution from the Electro Magnetic field pollution.

The brain wave listening when carried out in an environment void of the Electro Magnetic field pollution would mean awakening the third eye and the crown chakras which are the Spiritual links from the physical world. By unlocking the pineal gland, after a few weeks of brain wave transmission meditation, getting into a higher level of meditative state would not require brain wave in transmit anymore.

The true nature of our reality is then realized by focusing deep and reaching deep brain waves zones one can tap into the core of the universe's infinite knowledge.

This would in turn make our reality fit in together and make all the connections be observed. The potential to overcome hazardous effects that keeps many individuals from achieving this level of awakening include lack of proper exercising, poor diet, and diseases introduction into the body. Opening the third eye enhances the confidence of an individual and the method of achieving higher consciousness all of which meditation is an effective means of reaching.

Process of achieving this third eye opening and early experiences include feeling a light sensation within the first twenty minutes of the brain wave meditation which is felt at the location of the third eye Chakra.

This is the first step in achieving awakening the third eye. The boosting of the pineal glands makes it function during the first meditation. The stimulation of the pineal glands is similar to an exercise practice that takes place in the brain. With each meditation sessions, the toxins become removed and the individual becomes stronger and reaches a deeper level of extra sensory perceptions.

The slight pressure in the third eye Chakra region reduces after a few weeks, then the next effect is seeing vivid dark energy which looks like moving shadows or as others would put it, spirits but it has actually not been confirmed as to what it is exactly.

Immersion in warm water, in a semi dark room listening to the brain wave frequency enhances the meditation, some people claim to hear voices while others see the dark energy moving. These effects are subjective to individual differences

AWAKENING THE ETHERIC CHAKRAS

When the chakras are activated starting with the sacral Chakra, man is reminded partially about his Astral traveling although this is only a slight stimulation of the Chakra and man only even vaguely remembers.

This feeling is like flying through the atmosphere and comes in bits of different forms and the man might not fully comprehend it at the early stages.

As the solar plexus Chakra becomes awakened, the individual starts to become aware physically of the effects of the Astral World in his physical sense.

In the awakening of the heart Chakra, the individual becomes conscious of other people's happiness or sadness intuitively and often times, he feels the emotions they feel and can recreate the replica feeling in himself.

The awakening of the throat Chakra, wakes up the individual's abilities to hear voices vividly, and this voices make advices to him at times, he could possibly hear songs or some sounds he cannot describe and this ability is called being Clairaudient and is Developed in the etheric planes.

In the activation of the third eye Chakra, the man begins to see images clearly and have visions, some unexplainable, some of events occurring. During its early stages, the images are on form of flashes but eventually become full realized images which is referred to as clairvoyance.

This Chakra also makes the physical eye more advanced, improving the magnification and sight overall and helps one to examine images in contraction and expansion. Prior to this full realization of the clairvoyance, the individual is likely to see frequent flashes of images of the celestial, this is due to signals being received from vibrations from one Chakra or another.

This imagery would consistently show up until eventually the clairvoyance is fully achieved and the individual can clearly see images at will during meditation stages.

Depending on how deep a brain wave meditation is, an individual would see clear images and hear vivid voices from the celestial world when the exchange of energy forces is in play and the chakras active.

AWAKENING THE CHAKRAS BEFORE ITS TIME

For the majority, the teachings about the chakras and energy flow and all are just nay saying and heresy and thus most don't believe in it and would probably never get to awaken these chakras.

Well, in a sense, it is better for these individuals to not

awaken them and remain unaware of them as they remain laying in an inactive state as pertaining to their etheric use and not in connection to their physicality functionalities, as every human does require the chakras for normal existentiality as the energy flowing within them are required for normal activity and vitality as well.

Their spiritual qualities though, might never be utilized by the unaware and skeptics which is not bad as many, if not most of the people would end up living their lives without even having an idea what the chakras mean and they would still be fine Physically. It is the yearning for some spiritual connection that would be lost in people and the urge would go and remain unfulfilled in most of these individuals.

These regular people that never get to awaken these chakras and have them remain dormant are better off than those that awaken it prematurely before it's time. Awakening the chakras which are spiritual channels simply means attempting or even activating the Chakras before first developing a certain moral conduct which is more or less a necessity in unlocking the chakras in the first place.

Some of the effects can affect the individuals who

awaken these spiritual channels prematurely in harmful ways. It may lead to effects which may be manifested physically and thus leaving them in pain, and this is even the lenient effect as some other adverse effects could be more than just physical injuries and may cause permanent havoc to the chakras in etheric plane themselves. Another effect common with awakening it before its time is that it streams the energy flow downward instead of the normal upward flow and this would over supply some points, hence causing the traits associated with these points to be over exhibited in the negative sense because it is an unbalance in the Chakra and could eventually lead to wreaking havoc in the body system of the individual if he doesn't take into full caution.

Possibilities of the individual attaining supernatural qualities are true, but these abilities go out of his control and he eventually regrets unlocking the chakras without following suit of how to best go about it. Unlocking the chakras untimely also leads to the Christ spark over activating the entire body system and this results in the individual being overpowered with the traits which reaches first the traits attributed to negativity before the traits attributed to positivity. These traits would be greatly interwoven as one would come with the other, i.e., the positive with the negative such as incisiveness and brilliance associated with pride and cunning.

AWAKENING OF THE CHRIST SPARK

The inner layers of this fire gets subconsciously lit up in some case and this may not even require a planning, but in such instances, the glow is dull, it may start some motion by itself, but this is rare. When this happens, serious pain may be involved, due to the passages not being ready for it, it is normally expected to clear the passage by using up a considerable amount of etheric abilities and this is not usually achieved without a deal of pain or suffering.

At this point, it comes down to a junction of no-pain-no-gain, and while the processes involve pain, the suffering process is not directly dangerous or harmful to our being, it's just an indicator of new paths being created, those that does not exist before. When the arousal is accidental and not planned, it attempts to move up the interior sessions of the spine, moving through the path already trekked by its manifestation, both the lowest and the highest.

This upward movement is totally necessary when

possible but if it cannot be achieved, this is not serious need to worry, it will pop out to get expelled through the head into the immediate environment, this is not harmful but it will definitely cause a slight weakness in the body, this form of weakness has no permanent effect on the body and it will be gone within a few hours or a few days, all depending on the intensity of the whole process.

At the worst scenario possible, a loss of consciousness can occur but also, this is just temporary and will never lead to any permanent harm or death. All these dangers are not in any way connected to the upward rush in any sense, they are only connected to the possible of it turning downwards and inward. In occultism, the upward rush is known to make active the chakras and also establish strong connections between the astral and physical planes of the body, this connection is very paramount and cannot be underestimated. Once this spark gets to the center around the eyebrows and fully manifests, it comes with a power to hear, this hear is called voice of the master, with the master being the ego or higher self or advanced consciousness, it has also been noted as the voice of silence in several cases but regardless, this voice is an approval.

The pituitary body established all the communications

links required within, known as astral vehicle, through with all forms of messages are sent and received through stable paths without complications.

At this stage, it's not only this Chakra that is required, other chakras have to be actively awakened, that's the only way the sub planes can be linked responsively, from one force center to another, once this is achieve, the communication and links are swift.

This development cannot be rushed; therefore, it should not be rushed, it must be given the chance to play out. Hereditary and adaption also counts at this stage, according to records and researches, it has been proven that some Indians achieve this at first instance but the fact that their body is more adaptable naturally, but in most cases, this stage has to be repeated over time to achieve the connection. Repetitions is key for procuring the serpent-fire of the Christ spark since the passages are new at every time and every event of incarnation.

These repetitions become extremely easy over time has the body is no longer strange to new vehicles being developed but it must be noted that the processes are totally different for different individuals and that no exact result has to be expect in any case, for instance, there have been cases where the higher self was seen and not heard, this is due to the variation in the process and personalities.

Also, connection to the higher self has many levels, for individuals, it may mean ego and for the ego, it may mean monad power and also for the monad, it may mean a spontaneous epiphany of the logos, this is to show the possibilities and layers, nothing is fixed in a direct other and experiences may differ from person to person.

Chapter 3 Pineal Gland

Do you recall the location of your pineal gland? Well, it is right between your northern and southern hemispheres of your head. Oh-oh... And where is that, precisely? Easy – right at the position you can term the center of your brain.

Now, even when most of the things to do with your third eye are mental and spiritual, it may help somewhat to understand the physical nature and the scientific aspect and workings of your pineal gland. Of course, you may recall the pineal gland passing for the 'seat of the soul' and being able to regulate your sleeping and waking cycle.

In matters physiological, you may wish to know that your pineal gland has a lot to do with:

- Regulating your body temperature

- Controlling your skin color

- Controlling your hair color

- Controlling the color of your eyes

And what you may need to underline about the pineal gland with regard to the powers of the third eye include:

- Being responsible for generating dreams

- Regulating your emotions

- Enhancing your intuition

- Revamping your memory
- Enhancing your learning capacity

All this happens owing to the fact that your pineal gland is directly associated with your 6th chakra, that energy center in between your eye brows; the one they call ajna. And once the energy from your sixth chakra works in league with your pineal gland, then you are:

- Able to discern the reality from mere illusion

- Able to evolve and grow spiritually

- In a position to trust your intuition and benefit from it

- Able to enhance your intelligence

Are you eager to know something a little more interesting about the pineal gland?

Well, learned people of old took this tiny organ to be as useless as that piece of muscle in your abdomen – the appendix. Something that creation or the Divine just put there for lack of a better place to place it. But as you have already noted, the pineal cord has very important scientific and spiritual roles to play in your life.

Why not learn a little more about the pineal gland?

It is a tiny piece of muscle, as small as a pea, and it is within your brain's 3rd ventricle

It is named 'pineal' because it has a shape like that of a pine cone; which in Latin is called 'pinea'.

It establishes itself properly around the age of puberty

It happens to have its own cornea; its lens; and even its own retina – the same way your physical eyes do

It is the gland credited with producing the 'happy hormone' – serotonin

It is the gland credited too with producing the 'hormone in charge of darkness' – melatonin

It has a role to play in matters of sexual development

It plays an important role in protecting you from free radicals that are, obviously, harmful to your body

It is, however, susceptible to destruction and your apparent addiction to technology does not help matters touching on your pineal gland

At the time you are meditating, your pineal gland is seen to be working side by side with another hormone producing, pea sized gland, the pituitary, which is located at the lower part of your brain. How can you discern that, you may wonder? By the way the two tiny glands are seen vibrating in unison.

The pineal gland is credited with production of dimethyltryptamine, commonly referred to as DMT that substances that is linked with expanding your consciousness.

It receives heavy blood flow only 2nd to the all-important organs; your kidneys

It has the greatest accumulation of fluoride – no wonder it is calcified

It does not respond well to mercury fillings so if you care much about the health of your pineal gland, you may consider an alternative to mercury

You can decalcify the pineal gland somewhat by consuming alkaline water or water that is distilled. And with decalcification, your pineal gland does its functions better.

It is very sensitive to light and is stimulated by it

It is adversely affected by waves of extremely low frequency, otherwise referred to as ELF waves.

During astral projection or when you are trying to enhance lucidity or recalling a dream, it would help the working of your pineal gland if you unplugged every electronic device around you.

Where health is concerned, you can help keep your pineal gland in shape by consuming mugwort; wood betony; alfalfa; parsley; and even gotu kola.

Chapter 4 Meditation

Meditation is basically an age-old practice established in ancient Indian traditions. It is practiced with the goal of opening the mind for deeper intuition and perception. There are also several very powerful meditations developed specifically to open the third eye and strengthen the pineal gland.

Meditation also helps you control your thoughts and your mind, putting you, as the proponents of Buddhism believe, in control of your life. This is an extremely empowering gift to have. So many things in life are out of our control—but by learning to control our thoughts, we can respond to situations wisely and calmly and make better choices. This skill becomes even more pronounced when your third eye chakra is awakened.

How does Meditation Work?

When you meditate, your brain enters into an alpha wavelength state, (which is different from the normal beta wavelength state that the brain resonates with). In this quiet and relaxed state, the mind becomes more open to receiving subtle messages and insights from our third eye. The regular practice of meditation allows you to enter more and more easily into the alpha wavelength state and over time, you can receive deeper wisdom, knowledge, and information from the non-physical realm. It also helps strengthen spiritual gifts.

Types of Meditation

The types of meditation are varied and diverse. Zen meditation, Vispana meditation, mindfulness meditation, transcendental meditation, Taoist meditation, and mantra meditation are some of the most popular. There is also a type of meditation for almost anything, from relieving pain and stress to meeting your higher guides. But ideally, meditation should be approached with the goal of achieving inner calm and deeper awareness—and the sheer bliss of just being able to forget the world and relax.

Meditations for the Third Eye

Meditation allows us to switch off the thinking, logical mind. When the mind is quietened and enters an alpha level wavelength state, it then becomes a filter for subtle insights and messages from the third eye.

All types of meditation are effective for opening the third eye. Guided meditation and any sort of mindfulness meditation will work very well. However, the following are the most powerful for opening and nurturing the third eye.

Meditation 1: Trataka Meditation

This is an ancient meditation derived from the Tantra and Hatha yoga practices. In Sanskrit, Trataka means "to gaze" or "to look."

• This meditation requires you to sit perfectly still on the floor with legs crossed in the lotus position. If this is not comfortable, sit in a straight-backed chair where you can keep your spine straight.

• Close your eyes and breathe deeply from your

belly for two-to-three minutes until your body is completely relaxed.

- Focus deeply on the area of your third eye chakra. Continue to focus on the area for a few moments.

- With both of your eyes still closed, draw them upwards towards the inner eye chakra as if you are looking at it. You may feel a strain in your eyes as you try and hold them in that position. You will know that it is the correct position when you feel your eyes "lock" slightly above the bridge of your nose, and the position does not feel too strained.

- Keep your closed eyes in that position and slowly start counting backward from 100 (with about two seconds between each count).

- Keep your closed eyes focused on the third eye chakra until you have finished counting backward to zero.

- Draw your eyes back to their normal position and breathe deeply three times to ground yourself. Allow your eyes to return to their normal movement.

- Feel yourself become grounded and open your eyes. The meditation should last between ten-to-fifteen minutes.

Some people report that when doing this meditation, they can actually see their thoughts as if seeing a dream. You may feel warmth in the area of the inner eye, which indicates that it is attracting energy. In addition, not only is this a very powerful meditation for awakening the third eye, but it is also a great workout that keeps the eyes healthy.

Note: This meditation should be practiced in moderation to prevent the over-activation of the third eye chakra. Once a week will be enough to keep everything in balance.

Meditation 2: Body Scan Meditation for Third Eye Intuition

This meditation is specifically oriented toward increasing your intuition through the third eye chakra.

- Sit in a comfortable position with your back straight.

• Close your eyes and do the mindful breathing exercise in order to ground yourself. This should take two-to-three minutes, or until all the tension is released from your body and you feel completely relaxed.

• Start the body scan from the very top of your head or the crown chakra. Focus on this area until you begin to notice the sensations there. This could be tingling, pressure, a slight warmth, burning, or buzzing. Don't worry if you don't feel anything the first couple of times you practice this meditation. Your mind will become trained to pick up on these sensations over time.

• When you are ready, move down to the whole forehead area from the front to the back of your head. Focus on this area—again, noticing any sensations there.

• When you are ready, move down to the eyes, then the nose, the area above the mouth then the mouth itself. Spend a few minutes on each area and notice the sensations.

• Continue the body scan by moving downwards

and exploring every part of your body; chin, neck, shoulders, arms, torso, top of the stomach, lower belly, upper thighs, legs, and finally end with the feet.

• Do not react to or judge any negative sensations that you may feel. Simply acknowledge them and move on.

• If you want, you can repeat the body scan starting once again from the top of your head.

The meditation heightens the intuition by making you more aware of the subtle sensations in your body. You may receive certain insights or "aha!" moments as you are meditating—or even days after the meditation.

Meditation 3: Golden Ball of Light

• Sit in the lotus position or a comfortable chair with your back straight.

• Breathe deeply and feel the tension leave your muscles with every breath.

• Visualize a warm stream of energy flowing

through your body from the top of your head down to your toes. Continue to visualize and feel this energy slowly circulating around your body.

• Next, direct your focus to the third eye chakra and the warm energy filling the space between your brows.

• Visualize the energy coming together to form a rotating ball of golden light in the center of your third eye chakra.

• Focus on the rotating ball and the beautiful golden light that emanates from it.

• When you feel ready, allow the light to expand until it fills all of your third eye chakra. Visualize it expanding slowly until it finally emerges out of your forehead in a bright ray of incandescent golden light.

• Gaze at the beautiful ray of light with your inner eye and notice any colors or pictures that appear within it.

• Simply acknowledge what you see without

judgment.

- Now, still gazing into the light with your third eye, ask your third eye if it has a message for you. Take as much time as you need.

- When you are ready, bring yourself back to reality with deep breathing and slowly open your eyes.

Again, don't worry if you don't see anything the first few times you practice this meditation. The more you advance, the stronger the ray of light will become as well as the images and messages from your third eye.

Meditation 4: Third Eye Awakening and Decalcifying the Pineal Gland

- Sit in a comfortable position and allow your body a few moments to settle and relax.

- Close your eyes, take a deep breath, and hold it for as long as you can, feeling the fullness in your lungs. Exhale slowly through your mouth.

- Bring your full focus to the third eye chakra. If it helps, you can visualize it as a small ball of light.

- Allow your senses to become vividly and intensely aware of everything around you; any sounds in the background like voices or the hum of electrical appliances, the seat beneath you, the feel of your clothes against your skin, and any smells that may come to you.

- Allow your senses to fully experience all of these things while dismissing any thoughts about them.

- Visualize your third eye absorbing and processing all of these sounds, smells, and sensations.

- When you are ready, end the meditation by taking a few deep breaths.

This meditation can be practiced daily. It energizes both the third eye chakra and the pineal gland and heightens awareness and the senses.

Meditation 5: Mindfulness Breathing Cues

This is great meditation to keep you grounded throughout your day and regularly mindful of your third eye.

- Choose a certain cue from your daily life, such as whenever you look in the mirror or brush your teeth; when your phone rings or you have ended the call. It could be every time you look out of the window or hear a dog bark or a car horn. Just choose a cue that occurs regularly in your daily life—ideally, more than one.

- Each time they come up, breathe mindfully for a few minutes while focusing on your third eye chakra.

- Repeat the exercise whenever the cue occurs.

- This exercise allows you to relax and ground your overactive mind while also checking in with your third eye.

Tips to Get the Most out of Meditation

Here are a few suggestions to help you meditate better. These are not mandatory rules but just useful tips to consider.

Place. The ideal place to meditate should be relaxing and welcoming, with as little noise or disturbance as possible. It does not necessarily have to be indoors. Meditating in nature to the sounds of birds singing or waves sweeping onto the shore is a wonderful experience. The choice is up to you: just a calming environment that resonates with you.

Time. It is best if you are able to meditate at the same time each day; having a consistent meditation schedule really helps to ground your mind and creates a regular pattern of time-out for the body and mind. Many people find that having a regular meditation schedule gives them something to look forward to during a hectic day. Their meditation time is a quiet, energizing haven from the havoc of daily life.

Position. Whether you choose to sit on the floor or in a chair, the important thing is that you are totally comfortable. The ideal position is one where you can nod off if you want you. Always give your body time to settle down and relax before you start, as fidgeting during the meditation will break your focus.

• Try to clear your mind. Connecting with the third eye chakra and receiving information from the higher plane requires extreme clarity and calmness of the mind. This is easier said than done, especially if you are new to meditation. The best way to maintain clarity is to remain focused on the third eye for as long as possible during each meditation.

• Coming out of a meditative state is just as important as entering it. Never just open your eyes and jump up. Always bring your focus back to the physical world slowly and ground yourself with a few deep breaths until you are fully aware of your surroundings.

• Take your time. Each meditation should last for at least 30 minutes.

• Wear loose, comfortable clothing, and no shoes.

• Don't be alarmed when you suddenly receive a poignant message or thought, from your third eye. This may disrupt your concentration.

- Learn how to sit in the proper lotus position as it allows the best alignment of the body.

- Turn off cell phones, TVs, and other sources of distraction.

- Feel free to explore other forms of meditation such as guided meditation and meditating to nature sounds or music, or meditation that incorporates physical movement.

- Enjoy the experience.

Chapter 5 Healing Mind and Body Through Meditation

By regularly practicing meditation, you will allow your body and mind to get into the habit of relaxing completely while also giving yourself a chance to connect with your emotions. Meditation, when done correctly, has endless benefit for both your physical body and your mind. Not only does meditation help you to feel better where your mood is concerned, but meditation has also been known as a great tool for healing the mind and body (as well as aiding in the prevention of numerous health conditions and illnesses).

Stress-Induced Medical Conditions

Stress has been linked to one of the leading factors in causing depression, insomnia, headaches, weakened immune systems, and high blood pressure. Stress can also increase an individual's risk for heart attacks, erectile dysfunction, and problems with fertility.

Meditation can also be used to shrink neurons that are located in the brain's hippocampus. The hippocampus can regenerate and heal itself in the event that the individual is able to eliminate stress. The hippocampus is responsible for our memory, positive moods, and general learning capacity. To summarize: eliminating stress promotes immediate brain health.

Some say that illnesses are often rooted in our mind's or consciousness. With that in mind, by healing and relaxing our minds through the act of meditation we are able to eliminate the root of most illnesses (resulting in better health).

There are three types of spiritual healing that can be used to better one's physical and mental health: Chakra Healing, Reiki Healing, and Spiritual Cleansing.

Chakra Healing

The practice of Chakra Healing concentrates its focus on balancing one's health, spirit, and body in order to promote better physical health. Some of the techniques associated with Chakra Healing are chakra massage, yoga, chakra stones, and the use of essential oils. Gently massage the area in which the desired chakra system is located within the physical body. Chakra massage can help relax and strengthen individual chakra systems. Illness can be caused when a certain chakra's energy becomes stuck or stagnant, and various yoga poses have been known to allow this release of blocked energy. Yoga encourages your chakra energies to flow freely and fluidly throughout your body so the chakra system remains healthy (allowing your body to remain healthy and relaxed). Chakra stones (or healing crystals) can be used to relax individual chakra systems by applying the appropriate colors and vibration levels to promote the release of healthy, positive energy by the chakras.

You can achieve chakra healing through meditative practices too. A good way to achieve this is to choose a quiet area in your home where you will have minimal distractions from external stressors, noise, or disturbances. You can then turn on some soft, soothing music and listen to guided meditation audio files in order to help you to get in tune with your mind, body, and chakra system. Make sure to use a calm, soothing, comfortable voice as you read these exercises for recording. Also, it is important to stop for an adequate amount of time between each step in the guided meditation exercises so that you do not feel rushed when you play the audio file back and are performing the meditation practices.

Essential oils are often used in addition to regular meditation exercises or chakra massage and offer greater benefits when combined with these forms of chakra healing rather than being used alone. Below is a list of the seven chakras and the essential oils that are best for bringing relaxation and balance to them.

Chakra Stones

Chakra stones are also known as healing crystals. These stones are crystals that, when matched correctly with their corresponding chakra system, when placed on the body they draw out the negative energy from that physical area. Healing crystals, or chakra stones, are used to protect against numerous types of disease and are also used to cure certain types of ailments.

Below is a list of the seven chakras along with their corresponding chakra stones crystal type:

Root Chakra: Bloodstone, Tiger's Eye, Hematite

Sacral Chakra: Coral, Moonstone, Carnelian

Solar Plexus Chakra: Citrine, Topaz, Malachite

Heart Chakra: Jade, Rose Quartz, Green Tourmaline

Throat Chakra: Aquamarine, Turquoise, Lapis Lazuli

Third Eye Chakra: Amethyst, Purple Fluorite, Black Obsidian

Crown Chakra: Selenite, Amethyst, Diamond

Chakra Healing with Essential Oils

1st Chakra: Angelica, Frankincense, St. John's Wort

2nd Chakra: Juniper, Clove, Rosemary

3rd Chakra: Peppermint, Lemon, Marjoram

4th Chakra: Basil, Rose, Rosewood

5th Chakra: Sage, Blue Chamomile, Lemongrass

6th Chakra: Spruce, Elemi, Lavender

7th Chakra: Myrrh, Geranium, Sandalwood

Essential oils offer more benefits to your mental and physical health than simply relieving stress to help align the seven chakras. Essential oils have also been shown to balance hormonal levels, strengthen your immune system, improve respiratory issues, relieve pain, relax sore muscles, and heal skin conditions. As if these benefits were not enough to make one consider utilizing essential oils, these oils also reduce cellulite, wrinkles, inflammation, and fever.

Reiki Healing

Reiki healing is a Japanese method of spiritual medicine. This technique of spiritual healing is designed to reduce stress, increase relaxation, and promote healing. Reiki healing sounds complicated but in reality, the concept of how it works is relatively simple. Reiki healing works by flowing through the body's damaged areas of the energy fields and supercharges them with positive energy so that they may be balanced and healed. Reiki healing breaks down and destroys one's negatives energy (causing pain and illness) by increasing the energy field's vibratory levels.

Spiritual Cleansing

Physically cleansing the body of unwanted toxins is extremely beneficial to one's health, and has been a recently growing trend as a weight loss technique. Americans spend in average $33 billion each year on products designed to detox and cleanse the body in order to achieve weight loss. If you would be willing to try cleansing your physical body in order to achieve greater health and weight loss, why would you leave your mind clouded with unwanted toxins (in the form of stress and negative energies)? A spiritual cleanse can be as beneficial as a physical cleanse in order to achieve improved health and wellness. Spiritual cleansing techniques involved the release of thoughts and negative mental concepts in order to achieve mental clarity while promoting a better connection with one's emotions.

Chapter 6 Mindfulness Meditation

The higher the released energy flows, the greater the spiritual uplift the meditator feels. Fire sparks emanating from the mouth of the kundalini snake reach the hemispheres of the brain, stimulating them more and more to vigorous activity. The meditator begins to experience the deepest ecstasy, joy, and peace. It seems that the whole body is plunged into an ocean of happiness and bliss.

With the stimulation of the right hemisphere, hidden possibilities of extrasensory perception, such as clairvoyance, clairaudience, telepathy, providence, and so on, come to the surface. Consciousness begins to expand and go beyond its borders, opening up new dimensions of cosmic unity. The sense of self-identity begins to make quantum leaps into the ever-increasing orbits of the cosmic mind. This stage of comprehension of time and space is a reward to the adept for all his efforts.

Here are a few meditations that help rise to higher levels of consciousness and control internal energy.

Meditation on the clouds of light

Find a comfortable place to relax. Let your thoughts flow freely, come, and go; you are only an observer. Take a deep breath, hold your breath. Check for tension in the body. If you find such areas, free them - and on the exhale to get rid of everything that prevents you from completely relaxing. Take a deep breath again. As you exhale, release all energy and all your thoughts from the body. Take a deep breath. Feel new energy entering the body; you literally breathe in new possibilities and allow the body to become light. Relax more and more - until you stop feeling the body.

When fully relaxed, imagine a colorful mist vibrating around you. You yourself, being light, smoothly pass into this fog, just your being has a slightly higher density. Clouds of energy slowly float around you. Relax on one of them, feel safe. This cloud lifts you up and takes you to an infinite world. The boundaries between time and space are erased. You are immersed in a world of infinite beauty and endless possibilities. You are floating in the cloud, feeling how light you have become. Suddenly you see a giant rock below; the cloud softly and easily lands, you descend on a rock.

Feel the strength of the stone, feel the power emanating from the rock. You look back, and you see a big river. You cannot make out where it begins and where it ends. You are fascinated by the water stream. It is an endless river of energy, a river of life. You come closer to the water and try to examine its color, to feel it with your whole being. What sounds do you hear? You are the light, so you can safely enter the water, cross it, rush along with the stream, and when you want, stop.

Relax and try to realize what you need most at the moment. What is your main intention? What emotions will accompany you on the way to the chosen goal? Feel the energy of these emotions, feel how it moves through your light body, burns, pulsates. Inhale energy with your whole being. Try to see the paintings, images, symbols associated with it: they will appear in front of the inner eye themselves; you can only focus on them.

When you are completely filled with this energy, enter the river, dissolve for a moment in it, purify the energy, and then release it into the water. See how the energy cloud comes out of you, touches the water, and gradually disappears in the stream. Take a deep breath. Your desire merges with the source of life. Enjoy the river of life for some more time. Take a deep breath again and exit the river. Notice that the colored fog surrounds you again, and you rise up with it. You descend to the cloud and return. With each deep breath, you return to the outside world and feel peace and satisfaction.

Sacred Space Meditation

Relax, sit in a comfortable position. Close your eyes, calm your mind. Breathe slowly and deeply; breathing comes from the diaphragm. For a while, just breathe and pay attention to the spine. It is a pillar connecting earth and heaven.

Feel the energy being concentrated at both ends of this pillar. Let the flow of earthly energy move upward, exit the crown of the head, and disperse into the Universe. Together with the energy flow, all negative emotions, pain, anxiety, tension are carried away.

Your whole being is filled with peace. Let the mind be like the ocean, and thoughts - bubbles appearing on the surface of the water. You may remember your thoughts better, but for now, remain a simple observer. Breathe deeper, gradually slow down your breathing. With each breath, relax your body and mind more and more.

Feel the cool red fog enveloping you. It is not hot, not cold: you can only feel it with your skin.

Feel yourself on a cloud firm enough to hold you on yourself, but very cozy and comfortable. Each part of your body rests on a cloud: legs, arms, back, neck, head - all organs feel calm. The cloud begins to plunge slowly into the red fog, and you plunge with it. Immersion is very slow; you go deeper and deeper and relax even more. The fog begins to change its color: from brilliant red to red-orange.

Gradually, the orange color changes to yellow-lemon. Your body is also painted in lemon color. You are floating on a cloud that carries you to the green summer lawn. You can even hear the wind shaking the grass, feel the flowing blue light from heaven.

Blue light turns into purple; moonless night comes, dark, peaceful, quiet. The cloud you were floating on gently lands.

The fog disappears. You lie on your back on the green grass. You feel light blows of the wind; you can hear the faint chatter of night insects.

Wherever you are, there is always something that pulls you toward you. It may be someplace, person, impression. What you are thinking about may appear right next to you because you are in a sacred place of fulfillment of desires. Everything can change here, but any changes will occur only at your request. You yourself built this place, inhabited it. Rise, explore the sacred space in which you are. May you meet with something (or about whom) have long dreamed of.

After a while, you yourself will realize that the time has come to leave the sacred place. Say goodbye to what you saw, leave without regret, because you can always come back here whenever you want.

Lie on your back and again feel the fog enveloping you. This time it is dark, like a moonless sky. Feel the cloud again under your feet, arms, back, neck, head. It supports you - and begins to rise very slowly.

Breathe deeply, watch the gradual change of colors: the dark color of the sky turns into blue, cyan, green, yellow. All this time, you continue to rise slowly; yellow turns to summer orange, then red. Let your mind still float, and your body will slowly return to the tangible world. You begin to feel the floor with your back, to realize the room in which you are. You are coming back.

Understanding the Benefits of a Strong Meditation Practice

The mindfulness movement is rapidly gaining popularity in the Western world. If before meditation was practiced only by people who are fond of various kinds of spiritual practices, now it is considered the most common thing. Now in Europe and here in the USA, the phrase "I practice meditation" no longer causes a wary-detached attitude, as before. So what's the point? What are some of the benefits of meditation or mindfulness? Why are more and more people doing it?

Chapter 7 Awaken Your Inner Self

Meditation is a great way to become more mindful of your thoughts and to get in touch with your inner self. Doing so brings you the clarity of mind to determine what it is you want out of life. In this fast-paced world, we often forget to check in with our true desires in exchange for meeting deadlines and catering to others.

A simple practice of meditation every day can get you back in touch with your mind, opening doors and possibilities all around you. Getting started with meditation is easy. It does not require any fancy equipment or atmosphere. All you need is a quiet space, a willing mind and a little bit of time.

There are many different types of meditation, so finding something that speaks to you will be the goal. There is no right or wrong way to do it, so long as you feel refreshed and renewed with the practice. If you are new to meditation, it may help to have a few guided sessions to get a feel for it.

The idea is very simple, and can easily be done on your own. Find a quiet, comfortable room. Find a comfy chair or sit upright on your bed. Avoid laying down, as you may simply fall asleep. Dim the lights if possible and remove any distractions. Leave your cell phone and computer in another room.

Start breathing in and out, slowly and steadily, focusing on the sound of your breath. Put your energy into listening intently on this sound, and don't let your mind wander to other things. Just be at the moment. If it helps, using a guided meditation soundtrack or chanting can help focus the thought. Sometimes focusing on the breath actually quickens it, which isn't what we want.

This is really it. The goal is to relax your brain, giving it a break from the tireless thoughts of the day. You should feel relaxed and refreshed, ready to think fresh, positive thoughts for the rest of the day. With practice, it will become easier to get yourself to this state.

For more advanced practice, and to focus in on your inner self and your true desires, guided thought meditation can certainly help. Use the meditation time more actively and ask yourself to imagine what it is you want your life to

look like. Ask your mind to conjure up a detailed image of what that looks like. Ask for clarity and guidance to reach those goals.

This may not come easily, so don't become frustrated. If it has been a long time since you have listened to your inner self, it may be difficult to get in touch and really know what you want. With practice, those details will begin to emerge. Stay true to your practice every day, and soon you will be able to envision what it is you really need.

With meditation, you can also maneuver through your energy field. Once you get to a good state, begin to imagine that your body is a magnet, and envision the world around you as an infinite energy field. Everything around you gives energy. Look outside to see the trees and grass, the sky and the clouds. It all emits energy, look at it vibrating. Now imagine all of that energy drawing toward you, entering your body through the very crown of your head.

Feel it encircle your entire body. It enters from above but quickly engulfs your belly area, swirling around all of your organs, and soon finding its way to each finger and toe. It courses through you, invigorating every cell. Feel it wash every negative thought from your mind, and replace it with

purity and positivity.

Keep in mind that because energy is constantly moving and changing, you cannot expect your meditation to remain constant. Changing your technique and following your inner needs will help ensure that you are getting the most from your practice.

In case you need more reasons besides inner peace to practice meditation, studies show that regular meditation improves mental stability, improves concentration and productivity, enhances relationships and supports good physical health as well. It lowers stress, therefore reducing blood pressure and heart disease. The benefits are outstanding for such a simple practice. Why not get started today? Right now?

Awaken Your Intuition

Our natural intuition is what helps guide our decision making. It is the gut feeling we get when something doesn't feel quite right. The decisions made by intuition don't always make rational sense to the brain, but that is because we are listening to our inner wisdom, which has a broader scope of information to go on. Your intuition is something

that has always been with you and continues to try and catch your attention, but you are not listening.

You may be out of touch with your intuition if you are feeling generally unguided. You may feel as if even small decisions are difficult to make, and those decisions may lead you down a path that does not suit your best interests. If this sounds like the course of your life right now, it is time to get back on track by tapping into your natural intuition.

Being more mindful of your thoughts and subtle feelings throughout the day is a great way to get in touch with your intuition. We often ignore feelings of discomfort or dissatisfaction for the perceived greater good. We continue to go to jobs we don't really like for the sake of affording the bills. We continue to see specific friends even though they don't bring out our best selves. It is often easier to carry out these comfortable tasks to make things easier, as change can be difficult.

Now is the time to embrace the idea of bigger and better things. Are you truly happy with your job? Your circle of friends? Do you like the way you feel waking up in the morning, or do you feel unhealthy? Being honest with yourself will help make those tough decisions much easier.

Stop burying those intuitive feelings and let them bubble to the surface.

If you aren't sure exactly how to simply 'listen' to yourself, try doing more creative things to get the juices flowing. This could be anything from keeping a journal of your thoughts and feelings, to various types of art. It could be gardening and connecting more deeply with nature, or simply being more attentive to your thoughts.

Being creative is an activity of the spirit. When we do things like balancing the checkbook or do household chores, there is already a basic template for how it should be done. The framework for these tasks is always the same and doesn't allow any opportunity for the brain to stretch beyond its current capacity. However, creating something out of nothing is an exercise, something that requires inner strength, confidence, and guidance.

If you have ever written a book or created a piece of art, you may understand this feeling. Beyond the physical act of typing away at your keyboard or applying paint to a canvas, you actually go into a sort-of trance as you work. Your analytical brain takes a break, and your creative brain goes on autopilot. The result is a piece of work that has come directly from your inner spirit, something your analytical brain could have never imagined.

Once you find something creative that you love, let your spirit take off. Do whatever it is your spirit compels you to do. Experiment with new types of paints, try clay, take a hike in a new area, whatever the case may be. Learning to follow this intuition in a controlled environment actually trains you to let intuition take over when it really counts. As you practice these skills, you will realize that they have the same application in everyday life.

Your job can be run the same way. Allow some creativity to hold your interest, and if your intuition is leaving you blank, maybe it is time to make a shift in your life. Asking for new assignments that compel your creativity and intuition become your new art, and success is sure to follow. Remaining stagnant and following the same pattern does not allow that intuition to grow and change, which it will naturally want to do.

No matter how you choose to listen, harness the power of your intuition and don't be afraid to follow it. The biggest mistake you can make is hearing your intuition and squashing its power by not making any necessary changes. Life is all about flow and change. Staying stagnant and refusing to make important decisions do not keep us in good pace with the energy of the universe. Learning to fully function with intuition as our guide will ensure we are abreast of all of the positive things that may come our way.

Chapter 8 What Are Clairvoyant Capacities?

A clairvoyant is an individual who purports a capacity to see data avoided the ordinary faculties through extrasensory recognition (ESP) or is said by others to have such aptitudes. It is likewise used to depict showy entertainers who use methods, for example, prestidigitation, cold perusing, and hot perusing to deliver the presence of such capacities. It can likewise signify information on the psyche to impact the world sincerely and to the supernatural powers supposedly affirmed by those, for example, Uri Geller.

THE DIFFERENT PSYCHIC ABILITIES

1.   Perceptiveness

The broadly known mystic capacity, hyper vision, signifies "clear observing" and includes seeing what can't be seen by our physical eye. This could be objects, creatures, individuals, or inconspicuous spirits. Individuals with these forces can likewise "see" occasions, for example, those that happened before, those that are going on now, and later on.

2. Clairaudience

Clairaudience alludes to "clear hearing" and includes hearing sounds and voices that can't be heard by the physical ear. It envelops of hearing voices as addressed by spirits, voices inside the head, from creatures, and even sounds that originate from dormant things.

3. Clairsentience

Clairsentience is otherwise called "clear inclination," which includes the capacity to feel vibes that the five physical faculties can't distinguish in the material world.

For instant: you meet someone, and you feel the feeling of fear or sorrow immediately. It works related to climate perusing.

4. Clairalience

Clairalience signifies "clear smelling," and incorporates having the option to smell a fragrance that cannot be identified by our physical nose.

For example, somebody with this trait out of nowhere see the aroma that a carcass put on at the hour of their demise; or smelling blossoms or even consumed motivations when he/she goes into a room although there are no roses or motivators present there.

5. Clairgustance

Clairgustance alludes to as "clear tasting" and includes tasting something that is not in the mouth.

A model would act as a sample of blood when you pass by a house where somebody was being butchered.

6. Claircognizance

Claircognizance otherwise called "clear knowing" and includes quick knowing or having a hunch all of a sudden.

A model; Having this force gives you moments of mindfulness about individuals or events. An illustration is a point at which somebody is at serious risk or that the individual is being viewed, and each time this feeling is felt, their instinct is in every case right.

7. Astral Projection

Astral projection depends on the possibility that an individual has a spirit or soul self-destruct from the physical body. The capacity is gotten an out of body experience wherein the astral body or the soul isolates itself from the physical body and can go to any place it wishes.

Astral projection, for the most part, happens during reflection just as when the physical body is snoozing.

8. Air Reading

This capacity depends on the possibility that each individual has a climate that issues them. This quality is seen in various hues and is situated around 16' to 18" from the body. An environment is characterized as an electromagnetic field that every single living being has, which speaks to an individual's character, character, destiny, and soul.

Individuals who can peruse quality, can quickly let an individual's temperament, regardless of whether they are intrinsically fortunate or unfortunate, be known.

9. Programmed Writing

Individuals with this capacity can make written reports that originate from the profound world—otherwise called psychography.

The individual loses control of their cognizance and permits spirits from an excellent source to dominate and compose on paper what it plans to impart.

10. Divination

Hyper vision is the method for posing inquiries. With the utilization of stately apparatuses, answers are given, and it is one of the sorts of clairvoyant powers that can rapidly be learned and aced.

Various types of divinations incorporate the utilization of gem balls, runes, tarot card readings, and soul sheets.

11. Vitality Healing

This is a sort of elective medication wherein vitality from a healer is being moved to someone else, hence animating their average capacity to mend itself.

It tends to be finished with the healer genuinely contacting the patient, or hands-off recuperating where the healer just puts his hands over the patient's body. At the same time, separation mending should likewise be possible where a healer thinks and moves vitality to someone who isn't truly present.

12. Mediumship or Channeling

Mediumship or Channeling is one of the most known

and most dangerous sorts of mystic forces. It includes utilizing your body as a way to speak with a profound world. Mediums permit spirits to assume responsibility for their body to have the option to impart in the apparent world.

The underlying reason for mediumship is when individuals who've lost friends and family need to speak with the expired for the conclusion.

13. Remote Viewing

The individuals who are creating mystic aptitudes will find this is one of the numerous clairvoyant abilities that can be learned and aced.

Data that is accumulated by the clairvoyant usually is not straightforward and comes in images, examples, or energies, and the watcher deciphers them.

14. Precognition

Precognition is the capacity to see occasions of things to come. This includes seeing incidents in their fantasies or flashes of thought. These warnings are generally irregular and capriciously challenging to control.

15. Mystic Surgery

One of the most disputable mystic capacities, it is polished in the Philippines and a few pieces of Brazil. The procedure of clairvoyant, medical method includes making a mystic cut on the body and "pulling out" harmed tissues inside the body joined by a petition or melody to the supernatural world.

16. Psychometry

Otherwise called psychoscopy, psychometry is the capacity to assemble data about a spirit when you contact an article that they recently possessed.

It depends on the possibility that individuals move their profound energies to items and desert these energies, permitting the mystic to get impressions.

17. Scrying

Scrying is the capacity to get clairvoyant messages with the utilization of an instrument, for example, a precious stone ball or a mirror. It is expertise normally aced by seers or soothsayers.

18.   Retrocognition

Retrocognition is the capacity to see occasions that have occurred beforehand.

19.   Supernatural power

Have you at any point seen films wherein someone can move objects without contacting them indeed? That sort of supernatural force is called supernatural power. It is the capacity to move lifeless things and, in any event, living things with the intensity of the psyche.

The most mainstream and collective expertise appeared by the individuals who have supernatural power is twisting spoons.

20.   Clairvoyance

Clairvoyance is the ability to understand minds, just as speaking with someone else through his brain. It likewise includes the capacity to control the other individual by sending messages through the account.

Some portion of clairvoyance is likewise clairvoyant correspondence with creatures where pet mystic "talk" to animals through vitality channels that exist between spirits by sending them pictures or sentiments.

Chapter 9 Benefits of Astral Projection

The benefits of astral projection extend beyond our material existence. You might decide to attempt traveling in the astral plane out of a sense of curiosity, religiosity, or eagerness for a supernatural experience. Or you might in fact want to find some answers about yourself, or something that happened or happens to you. Whatever your reason might be, you will receive much more than you hoped for. Because the profound modification that astral projection can cause in your being, influences not only your mental and emotional perceptions of life, death, and meaning, but your physical world as well. Below, you will find the 10 most important and precious rewards you will gain in your spiritual journey.

1.   Metaphysical Awakening

Living in a universe governed by laws, and self-imposed, or otherwise imposed boundaries can feel a bit frustrating or stifling at times. Making a connection with your astral self, and awakening your divine perceptions, shatters all the limits that restrict you in the material world. If you are a faithful person, this will directly affect your spirituality, and facilitate a direct bond with your adored one(s). If, on the contrary, your belief vibrates in the energy flow scattered within your being, you will reach the deepest levels of self-awareness and the most intimate knowledge about your being's meaning. This effect depends on your personal ideology, but its ultimate contribution is the same: producing the unswerving liberation of your metaphysical consciousness.

2. Enhanced Imagination

Because it continually provokes your ordinary views and your creative potential, by means of visualization, detailed examination and concentration on natural or fantastic elements, astral travel augments your imagination. The more you practice it, the more you will be inclined to break free from the common paths and patterns of thinking, and the immediate result will be seen in your productivity. Imagination is what we engage to evolve beyond our bodily confinement, but it's also the essential tool for finding real life solutions for various types of problems. So this considerable advantage will greatly reflect in your real life choices too, and it can only lead to positive and prosperous outcomes.

3.   Extrasensory Abilities

Properties such as healing, telepathy, and foretelling are usually characteristics in legends, fairytales, and intensely debated accounts. The truth is, all of them are attainable. Through astral projection, as you align and unite your constituent parts, the astral and physical bodies, you remove all the emotional blockages that impeded you before from grasping your surroundings beyond mundane intuition. As you become skilled in traveling in higher energetic levels, and the frequencies on which you emit and receive signals from the bodies around you advance, it is possible to communicate with other beings at mystic levels. Whether they reside in the material or spiritual realm, you can bond with them, and influence their health state and yours, be it corporeal or emotional.

4.   Liberation of Death Fears

How many times have you looked up into the sky and wished you were a bird, free of your gravity obeying bodily mass, able to fly up high? And how many times did you tremble within, at the thought of your inevitable ending on this earth? You've surely wondered about death and dreaded its apparently decisive power. When you fly into spiritual worlds you only dreamed about, you not only fulfill a dream of unrestrained-to-ground liberty, but you also release yourself from the fears of the finale. Because you discover that it's really nothing to fear, but rather to embrace. It's a weightless flight, an unbounded journey, during which regrets of lost time and longings for faraway spaces never occur. As time and space and outer laws don't exist anymore, the only barriers are the ones your spirits sets.

5.   Life after Death Confirmation

An out-of-body experience doesn't just disclose that there is nothing to fear about the final detachment of your spiritual body from your physical one, but also reveals death is the final stop for your worldly shape. It's basically an astral projection that isn't followed by returning to your material form, as the silver cord that kept you tied to it has broken. Your very essence, the soul, lives on, and, if desired, it can actually return in another suitable earthly figure. Or it can fly up into your personal heaven and live happily there for an eternity.

6.   Personal Growth

Most of the people that went through near-death experiences, or other similar involuntary out-of-body incidents, declared how their perspective on living and its quality changed. Traveling in the astral plane not only consolidates your self-assurance and incites unsuspected powers and abilities, but it also elevates you. If our personal development was a pyramid, the ideal state would be reached at the top. How many people expect to actually touch their highest aspirations? And how many actually do? It is easy to respond to these questions if you consider that most of them never progress beyond earth-bound circumstances. But when one dwells and ponders beyond that, the respect for life in its complete unfolding will sharpen. And so will the empathy and the love for self and others, which is what helps guide your steps to the highest level of the pyramid.

7.   Time Travel

Remember, time and space are material representations, and valid only for a universe whose mass can be evaluated. Since in the astral plane, time doesn't exist, you can move in whatever dimension you wish. So, going back or forth, moving between past and future, while your physical body is caught in the present is not an unrealistic objective anymore. From ancient times to the Renaissance, and from there all the way to current times and a futuristic after time, you can visit them all. Obviously, this will not happen on your first attempt at astral projection, because your skills must be suitably developed. Still, this is possible.

8.   Retrospective Comprehension

By traveling in time and space, even getting to meet yourself while in earlier lives, you can obtain explanations for the way you are, who you are, and what your actual purpose is for your actual existence. Or you can simply find out something from the not faraway past, something that perhaps occurred in your childhood, and you want to explore and understand it. Whatever your aim, through astral projection, you can better realize a meaning, or a fact that formerly might have seemed senseless, distressing, or too dull.

9.   Tonic Relaxation

As you get in tune with yourself, and practically solve the mysterious puzzle of your own biography, you will gradually achieve an unparalleled state of relaxation. No disturbance will affect you as it used to before, and no obstacle will ever afflict you that much to make you feel defenseless and defeated. A peaceful sentiment will accompany you wherever you go, as long as you maintain a smooth communication with your spiritual self, and banish all the passing and damaging concerns.

10. Complete Self-Coordination

Because your energy flow is uninterrupted and your every pore, whether physical or spiritual, is coordinated with the surrounding ones, your inner organization will be impeccable. And it will reflect in your outer one accordingly. Discipline and orderly arrangement are key factors for achieving success and fulfilling aspirations, as perseverance is usually associated with them. Through astral projection, you will acknowledge exactly what you are looking for, the means to obtain it, and you will structure your endeavors to satisfy your inner and outer purposes.

Chapter 10 Psychic Abilities

Now, how do you enhance these abilities? Well, just like with any other skill, you simply have to keep on practicing them. When you say practice, it means actually putting it into real application. The best way to practice is to incorporate your psychic abilities in your everyday life.

So, how do you live with psychic abilities? Simply make them a natural part of who you are as a person. After all, there is no good reason for you to hide them. However, it should be noted that you should not boast about your abilities, and you should not use them for evil purposes. Let us now discuss effective ways on how to enhance your psychic abilities by making them a part of your everyday life:

When you take a bath, do not just clean your physical body, but also make an effort to cleanse all negative energies of your astral body. Visualize that as you clean your physical body, you also clean all negativities and impurities in your soul. See and feel the negative energies being washed away by the water and go in down the drain.

Visualize yourself shining brightly.

If you have time to focus on your breath, then you can cleanse and charge yourself at any time. As you inhale, visualize positive energy entering your body. When you exhale, see and feel the negative energies being released from your body.

When someone calls you on the phone, take a moment to define who it is. Close your eyes or just focus, listen to your intuition, and then focus on who it is.

When you are engaged in a conversation, do not just listen to the words that the other person is telling you. You should also connect to them on a deeper level by using your empathic ability. Use whatever technique you may find helpful or necessary.

Make sure to make time to meditate regularly (every day). Meditation plays a very important role in your spiritual development, especially in the awakening of the Kundalini.

When you see an interesting object, especially if it is an old object, hold it in your hand, feel it, and allow your intuition to tell you the history of the object. This ability is known as psychometry.

Start using your intuition. This does not mean that you should no longer use logic or reasons, but you should also pay attention to what your intuition tells you.

Improve yourself by working on corresponding chakras.

There are many ways to incorporate your practices in your daily life. The problem is that there are people who simply do not take the efforts to practice their abilities. It is also advised that you give yourself even just an hour from time to time to do nothing but to practice your abilities. You do not have to develop all your psychic abilities all at once. If you want, you can just focus on one or two abilities at a time.

The more that you make good use of your abilities, the more that you can develop them. The key here is repetition. This is why continuous practice is very important. You also have to give it your focus and attention. Always do your best.

Psychic games are a good way to have fun as you learn and develop your psychic abilities. You do not need to be so serious when you enhance your abilities. In fact, you will notice that you are more effective when you are having fun. When you are having fun, you are charged with positive energy, which is the best state to make use of your psychic abilities. Let us now discuss notable psychic games that you can try:

- Red or black

For this game, you only need to use a deck of ordinary playing cards. Playing cards have two colors: red and black. You just have to guess the color of the cards. To do this, you can rely on your intuition, divination, or even micro kinesis. Use whatever ability would apply and the one that you want to develop.

Shuffle the deck of cards and put it face down on the table in front of you. Now, predict or divine the color of the top card. Is it red or black? Say your answer aloud and then check if you got it right. Since a deck of cards only have a limited number pertaining to each color, it is advised that you reshuffle the whole deck after every two or three guesses/attempts. Again, you can use any ability of your choice. For example, if you want to apply psychometry, then you might want to touch the top card and try to get some sense impressions to help you predict its color correctly.

- Dancing candle

This is a game to help you develop your ability to project energy. For this exercise, you need to use a candle. Light the candle and focus on it. You need to make the flame lean in the direction of your choice by projecting energy to it. The idea here is to push it with energy. So, gather energy on the palm of your hand. Once you feel that you have enough energy, you should position your hand towards the candle with the palm facing outward.

Now, slowly move your hand to the flame and push it with the accumulated energy. The flame should lean/bend as you push it with energy. Remember not to put your hand close to the candle flame. If you want a more advanced version, then you can simply project energy directly to the flame without accumulating it in your hand.

• Pendulum swing

This game presents many opportunities as it can be used to develop different psychic abilities. But first, what is a pendulum? A pendulum is any weighted object that is suspended on a chain or string. You can buy many beautifully designed pendulums from metaphysical and occult stores, as well as online. You are also free to create your own pendulum. It is easy to make your own pendulum. For a basic pendulum, you can use a thread and a needle. The needle will act as the bob of the pendulum. Hold the end of the thread with your hand and allow the pendulum to hang freely. It should be still before you use it. This pendulum is very sensitive to energy, so be careful not to move it. Another option that you have is to tie the end of the thread to something so that you would not have to hold it anymore. However, if you are using it for divination, then it is advised that you hold the string of the pendulum in your hand.

If you want to use it for divination, then you can ask the pendulum questions that are answerable by yes or no. However, the first thing that you need to do is find out how the pendulum responds to say yes, as well as how it moves to signify a no. This is easy to do. As you hold the pendulum and have it hanging still, say, "Show me yes." The pendulum will move. Take note of how it moves. Is it in a clockwise, counterclockwise, or any other pattern of movement? Once you have the movement for a yes, you can ask her it would move for a now, "Show me no." Again, take note of how it moves. Once you understand how it moves for yes and for no, then you can start to ask it questions. This is a simple kind of divination with a pendulum, which can be very effective if you practice it long enough.

You can also use the pendulum to develop your other abilities. For example, you can to the end of the thread somewhere and have the bob hanging still. Now, you can project energy or even use telekinesis to make the bob (needle) move. Use whatever ability you want to make it move.

- Projection

This is a good game to play with a friend. This will help you learn to project prana more effectively. The first thing that you should do is to identify who will be the sender and who will be the receiver. The receiver should close their eyes as the sender projects energy to them. The receiver should tell which part of their body the energy is projected. If you want to take it a step further, you can also add a certain quality to the energy, and the receiver should be able to identify it. This game can develop your skill in projecting energy (sender), as well as in increasing your awareness of energy (receiver).

If you ever make use of negative energy, be sure to do some cleansing afterward. It is not good to keep any negative energy in your system. When you play this game, it is important that you and the other person are very honest with each other, as you need to know if you are able to send and receive energy properly. If nothing seems to happen on your first few tries, do not be discouraged. Just keep on practicing.

To take it a step further, you can try merging your energy and projecting it to someone or something, and see what happens. If you ever do this, it is advised that you only make use of positive energy, as it is never a good idea to send out any negativity to anyone.

- Shielding

You can ask the sender to project negative energy to you. However, before that, you should first surround yourself with a shield. This way, you can test just how effective your shield it. So, how do you create a shield? There are many ways to make a shield. The most common shield is known as the bubble shield.

To create this shield, simply imagine a strong bubble of light surrounding your body. Be fully convinced that it will protect you from all psychic attacks and negative energies. Charge it with energy as much as you can. Take note that the lifetime of a shield is only as good as the energy that you feed it. Therefore, if you feel like your shield is getting weak, you should recharge it again with energy. Normally, a regular shield lasts for about three to five hours before it will need to be recharged. You can also switch roles with your friend so you can also try to project another against their shield. Feel free to make adjustments or modifications to increase the power of your projection and your shield.

Chapter 11 Chakra Meditation

Maybe you consider reflection a demonstration of sitting leg over leg and murmuring to oneself. All things considered; this isn't all what contemplation is about. You will discover a wide range of types of contemplation that help you in unwinding and diminishing pressure. Chakra is a particular type of reflection which starts from Hindu convictions. Today, the specialty of chakra reflection has spread to each edge of the globe.

Chakra Meditation is a type of reflection that comprises a lot of unwinding procedures concentrated on bringing parity, unwinding and prosperity to the chakras. "Chakra" is an antiquated Sanskrit word that implies vortex or wheel that can be followed back to India.

Chakras are the human body's seven primary vitality focuses with every one relating to singular organs that administer our particular body parts in addition to different regions of the mind. They are situated alongside a hormonal organ along the human spinal segment.

Chakras can wind up blocked and if even one of the 7 Chakras ends up blocked, it sets us up for physical and passionate an issue which is something nobody needs.

How Do Chakra Meditation Techniques Work?

Our wonderful and puzzling universe circulates its awesome life-power vitality to the earth and to our organs and organs situated all through the body and circulatory system. This life-power vitality is key so as to acquiring ideal prosperity and wellbeing. It's accepted that since the chakras are interrelated, they intently influence each other, by attempting to accomplish the ideal degree of equalization.

Make Each Cell in Your Body Stir and Celebrate!

A large portion of us has vigorous squares and awkward nature just as vitality attacking propensities that keep us from getting to our full essentialness, which leads us to feel depleted, dispersed, dull... even sick.

The Benefits of Meditation

In the event that new to meditation, questions

concerning a capacity to do it can surface, bringing up issues like "How would I consider nothing?" or considerations like "I can't do that." It can appear to be odd to attempt to discharge ourselves from the pending negative issues in life by a what may appear to be a straightforward demonstration of sitting idle, particularly when compelling passionate battles can mist our psyche.

It very well may be hard to clear your head when such a great amount of weight from the outside world is by all accounts pulling you down, yet is significantly progressively fundamental during these unpleasant stages throughout everyday life. When I began ruminating, another point of view on life conquered me. These are only a couple of proposals from an energetic tenderfoot that may enable somebody to start a remunerating routine with regards to reflection and mindfulness.

Checking through breaths, one practice that has helped me keep my brain in the ideal spot when reflecting is to check during breaths. As I breathe in, I check until I've finished breathing in, by and large around eight for me, yet can be anything relying upon how quick or moderate you tally. As I breathe out, I tally to a similar number, arriving at eight when I've finished my breath out. Rehashing this procedure, I tally to eight breathing in through my nose and after that considering to eight I breathe out through my mouth.

Cool air in/warm let some circulation into. I have likewise thought that it was gainful to focus on my breaths as cool, positive vitality filling my lungs and leaving as warm, negative vitality that has been stockpiled inside being discharged. Every breath is imagined, envisioning the positive, new cloud streaming in through my nose and pushing the negative, stale cloud out as I breathe out through my mouth.

Concentrate on a solitary item. Another training that can be utilized to encourage contemplation is to concentrate on a solitary article. The item can be anything. I most normally picture a solitary light lit in a dim live with nothing else around. I watch it glint as contemplations go through my brain, mindful of them however giving no consideration. As I get it, this sort of contemplation has really been utilized to help with recuperating explicit pieces of the body.

Use sound for ruminating. A bit much, yet something that has helped me out a lot, playing a sound can help with "timing " sessions, liberating me of considering to what extent I've been thinking. Here and there the utilization of sound can get you more profound, quicker, however, I have a houseful with five youngsters, so putting on earphones and covering up for twenty minutes is once in a while the main route for me to work on contemplating.

Practice each day. The increasingly more you accomplish something, the simpler and simpler it gets. This remains constant for reflection, as well. Doing it consistently builds up a sound propensity for taking a vital break and recognizing the present, excessively effectively overlooked with our bustling timetables in this day and age. Practice each day and see what opens up for you.

I'm still new to the act of reflection, so I comprehend the anxiety with newness. Be that as it may, I can't overlook the advantages of reflection as they are read and experience for myself, further supporting the idea we are in charge of our own condition. Also, as I proceed with my routine with regards to contemplation, I am charmingly astonished by the positive vitality I feel when setting aside the effort to find myself.

The Health Benefits of Energy Healing

It's extremely fascinating to take note of that dependent on a distributed American Heart Association's examination in November of 2012 about the effect of pressure decrease projects utilizing reflection the discoveries demonstrated that contemplation extraordinarily lessens stroke, cardiovascular failure, passing, outrage levels and the dangers related with coronary supply route illness.

The aftereffects of the program are very great with the members who contemplated two times per day for times of 20 minutes every day. They had the option to diminish coronary episode and stroke hazards by 48 percent. Furthermore, they likewise diminished their annoyance levels. It's intriguing to take note of that the more continuous the contemplation sessions, the higher the positive medical advantages for the members.

Adapting to consistent outrage is very damaging to the brain and body. There are sure things that one should relinquish, or leave if there's no desire for change. To refer to one model, poisonous connections are not just fatal; they are a hindrance to recuperating.

Chakra Meditation Music and Chakra Colors to Meditate

Music is another control that is additionally utilized in adjusting the chakras. Notwithstanding the music, the chief has included numerous wonderful and brilliant pictures. These chakra vitality hues are likewise a significant mending segment.

A case of chakra hues incorporates green which identifies with the substance and discharges genuinely stifled injury. Another powerful shading is indigo for the third eye that encourages us to see flawlessness no matter what. Blue is likewise utilized with throat chakra reflection and the declaration of truth through discourse.

Different methods used to help reflection incorporate guided symbolism, body unwinding, perception and breathing strategies. Regardless of whether you understand it or not, your Chakras are grinding away inside your body always. They impact your psychological just as your physical state. By giving extraordinary consideration to these zones, you can impact them to improve certain parts of your life.

Chapter 12 Guided Meditations To Rebalance Your Chakras And Pineal Gland Activation

"How can you improve your mental skills? "Meditate" "Everyone advocates meditation as the ultimate key to improving mental skills. Some even explained how easy it is to increase your strength with different meditation postures. "But why didn't everyone make it?" "Because everyone misses the key!" What is the key How to channel energy? You need to focus energy on your third eye chakra. The third eye chakra (between the eyebrows) is the energy center that is most closely related to your mental performance. This chakra is the portal to improve your psychic skills. This is where you should really focus your attention and energy. The third eye chakra has the ability to see beyond the obvious. This gives us access to the area of intuition and clairvoyance. The third eye, also known as the sixth or agya chakra, is said to be the chakra for higher spiritual intuition and the one responsible for the development of psychic powers such as telepathy and out of body experiences. However, you need determination and patience to really open your sixth chakra. Before you take steps in a guided meditation to open the third eye, there are a few basic guidelines to consider. First of all, you have to allow some time for the guided third eye-opening, at least five to ten minutes. A comfortable, quiet place where you can relax and feel grounded is also important so that you can easily enter a higher level of spiritual awareness. Also, make sure that you are not too tired, hungry, or full and that all your needs have been met before meditation to avoid unnecessary distractions from the session. As with all meditations, do not strain or force your chakras to achieve the desired effects. Any guided meditation to open the third eye begins with you sitting comfortably, either with your legs crossed on the floor or in a chair with your feet flat on the floor and your spine straight and relaxed. Take five deep breaths to open and replenish your lungs. Remember to inhale and exhale gently and deeply with each breath. Put your hands on each other to facilitate the flow of energy. Then close your eyes and focus on the point between your brows on your forehead where the third eye is. Your eyes should, of course, move upwards without you having to open them. Hold this position for about two minutes. Using a mantra to say om can also help. Keep this state even if your mind wanders or you feel uncomfortable. If you get distracted, just do your best to return to your earlier state of concentration.

When you do guide meditations to open the third eye,

your sixth chakra is definitely activated and eventually brings you the small changes, such as deepening perception and development of the "sixth sense", to let you know that you are actually opening your third eye to have. As long as you continue to practice your chosen meditation in the same place and at the same time, you will definitely achieve this step of spiritual enlightenment in time. If you're looking for more information on how brainwaves, binaural beats, monaural beats, or isochronous sounds can help you relax, fall asleep, have better dreams, or just feel less stressed. Ajna chakra and head chakra are considered the third eye, while meditation techniques are performed for the third eye. The third eye meditation method is one of the guided meditations that help to experience peace and relaxation in life. All in all, various guided mediations are accredited to experience the stages of self-realization in life, to know wisdom, ESP, and intuition for life. Guided meditation by opening the third eye improves your intuition, strengthens psychological power, ensures health and well-being, and even promotes a positive outlook on life. The third eye is said to be an eye that has a connection with your soul that guides your future goals and path in a positive way. The guided posture to open the third eye helps you open your third eye, which is very spiritual by nature.

It's pretty easy to follow this guided meditation

technique at home. You can sit cross-legged on the floor or against a wall by slowly aligning your spine with the back of your head. After that, you must stay straight (upright posture) and slowly raise your chin in this posture. If you hold this posture with a deep breath for five minutes, you can really relax. Thus, opening the third eye of the guided meditation without a visual display is very easy to do. There are several advantages of guided meditation when opening the third eye, such as improved memory, good concentration, strong willpower, good circulation, sharpened intuitive performance, good sense of wisdom, good health signs, and optimism. It also helps reduce stress in your life by experiencing relaxation in a healthier way. Spending only 20 minutes of your day in this natural workout posture can benefit your health as immunity and blood pressure are improved. "If you want to learn more about how brainwaves, binaural beats, monaural beats, or isochronous sounds can help you relax, fall asleep, have better dreams, or just feel less stressed, check out this great resource.

Not everyone knows that we actually have three eyes. We humans have two physical eyes, but we also have a third spiritual eye, also known as Anja Chakra, and this eye is as important as the two physical eyes that we have. It has been reported that those who accessed their third eye had visions or even an astral projection. People who have access to their third eye are also called "seers." Well, actually accessing your third eye is a difficult process, but it's worth it. There are many different techniques to open the third eye. A few of the most common ways are meditations. The first thing you must do is sit down in a comfortable potion and try pretty much anything to dream. You want to focus on that peaceful place in your head. It will take some time to find the location that may not have been reached the first time. However, this is the case if you stay focused and relaxed. Once you find that your mind is clear and you find yourself in the place of peace where the third eye is, breathe in and out to keep yourself relaxed. You will start to feel the relaxing sensation and recharge your batteries when you awaken your chakra. With this relaxation and energy, your third eye should now be visible to you. They say that once you come into contact with your Anja chakra, your body and mind work together to form a large, powerful, harmonious sense organ. After accessing your third eye, it is a multi-sensory organ that perceives energy patterns or frequencies. The data is also returned in overlay information about your other senses. Once your third eye is open, it is a very powerful skill and can give you a better understanding of yourself and the relationship you have with the universe. However, people with lower vibrations and lower auras can benefit from the course. It was stated that if you do not understand and develop properly, it can confuse and lose your mind very much. People who have no understanding tend to run away or hide from the skills or strange descriptions. When you open it, you open your mind to many different phenomena around us. Fortune tellers and seers use this ability to make connections and answer questions. There were many ways that the third eye was used to improve your life, give insight into your path, and gain universal wisdom.

The spiritual development of a person depends very much on the functioning of each chakra. If even a single chakra is out of balance or blocked, the entire system is affected and hinders clear thinking and healthy living. Chakras are multidimensional and conduct energy between three bodies, namely physically, mentally, and emotionally. Seven chakras are in our body, the first is at the base of the spine, and the seventh is at the crown of the head; all five chakras are in between. The process of opening and cleaning the chakras always starts with the lowest chakra, and you gradually move up towards your crown chakra. It is very important to note that once all the chakras are open, you must also close each of them by moving down. So if you are looking for ways to open the third eye chakra, you will find many techniques to guide you through each step. Here we will debate the simplest form of meditation to open the third eye chakra. The overall process success essentially depends on your breathing technique. Close your eyes, and take a deep lungful to relax your body. Once you have reached a state of complete rest, try to focus between your brows with your eyes closed. You will soon see a beam of light and feel your eyes go up. Try to practice this regularly and make it part of your daily routine. It will help you to illuminate and convert all of your negative energy into positive energy and help you to achieve spiritual enlightenment.

There are many tried and tested ways that can open your heart, such as meditation, but it takes discipline to turn thoughts off and commit to the times. Golden DNA Activation is an effective and self-updating protocol for opening the heart without years because the effects start immediately and develop over time. Once a person opens their heart with golden DNA activation, they experience extreme joy. You feel more connected to the Source / God and your higher self. This joy creates new compassion. If you have not yet opened your third eye, the sixth chakra, DNA activation, creates inner vision. When you look at past events that have caused you pain and suffering, your heart is working from a compassionate perspective that makes it easy for you to forgive others and yourself. Self-compassion is the most effective way to heal internal violence against yourself and humanity. When you allow yourself to see more and forgive more, your body fills with real light. Essentially, joy solves old problems and blockages that are stored in the heart and creates space for light. An open heart is a frequency, just as a closed heart is a frequency. You've probably heard of The Secret, which the law explains how we pull things into our lives. Once you open your heart, your ability to manifest desires becomes faster and easier as joy becomes a rocket launcher for your ideas, goals, and desires. Your manifestations return to you in the form you desire. You experience a whole new reality. The golden DNA activation opens your heart, increases your frequency for joy, and opens the door to new possibilities. Golden DNA activation is the way to bring peace to humanity.

Some people get shaky when they see the word meditate, some people find meditation a lot of work, difficult or even impossible, but they can relax. If you are awkward with the thought of meditation, just work on relaxation. Relaxing calms the mind and facilitates the flow of spiritual communication. You probably have a good idea of how best to relax. Some people prefer to relax without activity, while others can relax better when they do something. That could be gardening, walking, jogging, or even cleaning. Do whatever helps you decompress so your mind can dream. You may want to ask a question that you then open to get the answer. You may be asking what you need to do differently in your relationship. As you relax, let the answers come to you. They can take the form of seeing, feeling, hearing, or thinking. Just be open to communication and trust in it. You may want to write your thoughts down when you are done relaxing.

Chapter 13 Mediums and Intuition

The most important thing you should know is that all of have some amount of intuition within us. This intuition depends upon a variety of factors. Every single one of us is intuitive at some form or manner. Intuition is believed to be the gut feeling or something that has been hidden in our soul and our subconscious. It is believed to be a strange mysterious wisdom that surfaces during certain times. Research and studies have shown that most people are born with an intuitive sense and everyone has the sixth sense. This sixth sense is not often paid attention to because studying it is quite difficult.

The sixth sense is more pronounced in some people while it is blurred or dull in some others. Everyone is not a medium however everyone does have the power to become mediums. Think of it as someone who has the talent to learn something like playing an instrument, everyone can play an instrument, but not everyone can play it exceptionally well. Similarly, mediums are of two categories. They can be born or they can be developed. A person who has the natural ability to perceive the sixth sense are called naturally born mediums and those who develop and fine tune their sixth sense as they progress are called latent mediums.

Latent mediums are those who have a higher sensitivity towards the sixth sense. They have a slightly higher intuition level as opposed to regular beings but their intuition intensity is a lot lesser as opposed to naturally born mediums. They have a form of natural inclination towards intuition and this is why some people have a good gut feeling. While it might not be so apparent, the skill can be developed over the course of time. This requires some amount of natural skill. Development of your sixth sense requires time and arduous effort

Now the question arises how exactly can one person tap into their sixth sense? How can one person tell how good their intuition is and how can they identify themselves as a medium? The answer to all this might seem like just mere meditation, however unlocking your psychic powers and intuition has so much more to do with just mere meditation. Meditation is just a small part of the exercise. There are many processes you will need to undertake for you to be able to refine your sixth sense. This does not just imply contemplation, meditation and challenging your core beliefs. Even your outlook and the company you keep might require changing if you ever want to truly develop your sixth sense.

How to develop your sixth sense and what are some processes you can easily follow to get it developed. Intuition is inner wisdom and in order to develop this inner wisdom, you would require patience.

Some of the easiest ways through which you can tell if you are a medium is if you have experienced the following:

1.   As a child did you ever have a fear for the dark because you feel something lurking in the shadows?

2.   Did you ever feel like you never managed to fit in and you felt disconnected to people?

3.   Did you explore spirituality and metaphysics and develop a fascination for supernatural beings and energies from a young age?

4.   Do you sometimes see beings or spirits? This could take the form of light sources or energies or even spheres that float in air.

5.   Were you more sensitive towards energy and could you detect emotions and feelings of people?

Your consciousness needs to be purified

One of the first steps you need to do when you want to increase the power of your intuition is to clear and purify your consciousness. This implies getting rid of all the things that hold you back. You can only develop a good intuition if you clarify and purify your mind. When you hold a lot of negative aura within you, it is going to block your third eye. This can result in your intuition to become weaker. Resentments, ill feelings and personal troubles should be let go of. You should be able to let go of the past and forgive yourself for the mistakes you have committed.

Channel all your negative emotions into something constructive. You can choose to write down your feelings to reduce the intensity of them. Try your best to get rid of feelings of remorse, regret, anger, jealousy and unhappiness. Make a conscious effort to detoxify yourself from these. Make room for more positive feelings and good thoughts. Cultivate feelings of happiness, peace and harmony. Forgive all the people who have wronged you and practice kindness and humility. Have a positive attitude and look at the bright side of the things. These are often easier said than done but make an effort to be a better person.

1   Get a Spiritual Mentor or a Guru to Help You

If you truly want to develop your intuition then it is a good idea to get a spiritual guru or someone who can help you develop your intuition. It is a good idea to find a spiritual person and the effort will pay off eventually. This is because you will get better wisdom and insights when you have someone who will guide you. Most spiritual gurus would have gone through what you went through and will be able to help you in your journey. You can get tips and points from them to cultivate your intuition. They would have undergone a similar experience and hence they will be able to channel your thoughts a lot better.

One of the most prominent points to note when looking for a spiritual guru or a teacher is to find someone who does not charge an exorbitant rate. If the person you have narrowed down to charges a high fee or demands for materialistic things then you would have gone to the wrong place. A guru needs to be someone who is inwardly as well as outwardly spiritual. He or she must not lay emphasis on material gains and must be more interested to take you as their disciple and reform you over scamming you off your money. Basically they should have a good value system.

The second aspect to consider when looking for a teacher is someone who has attained spiritual awakening. You might find a lot of people who are treading the path you are currently walking however these aren't helpful. Find someone who has been spiritually awakened and someone who has developed their intuition. The person you choose as your teacher or guru must be one who has attained the powers that you are looking to achieve. If they haven't then it will be difficult for them to guide you and you will be stuck in the middle ground and unable to access your true potential.

Also look for someone humble. When searching for a teacher the person must reflect the qualities that you are trying to attain. They should be at peace with themselves and should be able to channel your energy well. They should also exude positive thoughts, harmony and serenity and must not have negative thoughts and ill feelings. They should be collected and calm. Be aware of several fake teachers out there. There are many people who would claim that they would help you but really won't. The guru or teacher must be enlightened and humble. They should not be patronizing nor should they be haphazard.

2   Start to Cultivate and Enhance Your Vision

By cultivating your vision, we imply that you look both forward and backward to see the past, present and future. Be able to understand your past and analyze the experience. This also means that you should try and understand the past of others. Develop an empathetic attitude. This will help you understand the path a person has taken, their choices, their decisions, how these impacted them. Understand that everyone has had different experiences both in their current and past life. Develop a deeper sense of understand towards yourself and towards other people and you would be able to see the past.

Start by developing your memory. When you have a powerful memory and are able to recollect details. This will help you see the past. You need to be able to know what you did a few hours ago. If you do happen to visit a psychic, they are likely to be able to tell what you have done in the past life and what kind of a person you are. When they tell you such things it is a good rule of thumb to put them to test and ask them what you did a few hours ago. If the psychic is incapable of telling what you did a few hours ago then be assured that they are incapable of telling what you did in your past life. Intuitive people are able to tell what kind of a person you were in your past life but the trick isn't to be able to just feel the past of the people but to be able to visualize the past. You must have much more than just an idea of how the past of the people looks like.

3   Fine Tune Your Healing Abilities

Develop your ability to heal people. This is done through a variety of ways. You need to become a genuine person at the forefront. Start by wishing nothing but happiness upon people. Wish them well and be honest to them. Start to visualize the energy of the person especially the Prana energy. Under stand every connection in the body. The Prana energy when weak can affect the body. Understand the mechanics of this connection and make use of it to heal the physical form. Practice Reiki to channel healing chakras and harness positive healing aura through your body. This will help you heal others and create a spiritual barrier that makes you stronger.

4   Sharpen and Cleanse Your Five Senses

In order to develop your sixth sense you will need to

sharpen your other five senses. Make yourself more sensitive to all the senses. Stay away from negative substances and those that could harm your other five senses. Clean and purify your five senses and take care of them. Watch only positive things, read positive things and write and preach positive things. Eat healthy and good food and avoid eating junk. This way you will be able to slowly but surely cleanse and sharpen your five senses.

6.   Follow a Schedule and Maintain a Regime

Start by having a good healthy outlook in life. If you want to develop spiritual awakening and sharpen your intuition you can only do so if you make the required changes in your life. Be disciplined and practice what you preach. Sleep at a stipulated time everyday and wake up at the same time everyday. Eat healthy food and commit yourself into practicing everyday. Wake up and meditate for a while everyday. If you want to awaken your third eye you need to be focused and that should be your end goal. If you are lazy and uncommitted you will not attain liberation.

Chapter 14 Reiki Practice

Reiki is not an intellectual discipline, nor does it require any special talents. It's a tradition and practice that anybody can learn; there is no age limitation, so young children can learn the techniques as equally as older people. The Universal Energy that Reiki harnesses is a natural source of power that we all naturally have access to. For these reasons Reiki is one of the most accessible forms of healing but, at the same time, learning the practice can have some pitfalls. While practitioners and Reiki Masters are clear that Reiki is a pure form of healing which exists outside individual talents or aptitudes, they are also clear that the ability to perform Reiki must be passed from master to apprentice.

Reiki Levels.

There are three levels of Reiki practice; the first degree of Reiki training relates to the "hands on" element of the healing practice. The second, more complex, degree of Reiki teaches students to practice distant healing. The third and final degree is that of Reiki Master, at this level you become proficient in the practice but also are qualified to pass the skills on to others.

The first level of Reiki training requires what is called an "attunement" and this needs to be conducted on a face-to-face basis. In reality much initiation training is completed in group sessions. While one-to-one training is equally effective, most students find that group sessions are a better approach as they are less costly and also offer the chance to practice Reiki for real with a wider set of individuals. As in many other types of training, group work is invaluable as part of the learning process itself.

There is no standard approach to teaching Reiki at the first level, although most courses will take place over eight to twelve hours, or one to two days. Teaching, practice and time for reflection will be involved in the course. Many courses will teach the students the basics of Reiki during this period; self-care techniques should be part of the process as should the hand placements used in Reiki. Spot therapy should normally be covered in the sessions.

At the first degree of Reiki training several initiations should also take place. These are delivered by the Reiki Master, usually numbering four in total. The purpose of the attunement process is to open the crown Chakra and the palm Chakras, to allow the effective flow of healing energy. While it is possible to complete these actions alone it may take many years in order to achieve the desired result. In reality, the Reiki Master acts in part as teacher and in part as a "mechanic", fine tuning your abilities to vibrate correctly with the Universal Energy in order to be able to heal correctly.

As mentioned above, Reiki is not about innate talent but simply about being "programmed", or tuned, by a master to be effective at transmitting healing energy to the self and others. The first level of Reiki training is suitable for anybody who wishes to practice direct hand-healing on themselves or on friends and family.

At each level only one attunement is required and once you have Reiki it doesn't dissipate or wear off. You will have the ability to conduct Reiki healing for life. The experience is often a deeply spiritual one and can have a profound impact on an individual. Many people will find that their psychic abilities also increase post-attunement and this can be a life-enriching experience.

How Does Attunement Work?

The process of attunement is in no way a dangerous one and is generally beneficial to the physical and mental health of the student. However, the attunement can prompt a cleansing process in the student's own body and mind. The result is that toxins stored in the body can be released and removed from the system. In many cases, prior to taking a course in Reiki it's advisable to undergo a period of cleansing, fasting and purification. This is often recommended by the Reiki Master and it's believed that by undertaking this the attunement can be more effective when it is completed. As a simple guide the following is recommended before taking any Reiki training.

- Avoid meat, fish or fowl, simply eating a basic vegetarian diet for three to four days.

- Drink only water or fresh juice for the same period, avoiding alcohol, coffee or tea.

- Avoid sweet foods and chocolate.

- If you smoke, cut down or, better still, stop.

- Meditate daily for an hour or, if you find meditation difficult, simply spend an hour sat quietly, letting your thoughts flow as they will.

- Avoid TV, radio or the Internet. Spend as much time outside in the fresh air as possible, observing the world around you.

Second and Third Reiki Levels

The higher levels of Reiki are more complex methods and involve training as a Reiki Master. There is a serious level of commitment involved and, particularly with the latter, the practice of Reiki at these levels is very much about making Reiki a part of your daily life. The original concept of Reiki established by Usui was a spiritual tradition, linked to a concept of enlightenment and the way of life of monks in many Eastern Traditions, particularly Shinto. However, for many people, both the second and third degrees of Reiki offer a profoundly spiritual experience and can be beneficial to both you and to the wider world.

The Second Level of Reiki.

The second level concentrates on remote healing. This

can be an appropriate level to achieve for those who wish to work as healers on a more professional basis. Remote healing replaces the need to directly work with clients, friends or family on "hands-on" basis and connects the healer to the Universal Energy on a mental basis. The Attunement process is very much the same as with the first degree of training and simply is designed to "tune" you to the correct frequency of Reiki. Again, this is for life and once you have correctly attuned to this level the ability to conduct Reiki remotely will remain with you.

The Third Degree of Reiki.

The third degree of Reiki Training is that of Master; in the past this training was normally only offered by invitation. Existing masters identified the most apt students to become Reiki Masters. Today, many Masters will happily work with students to achieve this level. It is as a Reiki Master that you are able to train others and initiate them into the tradition. The process can be longer and takes the form of an apprenticeship with an existing Reiki Master. The life of Reiki Master is not for everyone but it is very rewarding. In most cases many initiates into Reiki will find that the first and second degrees are the most appropriate to them, in order to conduct healing on themselves, family, friends and the wider public. The third degree of training will be most suited to those who have developed a deep understanding of the principles of Reiki and it may be a path that they wish to take after many years of practical Reiki experience and delivery.

Finding a Reiki Master.

Reiki is a religious, spiritual tradition and, sadly, like all such traditions it is open to abuse by the less than honest individuals. As the Internet has developed there has also been the tendency (opportunity) for such individuals to promote themselves as Reiki Masters. As there is no internationally recognized qualification for this role, nor any absolute set of standards for imparting Reiki, this means that finding a genuine, qualified and talented Master can be a fraught and complex process.

The original Reiki Tradition was introduced to the West by a Master known as Mrs Takata, the Reiki teaching center established by Mrs Takata continues to operate and Masters who have trained under it have continued to train others. This lineage from Usui is important, as Reiki is passed directly from Master to student. As there are many willing to pose as Masters, and equally willing to lighten your soul of financial burdens, it's important to take some precautions when choosing a course and a Master. Some simple questions and steps to put in place are listed below.

Are You Ready for Reiki?

This is an important consideration. Before setting out on your path consider the following questions;

•   Do I feel ready to study Reiki and make it part of my life at present?

•   Am I able and willing to commit time and energy to Reiki practice?

•   Ask yourself if the Master feels "right" for you.

This last point is important and it's very much a case of intuition. Reiki already flows through you and it will offer a great deal of guidance before you have trained. Simply meditate on the question, quietly examine it, and go with your gut instinct.

Is the Master a Genuine Master?

These questions should be ones that you consider asking to establish how genuine the teacher in question is. Some are also useful as a guide to establish the teacher's experience and mastery of Reiki.

- How long do your classes last and what is covered?

- What should I expect to gain from the attunement?

- What is your level of training? Hands on Reiki training only is sometimes conducted by people who have attained this level only, but it's preferable to receive Reiki training from a master.

- When did you complete your own training? This helps you to establish the individual's level of practical experience.

- How do you practice Reiki on yourself? This is important as someone who works consistently in Reiki self-care will have a deeper, more profound connection with the Universal Energy.

• Where did you receive your training and from whom? Important in establish the Usui "lineage" of your Master.

• Could you describe Reiki to me, what it means and how it can be of use to me as an individual? A true Reiki Master will be able to answer this quickly and easily. They'll point out that Reiki is not really designed just to benefit you but should be used in a much wider sense!

• How much does the training cost, will accommodation and food be provided? This is a purely practical consideration and one that your Root Chakra should prompt anyway!

These are simply basic questions that genuine Masters will have no trouble in answering. You may feel additional questions are appropriate and, if you feel they are, then they are probably important. There is a strong level instinct in Reiki, the more you are able to go with this, the more likely it is that you are suited to Reiki practice in the first place!

Masters who take Offense.

Don't worry if you feel that these questions are rude, intrusive or arrogant. A Reiki Master will not, under any circumstances, take a poor view of a questioning individual. They'll be happy to answer questions and these questions will also help them to understand your intent and your suitability for Reiki. Those who are more interested in your money than your spiritual path are the ones who will take the most offense at a questioning soul! Those who wish to benefit you in Reiki practice and development will be happy to discuss their training in great detail.

Chapter 15 Energy Healing

Managing your inner energy requires a bit of maintenance, just as with choosing a healthy diet. The activities you choose to do, both physical and mental, play a role in the health of your inner energy, or your Chi, as it is called in Eastern medicine. Energy healing does not require a lot of money or time, but it does require some effort and, for beginners, guidance from an experienced healer.

Let us begin with the simplest method of all: energy transfer. This is simply manipulating the energy around your body to get it flowing. Energy naturally flows in a circular pattern throughout your body but can get blocked, building up in some places, and starving others. Think of this energy as your blood, coursing through your veins. A blockage can cause catastrophic problems within the system if it cannot be unblocked.

Energy transfer is a simple thing you can do every day to keep your energy flowing, and it is a great technique to add to your meditation practice. It is possible to move energy through your body by thought and gentle touch. The key is to recognize where this blockage may be occurring, so you can pinpoint that area. This may be a physical symptom, like pain in your shoulders, or a stomach ache. Simply sit still, place your hands gently over the afflicted area.

For example, if your stomach is upset, place your hands gently on your belly. Imagine that energy from all over your body is collecting in your hands, almost to the point where they tingle. Next, think about that energy flowing from your hands, into your belly, and washing it with health.

It will take a bit of practice to feel the effects of this technique. It takes a good deal of concentration to harness that energy and redistribute it properly. If you are new to meditation and energy work, seek the help of a professional. It is possible to do energy work on another person and to feel the effects, you may need to harness energy from another.

A professional Reiki practitioner will be able to help you determine where your energy needs improvement and can help open the lines of spiritual communication again. Reiki is open and beneficial to everyone, including those who may be skeptical of its benefit. Energy does not care about skepticism and will work regardless of belief.

Reiki is not a religion, and therefore, is truly open to everyone. You do not need to subscribe to any religious aspects of practice, making it more of an open field, much like massage therapy or acupuncture.

Whenever you are working with a practitioner in such a personal way, it is important to trust and feel comfortable around this person. There are people you may not click with, and others you do. If your first Reiki session doesn't seem quite right, don't give up. Give the benefit of the doubt and try again, or find another practitioner.

Acupuncture is another great way to remove energy blocks and get it flowing again. This ancient practice originated in China around 6000BC. Instead of needles, practitioners used sharpened animal bones to target a number of pressure points around the body.

Adding pressure and a skin prick to an area of concern causes the body to send blood flow and energy to that area for healing. This flood of energy unblocks the system, and the symptoms can be relieved. Acupuncture can be used to treat just about any ailment, from physical pain to emotional trouble.

Because acupuncture requires a sanitary, sterile environment, it is recommended to only receive acupuncture from a licensed professional. Find someone who is licensed by your local health district and who has a proper education. It is possible to transmit diseases via these needles, so a practitioner who follows the rules and disposes of used needles is of utmost importance.

Moving your body is another great way to get that energy flowing. We have known the correlation between general exercise and good health for quite some time. We often associate a healthy person as one who moves their body regularly. Starting or improving upon an existing exercise regimen can certainly improve the flow of energy and overall health.

Not all exercise is created equal. Many people make the mistake of exercising certain parts of the body and not others. For example, a walker may work their legs and heart, but their upper body is largely unchallenged. A bodybuilder may focus on muscles but not cardiovascular strength. The majority of people focus too much on the exercise itself, and not the stretching.

In addition, exercise is usually not done with optimal energy flow in mind. People focus on the task, but not the purpose, when really, the idea is to create an open channel of energy flow, getting oxygen and blood to all areas of the body, including vital organs. There are some exercises that are better than others at this.

Yoga is a wonderful practice that has been catching steam in the exercise world in the last decade. There are many different versions and classes available, with different ideas for what is right. Really, none of them are wrong, just different. Some classes focus on the same set of poses, while others change the routine often, even others that focus mostly on meditation.

Find a method that speaks to you by trying different versions, and figuring out what makes you feel your best. The immediate effects of yoga are clear. Those who practice report feelings of euphoria and lightness within their bodies directly after practice, and for the rest of the day in most cases. The practice relieves stress, stretches your muscles and moves energy around.

Practicing yoga does require basic physical strength and capability but is also something that improves with practice. If you are in good health in general and able to move, it is a great option. If your mobility is limited, it is possible to modify poses as well.

Qui Gong and Tai Chi are both ancient practices that focus on the flow of energy. If you were to watch someone practicing either one, it might remind you of karate or other martial arts, but at a much slower pace. The hand and leg movements mimic traditional moves but in a constantly-flowing slow-motion way. It is really quite a sight, and the benefits of stress relief and physical exercise associated with this practice enhances energy flow.

No matter what type of energy healing you subscribe to, regular participation in something that helps keep your energies balanced is a must in this stressful world. Your energy can take a shift in one direction or another at a moment's notice. It is important to recognize this and make adjustments as necessary so that you may live your best life.

Chapter 16 Creating Positive Thoughts

Energy can neither be created nor destroyed. That is a basic law of physics. We can, however, change the type of energy coming our way. We can take negative energy and turn it positive with the power of thought.

If you relate to the person who always seems to be in trouble, with luck nowhere in sight, it is likely related to how you process positive and negative energy. It is possible to live in a place surrounded by negative energy and still have a great life. Other times, it is best to remove yourself from it altogether.

Let's start with the first idea of changing your circumstances simply with thought. Imagine that you are living in an apartment complex on the bad side of town. The building is full of people that regularly use drugs, don't have jobs and result in violence to express their feelings. In psychology, we often recognize that raising a child into an adult in this environment often means that the child will resort to a similar life of crime and drugs. It is what they know. What about the select few that rise above these challenges and live lives that are productive, drug-free and peaceful? What is different about them that allows this to happen.

This anomaly shows that the internal energy of a person, created solely by their desires, is stronger than the environment. We do not need to succumb to negativity, we can change it. We are not destined to live less than ideal lives if we are born into it, we have the power internally to pull ourselves out of it.

The first step in accomplishing this is creating positive thoughts. Thinking positive has the power to take the negative energy from the environment and turn it around. You have the choice to react negatively to a negative situation, or you can turn it around and find the good in it. It takes a great deal of consciousness, self-discipline, and drive to do so, but these are things all humans are capable of.

You can easily instill more positivity into your day by rearranging your thoughts. To get started, set aside a small chunk of time every day to assess your thoughts. It only takes about ten or fifteen minutes to create more awareness in your thinking. Simply sit quietly and think about the content of your day. Think about the exchange you had with the store clerk after waiting in line for what seemed like forever. Were you cordial, or did you let your aggravation show? How did the clerk respond to your actions?

Think about your daily exchanges, and come up with constructive solutions to consciously change your future actions. For example, if you were gruff and a bit rude to the store clerk, what can you do better next time? This is a stepwise process. First, you can change your outward reaction to the stressor. Say, keep your aggravation to yourself and choose to be courteous, despite the annoyance. Quickly, you will begin to realize that you get more positivity back when you put positivity out. You may even turn the clerk's attitude more positive as well.

Over time, you will find that it really only hurts you to have negative thoughts. You will start to understand that the small things in life that aggravate you and cause negative thoughts aren't worth the time. So what if the line is long at the grocery store? What harm is it really doing in the grand scheme of things? With these mini-epiphanies, you can then transform your total way of thinking.

In addition to taking time for thought assessment, be more conscious in your daily thinking. Be present in each moment and be conscious of the thoughts that begin to develop. When you recognize yourself being negative about something, try to stop that thought in its tracks. Redirect yourself and challenge yourself to find something positive about it. For example, while you are waiting in a long line, you have a chance to relax for a few minutes. You may also take that time to engage in conversation with the person in front of you. These are all good things.

The brain is a funny organ, in that it is really a creature of habit. Our brain makes associations as a way to process information that is coming in. We learn how to act in different situations, and when we learn what brings good outcomes, we repeatedly do it. Unfortunately, we often think negative thoughts about certain things as a way to deter yourself from acting in a certain way. For example, if you didn't like the taste of brussels sprouts the first time, your brain will elicit a negative reaction to the sight of them to deter you from eating them.

The good news is, it is possible to redirect these associations and change them. Using conscious positive thought on a regular basis actually change the way your brain works. Brain scans over time actually show that creating positive associations instead of negative ones creates more gray matter, and forces you to use more of your brain power. These are all great things. Hooray for positivity!

Being more present in your thought strengthens your brain as well as your spiritual connection. Understanding what makes you happy, angry and overwhelmed is a key to understanding what makes your inner self tick. Your resolve becomes greater, and you become a stronger person overall as you become more in touch with yourself.

It is, however, possible to be weak in this department. Until you are a fully-functioning, energetically aligned human being, it may be necessary to physically change your circumstances to help the process around. If the negativity around you is greatly affecting your ability to be positive, it may be time to make a change. The body and mind are only resilient to a point. If you are doing your best, but are constantly bombarded with negativity, it can be very draining, to the point of no return.

For example, look at a negative relationship. We often see others in mentally and physically abusive relationships.

We judge them, whether we mean to or not. How can they continue to let themselves be abused in that way? The reason is, this is likely not how the relationship started. Over time, the emotional investment in the relationship makes a person overlook the negative jabs and perceived 'mistakes' of the abusive person.

The continued negativity draws energy away from the abused until they have nothing left. Their self-esteem disappears, and any shred of positivity within them has been used up. There is nothing left but consuming negativity, something they cannot lift themselves out of without help. The general recommendation for people in this situation is to remove themselves from it, and that is exactly what you can do in any type of overwhelmingly negative situation.

Imagine that this negative situation was actually a physical sickness. You have struggled with a stubborn cold for weeks, with a nagging cough and general fatigue. Over time, you get worse and worse, more fatigued and sick. You would not simply live like this, would you? You would likely get help fighting the illness with medicine. Think of positivity as medicine for your negative situation.

Changing your internal view of yourself, your

surroundings and your situation is the first step to gaining enough self-esteem to rise above the situation. This may mean a complete upheaval of your current life, or it may mean looking for a new job. Either way, you are making positive strides toward the life you have always dreamed of living.

Chapter 17 How To Heal And Strengthen Your Third Eye

When you open up your third eye, it is going to make it easier for you to see things as they truly are. You will not just see things in an altered state or ones that are based on your personal experiences in life, but you will see things like they are without a filter. However, when there are some imbalances, even some smaller ones, it will end up creating some havoc on your psychological, physical, and emotional health.

The third eye has a lot of history behind it. This eye is sometimes called the Ana charka and it is the sixth of the seven basic chakras, which are also known as the energy centers, inside of the body. It is sometimes even called the conscience and it is believed to be in charge of the pineal gland along with how your intuition, imagination, memory, and vision work.

Imbalances of the third eye

There are times when an imbalance could happen with

the third eye. The mind of a person can sometimes go into overdrive if too much energy ends up coming in through this chakra. When the third eye is overactive, it is really difficult to concentrate on anything and in some people, it can cause hallucinations and other issues. On the other hand, when the third eye is underactive, it can cause you to feel fearful or you can procrastinate and be indecisive. Some people who have trouble focusing or keeping their cool under pressure will find that it is because there is a huge imbalance of the third eye chakra.

There are actually a lot of different conditions that can happen when there is a block or some kind of imbalance of this third eye. Some of these conditions that you may notice include:

- Sciatica

- Insomnia

- Migraines

- High blood pressure

- Anxiety

- Depression

If you are dealing with these issues on a regular basis, it may be time to do some work on your third eye chakra. There is most likely an imbalance that is going on so it is important to make the right changes to get them back in line.

Healing the third eye

One of the best ways to work on healing the third eye is chakra meditation. But there are a few other options that you can try to help out with healing your energy. Some examples of what you are able to do include sound therapy, acupressure, acupuncture, and Reiki. If you are a yoga practitioner, there are some asanas that are good for balancing the third eye, such as shoulder stands, forwards bends, and child's pose.

Essential oils can help out with the third eye, especially when they are placed right where the third eye is situated. There are a lot of great essential oils that can help out with the third eye including sandalwood, juniper, clary sage, rosemary, marjoram, and frankincense. You do not need a lot of these oils, and usually, they should be mixed with some other oils so they are not too strong and will irritate the skin. Adding this onto the third eye once a day, maybe during Reiki or during meditation will make a difference.

Another option that some people will choose to work with is some healing stones. These are popular because they are going to rely on the stone having the right vibration frequency and the same chakra color as the third eye that you are working with. When these stones are used in the proper way, they are able to clear out all of the negative energy in the body and can restore the proper energy flow as well. Some of the tones that can work well for this include purple fluorite, Lapiz lazuli, quartz, amethyst, and moonstone.

In order to use these stones, you would need to have them near you. Some people will choose to hold the stones near the third eye while they are doing the meditation. You can also consider having a necklace or other piece of jewelry with the right stone on you to help with the healing.

Foods for the third eye

Some people like to focus on their diet when it comes to healing the third eye chakra. They want to make sure that they are feeding the third eye the right things so that it can balance out and can keep their whole body healthy. To make things simple, you need to stick with foods that are purple to work on the third eye. These need to be naturally purple and blue foods or they will not help the third eye as much. There are many options that you can go with including purple kale, purple cabbage, purple pepper, blueberries, eggplants, and plums.

Since the third eye is associated with the pineal gland, it is important that you feed it a healthy diet if you want it to stay strong. When the pineal gland is not working properly, it can cause some issues with how well you can focus and even with anxiety and other issues. When picking out your diet, make sure that you are eating one that is free of pesticides, preservatives, and other chemicals so that you can stay healthy.

There are a lot of other things that you are able to do to help when it comes to your diet. Doing these things will help to make the pineal gland stronger and can ensure that the third eye is going to work the way that it should. Some of the things that you can do to help strengthen the third eye in terms of your diet include:

- Get rid of the fluoride: another thing that you can work on if you want to make sure that the third eye is going to work in the proper way is to cut out the fluoride. It is common that our water supply is going to have high amounts of this fluoride so add on a reverse-osmosis filter to the tap. You can also change out to a fluoride-free toothpaste as well.

- Apple cider vinegar: because it is rich in malic acid, this can be a good way to detoxify the whole body. It also has a lot of benefits so it can make your water more alkaline and keeps you healthy. Having a tablespoon three times a day, mixed in with some honey and lemon to help with the taste, can make it better.

- Eat foods rich in iodine: kelp and seaweed are good options for this. The iodine inside is able to help support your thyroid and can be important to remove some of the sodium fluorides that is in the body.

- Raw cacao: this has a lot of antioxidants inside of it, which means that it can counter the free radicals that are in our bodies. This will help to keep the whole brain healthy while stimulating the third eye and detoxing the whole body.

- Coconut oil: coconut is known to provide a lot of enrichment to the body, including to the hair and skin. It can also provide some good nourishment to the brain and will detox the pineal gland also.

- Herbs: there are a lot of herbs that can be beneficial to both the pineal gland and to the brain. Go for options like Gotu Kola, parsley, and Alfalfa sprouts.

- Vitamin K2: this is seen as the missing ingredient in almost every diet thanks to the unnatural ways that we process well. It can help to prevent calcification in the pineal gland, as well as in the various bones of the body.

- Vitamin D: when light has reflected the retina, it is going to stimulate the pineal gland. While you should never look directly into the sun, having your eyes look at indirect sunlight on a regular basis can help to make the pineal gland work better. Just being outside and getting plenty of sunlight can make a big difference.

As you can see, there are a lot of great things that you are able to do to help make the third eye strong. It is so important that we work to make the third eye as strong as possible, giving it a chance to provide us with insights into the other world, the spiritual world, while helping us to do well in our current world. When the third eye is not balanced properly, whether this is because it has too much energy going through it or too little, it is going to mess with us and our ability to function in the normal world.

The good news is that there are a lot of things that we are able to do to help stimulate the third eye chakra and get it to work out well. If you feel that your third eye chakra is not working the way that you would like, make sure to check out some of these options and learn how to incorporate them into your daily life.

Conclusion

Opening the third eye chakra is no simple task, and it will take a significant amount of effort and time from your end. But as you start to tap into its powers, you will discover new perspectives and abilities that can eliminate much of the stress, anxiety, worry, and fear that we tend to deal with in our day to day lives.

I hope this comprehensive guide has helped you understand what you third eye chakra can do for you and how you can reap its unique abilities. Always remember to heal your chakras and cleanse your spirit to minimize the risk of an overstimulated third eye and maximize the benefits of using the helpful capabilities that the Ajna chakra can give you access to.

We are often contained in our physical world, unable to see beyond the 5 senses, trapped in the reality of our ego and the self-centered mentality that we're bred to adapt. But by accepting our interconnectedness with nature, the world, the universe, and others around us, we can become far more effective leaders of our system, achieving optimal spiritual growth to achieve a purposeful existence. And it all starts with your third eye.

Namaste.